THE

PRIVATE LIFE

OF THE LATE

BENJAMIN FRANKLIN, LL.D.

LATE MINISTER PLENIPOTENTIARY FROM THE UNITED
STATES OF AMERICA TO FRANCE, &c. &c. &c.

Originally written by Himself,
AND NOW TRANSLATED FROM THE FRENCH.

TO WHICH ARE ADDED,

SOME ACCOUNT OF HIS PUBLIC LIFE, A VARIETY OF
ANECDOTES CONCERNING HIM, BY M. M. BRISSOT,
CONDORCET, ROCHEFOUCAULT, LE ROY, &c. &c.

AND THE EULOGIUM OF M. FAUCHET,
CONSTITUTIONAL BISHOP OF THE DEPARTMENT OF CALVADOS,
AND A MEMBER OF THE NATIONAL CONVENTION.

Eripuit cœlo fulmen, mox fceptra tyranni. TURGOT.

A Paris, ce grand homme, dans notre ancien régime, feroit refté dans l'ob-
fcurité; comment employer le fils d'un chandelier? LE ROY.

LONDON:

PRINTED FOR J. PARSONS, NO. 21, PATER-NOSTER ROW.

Printing Statement:

Due to the very old age and scarcity of this book, many of the pages may be hard to read due to the blurring of the original text, possible missing pages, missing text, dark backgrounds and other issues beyond our control.

Because this is such an important and rare work, we believe it is best to reproduce this book regardless of its original condition.

Thank you for your understanding.

TO

SIR HENRY TEMPEST,

)F TONG, IN THE COUNTY OF YORK, AND HOPE-END, IN
THE COUNTY OF HEREFORD, BART.

THIS LIFE OF

BENJAMIN FRANKLIN,

A STATESMAN,

A PHILOSOPHER,

AND A PATRIOT,

IS DEDICATED,

(AS A MARK OF HIS ESTEEM AND REGARD,)

London,
July 1, 1793.

BY

THE TRANSLATOR.

A 3

PREFACE

FRENCH EDITION.

I SHALL not enter into an uninterefting detail relative to the manner in which the original manufcript of thefe memoirs, which are written in the
Englifh language, came into my poffeffion. They appeared to me to be fo interefting, that I did not hefitate a fingle moment to tranflate them into French.

The name of Franklin will undoubtedly become a
paffport to a work of this nature; and the chara&er
of truth and fimplicity, difcernible in every page,
muft guarantee its authenticity; I have no manner
of occafion to join other teftimonies.

If, however, any critic choofes to difbelieve my affer-
ton, and is defirous to bring the exiftence of the
original manufcript into doubt, I am ready to verify
it, by means of an immediate impreffion *; but, as I

Thofe who may be defirous of reading the Memoirs of the
Privæ Life of Franklin, in the original, are requefted to leave their
name with Buiffon, bookfeller, Rue Haute-Feuille, N° 20.
The work will be fent to the prefs as foon as there are 400 fubfcriber. The price is 48 fols.

am

am not certain of the fale of a work written in a foreign language, I cannot publifh it in any other manner than by means of a fubfcription, large enough to
indemnify me for the money advanced.

That part of the *Memoirs* of Franklin in my poffeffion, includes no more than the firft period of a life,
the remainder of which has become illuftrious by
events of the higheft importance; it terminates at the
epoch when, after havng married, he began to render
himfelf celebrated by plans and eftablifhments of
public utility.

It is very poffible that he may have written more
of his hiftory; for the portion of it which I now
prefent to the Public, concludes, according to his
own account, with the year 1771.

If this be the cafe, the heirs of that great man will
not fail fome day to publifh it, either in England or
in Pennfylvania, and we fhall doubtlefs have a French
tranflation, which will be received by the Public with
great eagernefs; but I am perfuaded, that his family will not difclofe any other than the moft brilliant
period of his life; that which is conneﬅed with tle
memorable part he aﬅed in the world, both as a
philofopher and a ftatefman. They will never be
prevailed upon to narrate the humble details o his
early days, and the fimple but interefting aneciotes
of his origin, the obfcurity of which, although t en-
hances the talents and the virtues of this grea man,
mav yet wound their own vanity.

1   If

If my conjectures prove right; if the memoirs which they are about to publish under the name of Franklin should be mutilated; if the first part, so essential to readers capable of feeling and of judging, should be suppressed, I shall applaud myself for having preserved it; and the world will be obliged to me for having enabled them to follow the early developements of the genius, and the first exertions of the sublime and profound mind of a man, who afterwards penetrated the mystery of electricity, and disconcerted the secret measures of despotism—who preserved the universe from the ravages of thunder, and his native country from the horrors of tyranny!

If I am accidentally mistaken; if the life of Franklin should appear entire, the Public will still have the advantage of anticipating the interesting part of a history which it has long and impatiently expected.

The principal object proposed by the American philosopher, in writing these memoirs, was to instruct posterity, and amuse his own leisure hours. He has permitted his ideas to flow, at the will of his memory and his heart, without ever making any effort to disguise the truth, notwithstanding it is not always very flattering to his self-love—but I here stop; it belongs to Franklin to speak for himself.

It will be easily perceived, that I have preserved as much as possible the ease and simplicity of his style in my translation. I have not even affected to correct the negligence of his language, or to clothe his senti-

ments

ments with a gaudy drefs, for which they have no manner of occafion; I fhould have been afraid of be-reaving the work of one of its principal ornaments.

As thefe memoirs reach no further than his mar-riage, I have made ufe of other materials in order to complete fo interefting a hiftory; and I have alfo added a number of anecdotes and remarks relative to this philofophical American.

THE EDITOR.

ENGLISH TRANSLATION.

THE Life of the late Dr. Benjamin Franklin is, perhaps, a DESIDERATUM in modern biography; for the manner in which that ſtateſman and philoſopher, although deſtitute of birth, and of fortune, was enabled to ſtruggle into opulence and celebrity, cannot fail to excite the intereſt, and gratify the curioſity of a liberal and enlightened age.

But this work is eſtimable in another point of view; for it may be conſidered as a treatiſe enforcing the love of virtue and of induſtry, diſplaying the advantages ariſing from ſtudy, and exhibiting the moſt eaſy mode of acquiring literary and moral excellence.

Youth will be gratified by the early efforts of our Author's riſing genius, and old age comforted, at beholding that happy ſerenity diſplayed in the latter period of his life.

The Tranſlator would have preſented the world with this volume long ſince, had he not

been

been reftrained by a certain degree of delicacy, mingled with veneration, towards the family of this great man; for on being informed by a refpectable bookfeller in St. Paul's Church-yard, that the works of Franklin were about to be publifhed by his grandfon, he with-held the prefent publication for feveral months, in expectation of that event.

He begs leave to add, that, throughout the whole work, he has attempted a plain, fober, unadorned ftyle, as beft adapted to convey the Author's fentiments; and that, in the fecond part, he has fupplied fome erroneous dates, and cancelled a variety of unjuft reflections which were thrown out in England againft Dr. Franklin, during the late odious war with America, and but too haftily adopted by the French Editor.

Feb. 1, 1793.

CONTENTS.

PART

PART III.

THE

THE

PRIVATE LIFE

.O F

BENJAMIN FRANKLIN, LL.D.

PART I.

CHAP. I.

The Author's Reafons for undertaking the prefent Work—A Differtation upon Vanity—Some Account of his Anceftors—He difcovers that he is the youngeft Son of the youngeft Son for five Generations—Young Franklin is at firft deftined for the Church—His Father foon after takes him from School and employs him as an Affiftant in making Candles, &c.—He is defirous of being a Sailor—Some Account of his youthful Frolicks—Becomes greatly attached to Books—Is bound Apprentice to a Printer—Begins to ftudy Compofition—Adopts a vegetable Regimen—And is extremely fond of Difputation.

MY DEAR SON,

I HAVE lately amufed myfelf with collecting fome little anecdotes concerning our family. You muft remember the enquiries that I made among fuch of my relations as remained alive, when you were with me in England, as well as the journey I undertook for that purpofe. As I conceive that it muft be agreeable to you, to be acquainted with all the circumftances of my life and origin, many particulars of which are at prefent unknown to you, I

now

now mean to commit them to paper for your in‑ formation. It fhall be the occupation of a week's uninterrupted leifure, which I promife myfelf in my prefent rural ‑ retirement. Befides, there are other powerful motives, which impell me to this un‑ dertaking. From amidſt the poverty and obfcurity in which I was born, and in which I paffed my early years, I have raifed myfelf to a fituation of opulence, and to fome fhare of celebrity in the world. An un‑ interrupted feries of good fortune has accompanied me, even to an advanced period of life; my pofterity will therefore perhaps be gratified in learning the means which I have employed, and which, thanks to the affiftance of Providence, have fo well fucceded with me. They may alfo derive fome ufeful hints from my experience, fhould they ever find themfelves in fimilar circumftances.

This good fortune, when I refle&t ferioufly on it, which is frequently the cafe, has fometimes induced me to fay, that if the offer were made to me, I would again engage to travel over the fame courfe, from the beginning to the end. I fhould only defire the privilege of an author in a fecond edition, to cor‑ re&t fome of the errors of the firft. I fhould likewife wifh, were it in my power, to alter fome particular incidents and events of my life, for more favorable ones. However, if this condition were refufed me, I fhould neverthelefs confent to begin again. But fince to repeat life is impoffible, that which in my opi‑ nion moft nearly refembles it, is to recall all its par‑ ticular circumftances, and to render the remembrance of them the more durable, by committing them to writing. In employing myſelf thus, I ſhall yield to the inclination ſo pleaſing to old men, to talk of themſelves and their own actions; and I ſhall indulge it without being burdenſome to thoſe, who, from reſpect to my age, might think themſelves obliged to liſten to me, as it will be always in their option either to read or not, as they pleaſe. In truth, I may as well confeſs (as nobody would believe me if I ſhould deny it,) that perhaps I may in this gratify my ſelf-love. I hardly ever heard any perſon pro-nounce this preparatory phraſe: *I may ſay it with-out flattering my vanity, &c.* without its being imme-diately followed by ſome ſtrongly marked ſtroke, charactereſtic of that very vanity which they ſeemed deſirous to deprecate.

The generality of men detect this foible in others, however large a portion of it they themſelves may poſſeſs. For my own part, I pardon it wherever I find it, perſuaded that it is advantageous to the indi-vidual whom it influences, as well as to all thoſe who come within its ſphere of action. Conſequently it would, in many caſes, be by no means abſurd, that a man ſhould conſider his vanity among the comforts of his life, and give thanks to Providence that he is endowed with it.

And in this place let me acknowledge in all hu-mility, that to Divine Providence I attribute the happineſs I have hitherto enjoyed. It alone has pre-ſented to my mind all the means that I have made uſe of, and has influenced their ſucceſs. My belief

in

in this refpect induces me to hope, although I ought
by no means to depend upon it, that the divine
goodnefs will be continued towards me, either in
prolonging my good fortune to the termination of
my life, or in granting me ftrength to fupport any
unfortunate reverfe which may happen to me, as it
has to fo many others. My future fate is known to
Him alone, who holds our deftiny in his hands, and
who can convert our very afflictions into the fources
of our greateft happinefs.

One of my uncles, defirous like myfelf of collecting anecdotes relative to our family, gave me fome
notes, from which I have extracted feveral circumftances concerning our anceftors. From thefe I learn
that they lived in the village of Eaton, in North-
hamptonfhire, on a freehold of about thirty acres,
during at leaft three hundred years. My uncle could
not difcover how long they had refided there prior
to that period. It is probable they had continued ever
fince the time when, in imitation of their fellow citizens all over the kingdom, who then began to affume particular names, they took that of Franklin, which previoufly denominated a peculiar clafs
of people.

This inconfiderable property would not have fuf-
ficed for their fubfiftance, had it not been for the
occupation of a blackfmith, which continued in the
family down to my time, the eldeft fon being always
brought up to that trade; a cuftom which both my
uncle and my father followed, with refpect to their
eldeft fons.

Among

Among the enquiries I made at Eaton, I·found no account of their births, marriages, or deaths, prior to the year 1555, as the parifh-regifter extends no farther back than that period. I learned from it however, that I was the youngeft fon of the youngeft fon for five generations. My grandfather, Thomas, who was born in the year 1598, lived at Eaton till he was too old to continue his bufinefs, and then retired to Banbury in Oxfordfhire, to the houfe of his fon John, a dyer, to whom my father was apprentice. There my grandfather died and was buried; we faw his tomb-ftone in 1758. His eldeft fon Thomas lived in the family houfe at Eaton, and left it, together with the landed property, to his only ·daughter, who agreed with her hufband, Mr. Fifher of Wellingborough, to fell the whole to Mr. Efted, the prefent proprietor.

My grandfather had four fons who lived to be men, namely, Thomas, John, Benjamin, and Jofias. I·fhall mention to you fuch circumftances relative to them, as my memory furnifhes me with, not having my papers at hand, in which you will find more particulars, provided they have not·been loft during my abfence.

Thomas had learned the bufinefs of a blackfmith, with my father; but having fome natural genius, he improved himfelf by ·ftudy, in confequence of the advice of ——— Palmer, Efq. who was at that time the principal man in the parifh, and who encouraged all my uncles in the acquifition of knowledge. Thomas thus enabled himfelf to tranfact the bufinefs of

a fteward.

a fteward. He foon became a man of fome little confequence, and was one of the principal projectors of all the public enterprifes, for the benefit of the county and town of Northampton, as well as for the good of his own village. After having been a good deal noticed and protected by Lord Hallifax, he died on the 6th day of January, 1692, exactly four years before I was born. Could I remember the particulars of his life and character, as related to me by fome old people in the village, you would be furprifed at the analogy of many parts of them with mine : " Had he died," you would fay, " four years " later, one would have fuppofed that a tranfmigra- " tion had actually taken place."

John I believe was brought up a dyer of woollens.

Benjamin ferved an apprenticefhip in London, to a filk dyer; he was an induftrious man. I remember him well, for while I was yet a child he came to join my father in Bofton, and lived fome time in our houfe. A particular friendfhip fubfifted between them, and I was his namefake ; he lived to a very advanced age. He left two manufcript volumes in quarto, of poetry, of his own compofition, confifting of little fugitive pieces addreffed to his friends ; he had formed to himfelf a fyftem of fhort hand, which he taught me, but having never practifed it, it has long fince flipped from my memory. He was a pious man, and attended the fermons of our beft preachers, which he delighted in taking down in the expeditious mode adopted, if not invented by him, and of thefe he had collected feveral volumes. He

was

was alfo fond of politics, too much fo perhaps for his
fituation. I lately met in London, with a collection
he had made of all the principal political pamphlets,
from the year 1641 to 1717. Some part of the feries is manifeftly wanting, but there ftill remained,
eight volumes in folio, and twenty-four in quarto and.
octavo. This collection had fallen into the hands of
a dealer in old books, who knew me, by having been
a cuftomer, and brought it to me. My uncle apparently had left it with him, when he went to Ame-.
rica, fifty years ago. I found many notes written on
the margin with his own hand. His grandfon Samuel
Franklin ftill lives at Bofton.

Our humble family at an early period embraced
the principles of the reformed religion. Our forefathers remained faithfully attached to it during the
reign of Mary, and were in danger of being harrafſed
on account of their zeal againft Popery. They were
in poffeffion of an Englifh verfion of the Bible : In
order to conceal and preferve it in fafety, they be-
thought themfelves of faftening it with ftrings, in an
open pofition, to the infide of the cover of a night-
ftool. When my great grandfather was defirous of
reading it to the family, he reverfed the cover upon
his knees, and turned over the leaves, without un-
loofing the cords which faftened it. One of the children always remained at the door to give notice if he
faw the apparitor approaching ; this was an officer of
the fpiritual-court. On the leaft alarm, the cover of
the night-ftool was inftantly reftored to its proper
place, and the bible remained concealed underneath

it

it as ufual. This anecdote I had from my uncle Benjamin.

The whole family continued attached to the church of England, till towards the conclufion of the reign, of Charles the Second; an æra when fome of the minifters who had been difplaced as non-conformifts, having eftablifhed conventicles in Northamptonfhire, Benjamin and Jofias joined them, never again to feparate. The reft of the family continued in the Epifcopal church.

Jofias, my father, married early. He carried his wife and three children to New-England, about the year 1682. The conventicles being at that time under the profcription of the law, and their meetings frequently difturbed, fome confiderable people of his acquaintance refolyed to go to America, in hopes of enjoying the quiet exercife of their religion ; and he determined to accompany them.

My father had four more children by the fame wife in America, and ten by a fecond marriage ; in all feventeen. I remember to have feen thirteen of them at table together, all of whom grew up and married. I was the youngeft fon, and the youngeft of all the children, excepting two daughters.

I was born at Bofton in New-England. My mother, my father's fecond wife, was Abias Folger, the daughter of Peter Folger, one of the firft fettlers in New-England, whom Cotton Mather mentions in his ecclefiaftical hiftory of that province, as a *pious and learned Englifhman*, if I remember his expreffion properly. I have heard that he compofed feveral little

pieces,

pieces, though one only was printed. I faw it many years ago ; it was written in 1675, in familiar verfe, according to the tafte of the times and the country. It is addreffed to the then governors, and requefts liberty of confcience for the Anabaptifts, the Quakers, and other fectaries, who had recently been perfe-cuted. He attributes the war with the natives, and other calamities which at that time afflicted the country, to this perfecution, confidering them as fo many judgments of God, for the punifhment of this odious crime. He alfo exhorts the government to abrogate laws fo inimical to charity. This piece appeared to me to be written with a certain degree of mafculine liberty, and agreeable fimplicity.

My brothers were all bound apprentices to various trades. With refpect to myfelf, I was put to a grammar-fchool, in the eighth year of my age. My father deftined me for the church, and already confidered me as the chaplain of the family. The facility with which I learned to read in my infancy, (for I do not recollect the time when I could not read,) and the opinion of all his friends, who affured him that I would certainly become a man of letters, confirmed him in this defign. My uncle Benjamin likewife approved of it, and promifed to give me all his volumes of fermons, written in his own fhort-hand, as I have already mentioned, provided I would be at the trouble to learn it. I remained, however hardly a twelvemonth at fchool, although during that fhort period I had rifen fucceffively to the middle of that year's clafs, then to the top of the fame clafs, thence to the clafs immediately

immediately above, and I fhould have gone into the next, at the beginning of the enfuing year ; but my father, burdened with a numerous family, found himfelf unable, without much inconvenience, to fupport the expences of my education; befides, confidering, as I heard him fay in my prefence, the fmall encouragement that fuch a line of life affords to thofe educated purpofely for it, he renounced his original idea, withdrew me from my ftudies, and fent me to the fchool of a Mr. George Brownwell, to learn writing and arithmetic ; he was a fkilful mafter, who commonly fucceded very well in his profeffion, by employing only the gentleft methods towards his pupils. I foon learned under his tuition to write a good hand, but in arithmetic I made not the fmalleft progrefs.

At ten years of age I was brought home to affift my father in his bufinefs, which was that of a candle and foap-maker, trades, to which he had not indeed ferved an apprenticefhip, but which he had embraced on his arrival in New-England, finding that there was not fufficient employment for a dyer, to enable him to fupport his family. My employments confequently were to attend the fhop, cut the wicks for the candles, run errands, &c.

I difliked this trade much, and had a great inclination for that of a failor, but my father pofitively declared againft this idea. However, the neighbourhood of the water afforded me frequent occafions of exercifing myfelf both on it and in it. I learned early to fwim and to fteer a boat, and when I was embarked

barked with other children of my own age, they always gave up to me the management of the helm, especially on dangerous occasions. Indeed, I was almost always the leader of the party, and frequently brought them into mischief. I shall mention to you one example, which evinces an early spirit of public enterprise, although not indeed in this case consistent with justice.

The reservoir of a neighbouring mill was terminated on one side by a salt pit, on the bank of which we used to place ourselves at full tide, in order to catch small fish. As by frequently treading on it, we had rendered it a perfect mire, I proposed to construct a causeway on which we might stand dry and firm. I pointed out to my comrades a large quantity of stones, collected indeed for the purpose of building a new house near the salt-pit, but admirably calculated for completing our project: On the evening, after the workmen were gone home, I got together a number of my play-fellows, and by labouring diligently like so many ants, two or three sometimes assisting to remove a single stone, we carried the whole off, and constructed our little key. In the morning, the workmen were astonished at not finding their stones, which had all travelled to our causeway. The authors of this transfer being found out and detected, most of us received a correction from our parents; and although I demonstrated the utility of our labours, my father convinced me that nothing could be truly useful which was not strictly honest.

Perhaps

Perhaps you may be defirous to know what fort of a man my father was? He'had an excellent conftitution, was of a middling fize, but well made, very ftrong, and dexterous in performing whatever he attempted. He drew pretty well, and he knew fomething of mufic; his voice alfo was fonorous and agreeable; fo that when he fung a pfalm-tune, accompanied with his violin, which he fometimes did in the evening, it was truly pleafing to hear him; he likewife knew fomething of mechanics, and could occafionally ufe the tools of feveral trades. But his moft excellent quality was a found underftanding and folid judgment, of fuch matters as came within the jurifdiction of prudence, whether appertaining to public or private life. He was never indeed employed in the former, becaufe the numerous family he had to educate, and the moderatenefs of his fortune, kept him inceffantly employed in his profeffion; but I well remember that he was frequently confulted by our principal men, who came to afk his opinion relative to the affairs of the town, or of the particular fect to which he belonged, and they paid great deference to his judgement; individuals alfo often applied to him on their private affairs when involved in difficulties, and he was frequently chofen arbitrator between contending parties.

He was fond to fee at his table, as often as it was convenient, fome friends or neighbours of fuperior underftanding, whofe converfation was agreeable;

and

and he always took care to introduce fubjects either
ufeful or amufing, which might tend to inftruct his
children. By thefe means he early formed our minds,
to what was good, juft, prudent, and ufeful, in the
conduct of life., Never was there any enquiry concerning the difhes that appeared on the table, nor any
difcuffion whether they were well or ill cooked, in or
out of feafon, tafted agreeably or the contrary, or were
preferable or inferior to fuch and fuch others of the
fame kind. Thus accuftomed from my infancy to the
utmoft inattention to thefe matters, I have been all
my life wholly indifferent as to what kind of food was
fet before me ; and even now I pay fo little attention to
it, that a few hours after my dinner, I fhould be unable to fay of what it had confifted. In travelling I have
more efpecially found the advantage of this habit, for·
I have often met with people who, poffeffing a nicer
tafte than myfelf, becaufe they cultivated it more,
fuffered much on occafions where for my own part I
could perceive nothing wanting.

My mother alfo had a moft excellent conftitution.
She had fuckled all her ten children herfelf, and I
never remember to have feen either her or my father
afflicted with any complaint, except that of which
they died ; my father, at the age of eighty-feven, and
my mother of eighty-five. They were buried together
at Bofton, where, a few years ago, I placed a marble
tablet over their grave, with the following infcription :

                                          " Here

" Here Lie
" JOSIAS FRANKLIN and ABIAS his Wife,
".They lived together with reciprocal affection during fifty-
" nine years ; and without any settled revenue or lucrative
" employment, by means of affiduous labour, and honeft induftry,
" maintained a numerous family with decency, and brought up
" thirteen children, and feven grand-children.

" Reader, let their example encourage you to fufil with dili-
" gence the duties of your vocation, and'to rely on the affiftance
" of Divine Providence !
" He, was pious, and prudent,
" She, difcreet, and virtuous.
" Their youngeft Son fulfils his duty,
" In confecrating this ftone to their memory."

I perceive by my rambling digreffions that I am
old. I formerly wrote with more. method, but one
does not drefs for private company, as if they were
going to a ball. This is perhaps merely negligence.

To return, I continued to follow the profeffion of
my father, during two years, that is to fay, till I was
twelve years of age ; at that time, my brother John,
who had ferved an apprenticefhip to the fame trade,
having left my father, married, and fet up for himfelf, in Rhode Ifland ; I was deftined, according to
all appearances, to fupply his place, and continue all
my life a maker of candles. But my averfion to this
bufinefs continued, and made my father afraid, that
if he did not offer me fome more agreeable occupation, I would leave him and go to fea, as my brother
Jofias had done, very much to his diffatisfaction.
For that reafon he carried me to fee mafons, joiners,
coopers,

coopers, braziers, &c. at work, in order to try if he could fix my inclination on fome profeffion that would keep me at home. Ever fince that time it has afforded me pleafure to fee good workmen handle their tools, and I have often experienced the utility of what I had picked up in this manner, by its enabling me to do little jobs for myfelf when there were no workmen at hand, and to conftruct fmall machines for my experiments at the moment when the ideas I wifhed to realize were frefh and ftrongly imprinted on my mind.

My father at laft refolved to make me a cutler; he fent me a few days on trial, to Samuel, fon of my uncle Benjamin, who, after learning this trade in London, had lately fettled in Bofton; but the fum he exacted as my apprentice fee, not being agreeable to my father, I was again taken home.

From my infancy I was fond of reading, and I laid out in books all the little money I could procure. I was particularly delighted with relations contained in voyages; my firft acquifition was Bunyan's Works in fmall feparate volumes. I afterwards fold this, in order to enable me to purchafe the Hiftorical Collection, by R. Button, which confifted of about forty or fifty little cheap volumes.

The fmall library belonging to my father, confifted principally of books of practical and polemical divinity; I read the greateft part of them. I have often regretted, that, at a time, when I had fo great a thirft for knowledge, fome better books did not fall into my hands, as it was decided that I was not to

belong

belong to the church. He had alfo the lives of Plutarch, in which I read much; and I ftill confider the time fpent in perufing them, as well employed. I likewife found a work of Daniel de Foe, entitled *an effay on projects*, from which I received impreffions that may perhaps have influenced fome of the principal events of my life.

My inclination for books at length determined my father to make a printer of me, although one of his fons was already in that profeffion. My brother James had returned from England in 1717, with a prefs and types, in order to eftablifh a printing-houfe at Bofton. This bufinefs was much more agreeable to me than that of my father, although I had ftill a predilection for the fea. To prevent the effects that might refult from this inclination, my father was impatient to fee me bound apprentice to my brother. I refufed a long while; at length I allowed myfelf to be perfuaded, and figned my indentures at twelve years of age. It was agreed that I fhould ferve as an apprentice till I was one and twenty, and fhould only receive wages as a workman during the laft year.

In a fhort time I made great progrefs in this bufinefs, and became an ufeful affiftant to my brother. I had now an opportunity of procuring better books; the connections that I neceffarily had with the apprentices of bookfellers, enabled me now and then to borrow fome volumes from them, which I always returned very punctually and uninjured. How often have I paffed the greater part of the night reading in my chamber, when a book had been lent me in the evening, which it was neceſſary to return in the morning, left it ſhould be perceived to be miſſing, or ſhould be enquired after!

At length, a merchant of the name of Matthew Adams, a man of ſome abilities, and poſſeſſed of a good collection of books, who uſed to come frequently to our printing-houſe, paid ſome attention to me ; he invited me to ſee his library, and had the goodneſs to lend me ſuch books as I wiſhed to read. I was at this time ſeized with a ſtrong inclination for poetry, and compoſed ſeveral trifles in verſe. My brother imagining that he might find his account in it, encouraged me, and engaged me to compoſe two ballads ; the one called the *Tragedy of Pharoah*, contained an account of the ſhipwreck of Captain Worthilake and his two daughters ; the other was a ſailor's ſong, on the capture of a famous pirate, named Teach, or Black-Beard ; they were wretched in point of ſtyle ; mere blind-men's ditties. After they were printed, my brother ſent me to hawk them about the town ; the firſt had a prodigious run, becauſe it related a recent and much-talked-of event.

Succeſs flattered my vanity, but my father depreſſed my courage, by ridiculing my performances, and telling me, that verſe-makers were always poor. Thus I eſcaped the misfortune of being a poet, probably a very bad one ; but as the talent of writing in proſe has been of great utility to me in the courſe of my life, and has principally contributed to my advancement, I ſhall now recount to you, by what means,

C   in

in the fituation I then was, I acquired what fmall degree of ability I may poffefs in that line.

There was another young man in the town, a great lover of books alfo, called John Collins, with whom I was intimately acquainted. We had frequent difputes with each other; we loved argument, and liked nothing better than to be by the ears together. This contentious turn of mind, by the bye, is apt to become a very bad habit, which often renders a perfon infupportable in company, becaufe it can only be exercifed through the medium of contradiction; and, befides the animofity and trouble which it occafions in converfation, it frequently produces diflike, and even enmities, between thofe who have the greateft occafion to cultivate each others friendfhip. I acquired this turn at firft, by reading books on polemical divinity, when I lived with my father. I have fince obferved, that fenfible people rarely fall into this error, except thofe who belong to the law, the wranglers of the univerfity, and men of all profeffions who have received their education at Edinburgh.

There arofe one day, I know not how, a difpute between Collins and me, relative to the education of women; namely, whether it was proper that they fhould be inftructed in the fciences, and if they had talents to profit by ftudy? He fupported the negative, and afferted that that line was above their powers. He was naturally more eloquent than me; words flowed in abundance from his mouth; and fometimes in my own opinion, I was vanquifhed

more

more embarraffing to thofe againft whom I employed it.

I foon took much delight in it, and practifed it on all occafions ; and I became dextrous in obtaining, even from thofe who were much my fuperiors in point of knowledge, conceffions of whofe confequences they themfelves were not aware. I thus embaraffed them in difficulties, from which they could not extricate themfelves, and often obtained victories neither due to my caufe, nor to my arguments.

I continued to ufe this mode of difputation during feveral years ; however, I gave it up by degrees, only preferving the habit of expreffing myfelf in terms of diffidence and modefty; and when I advanced any doubtful pofition, I was careful never to ufe the words *certainly, undoubtedly,* or any other that might convey the idea of obftinate attachment to my own opinion. I would rather fay, *I conceive, or I fuppofe fuch a thing may be fo,* it *appears to me that I fhould think fo or fo, for fuch or fuch reafons ;* or, *I imagine it may be thus or thus, if I am not deceived.* This habit I think has been very ufeful to me, when I have been defirous of impreffing my opinions on the minds of other men, or of perfuading them to adopt meafures, which I have from time to time propofed to them ; and fince the chief ends of converfation are to *inform, or to be informed ; to pleafe,* or *to perfuade ;* I earneftly defire, that enlightened and well-meaning men, may not voluntarily diminifh the power which they poffefs of doing good,

C 4   by

by a pofitive and prefumptuous manner of expreffing
themfelves, which never fails to difguft their hearers,
to excite oppofition, and to deftroy all the purpofes,
for which fpeech has been beftowed on man.

In a word, if you are defirous of inftructing others,
a pofitive and dogmatical manner of advancing your
opinion, ferves only to provoke contradiction, and
to prevent you from being liftened to with attention,
If with a wifh to learn, and to profit from the
knowledge of others, you exprefs yourfelf as one
ftrongly attached to your own opinions, modeft and
fenfible men, who are averfe to conteft, will probably allow you to remain in peaceable poffeffion of your
errors.   In following fuch a method, you can rarely
hope to pleafe your auditors, fo as to conciliate their
good will, or to perfuade fuch as you are defirous of
inducing to concur with you, in your intentions. Pope
judicioufly obferves, that

> " Men muft be taught as if you taught them not,
> " And things unknown propos'd as things forgot."

He alfo advifes

> " To fpeak, tho' fure, with feeming diffidence,"

He might here have added a line, which he has inferted in another place, in my opinion, with lefs
propriety.

> " For want of modefty is want of fenfe."

If you afk, why I fay with lefs propriety ? I will
mention the two lines together :

> " Immodeft words admit of no defence,
> " For want of modefty is want of fenfe."

But

But is not the want of fenfe, when a man has the misfortune to be in that predicament, a fort of apo-logy for the want of modefty ? And would not thefe lines be more confonant to truth were they written thus :

Immodeft words, admit *but this defence*
That want of modefty is want of fenfe.

This, however, I refer to thofe who are better judges of thefe matters than I can pretend to be,

CHAP,

C H A P. II.

Young Franklin is eager to acquire Literary Reputation—He sends some anonymous Essays to his Brother's News-paper— The Origin of his Aversion to Arbitrary Power—He becomes discontented with his Situation—Leaves Boston—Embarks for New-York at the age of Seventeen—Arrives there, and sets out soon after for Philadelphia—Saves the life of a Dutchman—A Dissertation concerning the Pilgrim's Progress, written by the celebrated John Bunyan—Our Author cures himself of a Fever by drinking cold Water—Some Account of Dr. Brown—Arrival in PHILADELPHIA.

MY brother resolved in 1720 or 1721, to set up a news-paper ; it was the second that had been printed in America, and was entitled, " The New England Courant ;" the only one that ever appeared before, was the " Boston News-Letters." I recollect very well, that some of his friends wished to dissuade him from this enterprize, representing it as a scheme that in all human probability would prove unsuccessful, because, according to them, a single news paper was sufficient for all America. Notwithstanding this, there are now (in 1771) no less than twenty-five.

He however carried his project into execution, and I was employed in distributing the papers among his customers, after having assisted in printing and working them off.

There were a few ingenious men of my brother's acquaintance, who amused themselves by writing little

essays

effays for his paper, and this circumftance not only added to the credit, but augmented the fale of it. Thefe gentlemen often called upon us ;. I liftened to their converfation with great eagernefs, and heard them exult at the good reception which their writings received from the public. I was tempted to afpire to the fame kind of reputation ; but as I was ftill a boy, I naturally enough concluded that my brother would not infert any thing of which he knew me to be the author. I refolved therefore to difguife my hand-writing, and having drawn up an anonymous fpecu-lation, I put it that very night under the printing-houfe door. It was found next morning, and imme-diately communicated to the little literary club ; they read it in my own hearing, and I enjoyed the exquifite fatisfaction of knowing that it had obtained their ap-probation, and, that among their various conjectures concerning the author, they did not indicate a fingle perfon who did not enjoy a great reputation for ge-nius and abilities in the province. At prefent I am inclined to fuppofe that I was extremely lucky in my judges, and that they were not fo excellent as I be-lieved them to be. Encouraged, however, by their ap-plaufe, I wrote and fent to the prefs in the fame man-ner, feveral other papers of my compofition. all of which were alfo approved of, and I preferved my fe-cret until my little ftock of ideas was completely ex-haufted,

My brother from that moment began to have a lit-tle more refpect for me ; but he ftill looked upon himfelf as my mafter, continued to treat me as an ap-prentice,

prentice, and infifted on receiving the fame fervices from me as if I had been an utter ftranger. I, on the other hand, imagined that he required too much from me in many cafes, and thought myfelf intitled to more indulgence on the part of a brother. Our difputes were often referred to my father, and I am inclined to think that the other was either for the moft part in the wrong, or that I was the better advocate of the two ; for judgment was commonly declared in my favour : But my brother, who was choleric, ftill continued to ftrike me, a circumftance which I took in great dudgeon,

I have been often fince induced to think, that this harfh and tyrannical treatment, contributed not a little to imprint in my mind, that averfion for arbitrary power which I have retained during the remainder of my life.

In a fhort time my apprenticefhip became fo infupportable, that I fighed after an opportunity to fhorten it ; at laft one prefented itfelf in a very unexpected manner. A paragraph inferted in our paper, concerning fome political fubject which I do not at prefent recollect, happened to give great offence to the affembly. My brother was arrefted, reprimanded, and imprifoned, by the fpeaker, becaufe, as I imagine, he would not give up the author. I myfelf was alfo taken into cuftody, and examined before the council ; but although I did not give any fatisfaction to its members, on the fubject concerning which I was queftioned, they contented themfelves with admonifhing

me,

me, confidering me perhaps as obliged, in quality of an apprentice, to preferve my mafter's fecrets inviolable.

. Notwithftanding our private quarrels, my brother's imprifonment infpired me with much refentment. While it continued I was intrufted with the direction of the paper, and I had the courage to infert fome bold obfervations upon the conduct of his profecutors. This circumftance gave great fatisfaction to him, but his adverfaries began to look upon me in an unfavourable point of view, and to confider me as a dangerous young man, much given to libels.

The enlargement of my brother was accompanied by a very ftrange order from the affembly, directing, that " James Franklin fhould no longer print the news-paper, entitled, The New England Courant."

On this he affembled all his friends in our printing-houfe, in order to confult what was proper to be done in this conjuncture. Some propofed to elude the fentence by altering the title of the news-paper ; but my brother perceiving great inconvenience in this fcheme, it was at length agreed, that it would be infinitely better to print it henceforth under the name of Benjamin Franklin; and in order to evade the vengeance of the affembly, which might overwhelm him, under pretence of ftill printing this news-paper, through the intervention of his apprentice, it was decided that my inden-tures fhould be given up, with a complete and final dif-charge at the back of it, fo that it might be produced by me in cafe of neceffity ; but, that in order to infure to my brother the benefit arifing from my fervices, I fhould fign a new contract for the unexpired part of

3

the

the term, which fhould be kept fecret. This was a very frail arrangement. It was, however, inftantly put in execution, and the paper, in confequence of it, was printed for feveral months under my name.

At length, another quarrel having' taken place between my brother and me, I was determined to make ufe of my newly-acquired liberty, prefuming that he would not dare to produce the engagement into which I had recently entered. It was not honeft, however, on my part, to make ufe of this advantage; and I, in confequence, look upon this action as one of the firft errors that I committed ; but the irregularaity of it made but little impreffion on my mind, embittered as it was by refentment, on account of the blows which my brother's anger had often induced him to make me experience, although in other. refpects his difpofition was not naturally bad; perhaps my anfwers were fuch as to give him fufficient provocation.

When he perceived that I was refolved to leave him, he endeavoured to prevent me from working any where elfe ; he accordingly went to all the printing-houfes in the town, and prepoffeffed the mafter-printers againft me, who confequently refufed to give me any employment.

I then determined to repair to New-York, which was the neareft town where there was a prefs. After long confideration, I was confirmed in my defign of leaving Bofton, where I had already rendered myfelf odious to government. It appeared to me to be very likely, after the arbitrary proceedings of the affembly againft my brother, that any longer ftay there might

3   expofe

expofe me to embarraffments, and I had ftill greater
reafon to fear this, as my indifcreet difputes concerning religion, made me begin already to be looked
upon with horror by the *faithful*, who confidered me
as an Apoftate, or an Atheift.

· I accordingly came to a determination ; but my father being for this once on my brother's fide, I prefumed that if I departed openly, they would take the
proper means to prevent me.

My friend Collins undertook to affift me in my
flight. He made a bargain for my paffage with the
captain of a floop, belonging to New-York, to whom
he told that I was a young man of his acquaintance
who had an intrigue with a woman of bad character,
whofe relations wifhed to force him to marry her, and
that in confquence, I neither dared to appear, nor to
depart publicly.

I fold part of my books in order to procure a fmall
fum of money, and I then repaired fecretly on board
the floop. By means of a good wind I found myfelf
in three days at New-York, 300 miles diftant from
the place of my nativity, at the age of feventeen,
without the leaft recommendation, without even
knowing a fingle perfon in that town, and with a very
fcanty fupply of money in my pocket.

The attachment I had once formed to the life of a
failor was entirely evaporated, elfe I might now have
fatisfied my propenfity in favour of that occupation ;
but having another trade, and thinking myfelf a good
workman, I did not hefitate to offer my fervices to
the only printer in this town, old Mr. William Bradford,

ford, who had been fettled in Pennfylvania, but had quitted that province, on account of a quarrel with Governor Keith. He could not give me any employment, having but little to do, and being already provided with a fufficient number of men; but he told me that his fon, who was a printer in Philadelphia, had fome time fince loft his principal workman, Aquila Rofe, and that if I went there, he believed I might be employed by him.

Philadelphia is one hundred miles from New-York, but I did not hefitate to embark on board a fmall veffel, in order to repair by the fhorteft cut to Amboy, leaving my trunk and effects behind, which were to come to me by a circuitous voyage. In croffing the Bay we experienced a gale of wind that tore all our fails, which, by the bye, were very rotten, prevented us from entering the Schuylkill, and obliged us to bear away for Long-Ifland.

During the ftorm, a drunken Dutchman, who was a paffenger as well as myfelf, fell over-board. At the moment he plunged into the fea, I feized hold of him by the hair of his head, and drew him towards the veffel, fo that with a little help I contrived to get him once more on board. This immerfion feemed to make him a little more fober, and he foon after fell afleep, having firft pulled a book out of his pocket, which he begged me to dry for him; this happened to be a tranflation of my old favourite Bunyan into low Dutch; it was an excellent impreffion, on fuperfine paper, with copper-plate prints; a more favourable appearance than I had ever feen it affume in the original.

original. I have fince learned, that it has been tranflated into moft of the European languages, and I am
perfuaded, that, after the Bible, it is one of the books
which has been moft in circulation.

Honeft John is the firft I know of, who has mingled narrative and dialogue together; a mode of
writing very engaging to the reader, who in the moft
interefting paffages, finds himfelf admitted, as it
were, into the company, and prefent at the converfation. Defoe has imitated him with fuccefs in his Ro-
binfon Crufoe, his Moll Flanders, and feveral other
works, and Richardfon has done the fame in his
Pamela, &c.

On approaching Long-Ifland we found ourfelves
unable to land, on account of the furf on that part
of the coaft, which proved to be very rocky. We
therefore caft anchor and veered out our cable, fo as to
bring us as near as poffible to the fhore ; fome of the
inhabitants came down towards the fea-fide, and hailed
us, as we did them ; but the wind was fo ftrong and
the waves fo boifterous, that we could not underftand
one another. We perceived feveral fmall boats, and
we made figns, and defired them to come with one
of thefe and take us from on board, but they either
did not comprehend us, or our requeft appeared impracticable to them, for they foon after retired.

Night now approached, and nothing elfe was left for
us but to have patience until the wind abated ; in expectation of this event, the pilot and I determined, if
poffible, to get a little fleep. In order to accomplifh
this, we retired between the hatches, and rejoined the

.D   Dutchman

Dutchman, who was still wet. The waves, however, which now and then broke over the veffel, ran through the feams of the little quarter deck in such a manner, that we were foon nearly as much drenched as himfelf. We had but little repofe during the night, but the wind having become a little lefs violent next morning, we fucceeded in reaching Amboy before the evening, after having been thirty hours deftitute of provifions and deprived of any other nourifhment than a bottle of bad rum, the water on which we failed being falt.

I retired to bed early, with a very violent fever. I had fomewhere read, that cold water drunk in abundance, was an excellent remedy on this occafion : I accordingly followed the prefcription, and having fweated copioufly during the greateft part of the night, the fever left me.

Next morning I paffed the ferry, and continued my journey on foot. I had fifty miles to travel before I reached Burlington, where I had been told I fhould find a boat that would carry me to Philadelphia. It rained hard during the whole day, and I was wet to the fkin. Finding myfelf extremely fatigued about noon, I ftopped at a miferable public-houfe, where I paffed the reft of the day, and the enfuing night. I now almoft began to regret that I had ever left home, for my appearance was fuch, that I was fufpected of being a runaway fervant; this I perceived by the queftions put to me, and I began to think that I ran fome rifk of being arrefted as fuch. I however continued my journey next morning, without interruption,

tion, arrived on the fame evening within eight or ten miles of Burlington, and took up my quarters at an inn kept by a perfon who paffed by the name of Dr. Brown.

This man entered into converfation with me, during fupper, and finding that I had read a little, he teftified the livelieft friendfhip for, and intereft in my behalf: our acquaintance continued during the remainder of his life. I imagine that he had been what is commonly termed a Quack Doctor, for there was not a fingle city in England, or indeed in any country in Europe, of which he could not give fome defcription. He poffeffed a certain degree of learning and genius, but he was an Infidel; and a few years after, he wickedly attempted to turn the Bible into burlefque metre, as Cotton had formerly *traveftied* Virgil. By thefe means he reprefented a number of facts under a ridiculous point of view; this circumftance might have given great offence to weak minds, if his work had been publifhed, but it never made its appearance. I fpent that evening at his houfe, and reached Burlington next morning.

I had the mortification to learn, that the ufual paffage boats had fet off fome time before my arrival. This was on a Saturday, and there would not be a fimilar opportunity before the following Tuefday. I inftantly returned towards an old woman's houfe, who had fold me fome gingerbread, which I intended to have ate upon the water, and of her demanded what was to be done? She invited me to lodge with her, until fome new occafion fhould prefent itfelf, of embarking on board a veffel bound for Philadelphia; being greatly fatigued with travelling fo far on foot, I accepted her kind offer, When fhe heard that I was a printer, fhe endeavoured to prevail upon me to remain at Burlington, in order to follow my trade there. She was ignorant of the fums to be advanced, and the capital neceffary for carrying it on! I found true hofpitality under her roof. She gave me, with a very good grace, a dinner compofed of ox-cheek, and would accept nothing in return, but a pint of ale,

I thought myfelf fixed here until next Tuefday, but happening to walk that very evening on the banks of the river, I perceived a boat bound to Philadelphia, in which there was a great number of paffengers. They received me inftantly on board, and as there was little or no wind, we made ufe of our oars, Not being able to defcry the city, towards midnight feveral of our company affured us that we had paffed it, and would row no longer; the others not being pofitive as to our fituation, it was decided that we fhould proceed no farther; we accordingly made towards the fhore, entered a creek, and landed near an old palifade, the wood of which ferved us to make a fire, as the night (it being in the month of October) was exceedingly cold,

We remained here until day light; a perfon in company then recollected that the place where we had fpent the night, was called Sooper's Creek, a little above Philadelphia, which we foon after difcovered.

covered. We arrived there on Sunday, about eight or nine o'clock in the morning, and landed at the Quay in Market-Street.

I have thus entered into all the minute details of the voyage, and I shall describe, in the same manner, whatever occurred to me, on my first arrival in that city, so that you may be enabled to compare such very unlikely beginnings with the figure I afterwards made there.

CHAP.

C H A P. III.

—Franklin arrives at Philadelphia, deflitute both of Money and
Friends—He purchafes fome Bread, which he eats in the
Street—in this Situation he has a glimpfe of his future
Wife—He is employed in a Printing-Houfe—Some Account
of Keimer his Mafter—He becomes acquainted with the
Governor of Pennfylvania—Goes back to Bofton—Returns to
Philadelphia—Is accompanied by Collins—Their Quarrel
and Separation.

WHEN I arrived at Philadelphia, I was in my
working drefs, my beft clothes being in my
trunk, which was to come round from New-York,
by fea. I was befides very dirty, in confequence of being fo long in the boat; my pockets too were
crammed with fhirts and ftockings, and I am fure that
I muft have made a very ftrange figure.

To add to my mortification, I did not know a
fingle perfon in the town, and was even ignorant
where I could find a lodging. I was extremely fatigued on account of having rowed during the whole
night; I was alfo very hungry, and all the money I
had in the world, confifted of a fingle dollar, and
about a fhilling in half-pence, which I gave to the
boatmen. They refufed it at firft, becaufe I had
helped them; but I infifted on their accepting it. A
man is fometimes more generous when he has but
little money, than when he has a great deal : The
reafon

reafon of this perhaps is, that on fuch an occafion he is defirous of concealing his poverty. —

I proceeded towards the end of the ftreet, examining both fides of it at the fame time, with the utmoft attention, until I arrived at Market-Street, where I met a boy carrying fome bread in his hand. I had often made an entire meal of dry bread. I afked him where he had purchafed it, and went ftraight to the baker's, which he pointed out with his finger. I inftantly called for two or three bifcuits, thinking to find fome of the fame fpecies we had at Bofton; but I was informed that none of that kind was to be found at Philadelphia. I then afked for a three-penny loaf, but I was told that they had not any at that price. Being entirely ignorant of the different prices and kinds of bread made in this part of the country, I defired them to give me three-pence worth of bread, of whatever fort they pleafed. On this I got three large loaves; I was furprifed at receiving fo many, but took them neverthelefs, and having no empty room in my pockets, I continued my walk, with a loaf under each arm; as to the other, I held it in my hand while I ate it. In this manner I paffed along Market-Street, arrived at Fourth-Street, and paraded before the houfe of Mr. Read, the father of the young woman who was afterwards my wife. She happened at that very moment to be at the door, and had good reafon to think that I made a very fantaftical appearance.

After this I turned the corner into Chefnut-Street, eating my bread all the way, and having thus made a circuit, I found myfelf once more upon the Quay in Market-Street, within a few yards of the boat in which I had arrived. I defcended a few fteps in order to drink fome of the water of the river, and finding myfelf entirely fatisfied with my firft loaf, I beftowed the other two on a woman, who, with her fon, had been my companions on our excurfion by water.

Being now refrefhed, I again wandered along the ftreet. It was then filled with a number of perfons, all of whom were very neatly dreffed, and walked after one another, in a decent and orderly manner, always keeping the fame fide of the way. I immediately joined and accompanied them to the Quaker's meeting-houfe, near the Market. I fat down as the others did, and after having fpent fome time in looking around me, without hearing a fingle word uttered, being exceedingly fatigued with my labour, and want of reft during the preceeding night, I fell into a profound fleep. I remained in this fituation until the affembly feparated, when one of the affiftants had the complaifance to awaken me. This confequently was the firft houfe which I entered, or in which I flept, after my arrival in Philadelphia.

I now once more regained the ftreet, and continued to walk along the fide of the river; during my progrefs I attentively examined the faces of all the paffengers whom I met, and at length fixed upon a young Quaker, whofe phyfiognomy pleafed me: I accordingly accofted and befought him to inform me where a ftranger might be able to find a lodging?

We

We were then exactly oppofite the fign of the *Three Sailors.* "They receive ftrangers there," fays he, pointing out the place at the fame time with his finger, "but the houfe is not of good repute; if thou "wilt accompany me, I will fhow thee a better one." He accordingly conducted me to the *Crooked Billet* in Water-Street.

There I ordered a dinner, and while I was eating it, the people of the houfe put feveral queftions to me. My youth and appearance led them to fuppofe that I was a fugitive. After dinner my inclination to fleep returned again; a bed was accordingly prepared for me; I caft myfelf upon it, without undrefsing, and flept till fix o'clock at night, when they awakened and called me to fupper. After that I returned to bed at a very early hour, and flept without interruption, until the next morning.

As foon as I arofe I dreffed myfelf as well as pofsible, and repaired to the houfe of Andrew Bradford, the printer. I found his father, whom I had feen at New-York, in the fhop, and who by making the journey on horfe back, had arrived before me at Philadelphia. He prefented me to his fon, who received me in a very kind manner, and invited me to breakfaft; but he informed me, that he had no occafion for a workman at that time, being provided with one a little before. He added that there was another printer of the name of Keimer in the town, who had juft entered into bufinefs, and who might perhaps employ me; and in cafe of his refufing to do fo, he himfelf would moft willingly give me a lodging, and

3   a

a little work from time to time, until fomething bet=
ter might occur.

The old man offered of his own accord to conduct
me to the new printer's, and when, we had arrived
there, "Neighbour," fays he to him, "I have
"brought you a young man of your profeffion ; per=
"haps you may ftand in need of his fervices." Keimer
put a few queftions to me, placed a *compofing ftick* in
my hand, in order to fee in what manner I worked,
and then faid that he would give me employment in a
fhort time, but that at prefent he had no occafion
for me.

Looking upon old Bradford to be a perfon who
wifhed him well, and was defirous to ferve him, he
began to converfe with him about his prefent enterprife, and his future profpects. Bradford was careful
not to difcover himfelf to be the father of the other
printer, and as foon as Keimer told him, that he
hoped in a fhort time to have the greateft part of the
bufinefs of the town in his own hands, he by means
of feveral cunning interrogations and artificial doubts,
led him to difclofe the foundation of his hopes, and
the manner in which he intended to proceed. I was
prefent at, and heard the whole of this converfation,
and I was not long in difcovering that one of them
was an old fox, and the other a filly novice.
Bradford foon after departed and left me with Keimer,
who was exceedingly furprifed when I informed him
what and who the old man was.

I found that Keimer's printing utenfils confifted of
an old damaged prefs, and a fecond-hand fount of
Englifh

Englifh types, pretty much ufed, and which he himfelf employed at that very time in compofing an elegy
on Aquila Rofe, whom I have mentioned before.

This young man, who, to great abilities, united a
moft excellent chara&er, had been much beloved and
efteemed in the town: He was fecretary to the affembly, and had a very fine turn for poetry. Keimer
alfo made verfes, but they did not rife above medi-
ocrity. He could not, indeed, be faid with propriety,
to *write* verfes ; for it was cuftomary with him to
compofe them with his types, juft as they ftruck his
imagination, and as he worked without any copy,
had no more than one pair of cafes, and the elegy
was likely to occupy all his *letter*, it was impoffible
for any one to affift him. I undertook to put his
prefs, of which he had not as yet made any ufe, and
concerning which he was entirely ignorant, into
proper order, and having promifed to come back and
work off his elegy, as foon as it fhould be ready, I returned to Mr. Bradford's, who gave me fome trifle
to employ myfelf upon for the moment, and alfo my
bed and board.

A few days after this, Keimer fent for me, in order
to work off his elegy. He had by that time procured another pair of cafes, and a pamphlet to re-
print, upon which he inftantly employed me.

Both the printers of Philadelphia appeared to me
to be totally deftitute of the qualities neceffary to infure fuccefs in their profeffion. Bradford had never
been brought up to the bufinefs, and was exceedingly
illiterate. Keimer was a little better educated, but
he

he was no more than a fimple compofitor, and underftood nothing at all of prefs-work. He had been one
of the *French Prophets*, and he knew how to imitate
their fupernatural agitations. At this period of
our acquaintance, he profeffed no particular religion
whatever, but a little of all at times; he was very
ignorant of the world, and had a great deal of guile
in his heart, as I had occafion afterwards to difcover.

Keimer was very unhappy that I lodged at Bradford's, while I worked for him. He was indeed in
poffeffion of a whole houfe, but it was entirely deftitute of moveables, fo that it was impoffible for him
to accommodate me there. He procured me a lodging, however, at Mr. Read's; whom I mentioned before, and who was the landlord of his houfe.

My trunk and effects, having arrived at this time,
I dreffed myfelf fo as to appear before Mifs Read, in
a better plight than when chance firft difcovered
me to her, eating a loaf, and wandering along the
ftreets.

I now began to form an acquaintance among fuch
of the young men in the town as were fond of reading, and I fpent many very agreeable nights in their
company; I was at the fame time enabled to gain a
good deal of money by my induftry, and to live very
well and very contented, thanks to my frugality.
Thus I endeavoured to forget Bofton as much as poffible, and did not wifh that the place of my nativity
fhould be known to any perfon except my friend
Collins, with whom I kept up a conftant correfpondence, and who faithfully preferved my fecret.

A cir-

A circumſtance, however, occurred fooñ after that made me return home much fooner than I had at firſt propoſed. I had a brother-in-law of the name of Robert Holmes who was maſter of a ſloop, employed as a coaſter between Boſton and the Delaware. Finding himſelf at Newcaſtle, forty miles below Philadelphia, he there happened to hear of me, and wrote me a letter, in which he informed me of the ſorrow, which my precipitate departure from Boſton had occaſioned to my parents, and of the great affection they ſtill entertained towards me, aſſuring me at the fame time, that every thing would be accommodated to my entire ſatisfaction provided I returned, a proceeding, which he moſt earneſtly exhorted me to. In my reply to his letter, I thanked him for his good advice, but I at the fame time ſpecified the reaſons which had induced me to leave Boſton, with ſo much force and precifion, that he was convinced I was not ſo much in the wrong as he had at firſt imagined.

Sir William Keith, governor of the Province, was at this very time at Newcaſtle. Captain Holmes happening accidentally to be in his company, when he received my letter, took advantage of that opportunity to ſpeak warmly in my favour, and even to ſhow it to him. The governor read it, and appeared aſtoniſhed, when he learned my extreme youth. He obſerved that I was a young man, of whom great expectations might be juſtly formed; that I ought to be encouraged; that the printers in Philadelphia were all very ignorant in reſpect to their
buſineſs;

bufinefs ; that if I were eftablifhed there, there could
be no manner of doubt of my fuccefs, and that for
his part he would employ me to print for the government, and would do me every other fervice in his
power. My brother-in-law afterwards recounted all
thefe particulars to me at Bofton, but I was entirely
ignorant of them at the time.

One day as Keimer and I happened to be at work
together near the window, we perceived the governor
and another gentleman, who proved to be Colonel
French of Newcaftle, both very elegantly dreffed.
They came ftraight towards our houfe, and in a
few fecònds we heard them both at the door.
Keimer thinking the vifit intended for him, immediately went down ftairs to receive them, but the governor, after afking for me, afcended to the apartment
where I was ftationed, and with a politenefs and con-
defcenfion to which I had been hitherto unaccuf-
tomed, paid me many compliments, defired to be better acquainted with me, reproached me for not
making myfelf known to him on my arrival, and
infifted on my accompanying him to a tavern in
order to drink a glafs of Madeira with him and the
Colonel.

I muft acknowledge that I was not a little furprifed
at the honour now done me ; and as for Keimer, he
appeared in a ftate of ftupefaction.

I, however, accompanied the governor and his
friend, to a tavern at the corner of Third ftreet,
where he propofed over a glafs of wine, that I fhould
eftablifh a printing houfe. He infifted on the probability

bability of my fuccefs, and both he and Colonel, French affured me, that I might depend upon their influence and protection, and that they would unite their efforts, in order to procure me all the public bufinefs of this and the adjacent province. When I expreffed my doubts of my father's affifting me in this enterprize, Sir William told me, that he would give me a letter to him, and that he had no manner of doubt but that he would comply with his requeft. It was accordingly determined that I fhould return to Bofton by the firft veffel that failed for that port, with a letter of recommendation from the governor to my father. In the mean time, it was agreed, that this project fhould remain fecret, and that I fhould continue to work for Keimer as ufual.

The governor invited me to dine with him, from time to time; I looked upon this as a very great honour, and I was fo much the more fenfible of it, as he converfed with me in the moft affable, familiar, and amicable manner that could be imagined.

Towards the conclufion of the month of April, 1724, a fmall veffel prefented itfelf for Bofton; on this I took leave of Keimer, as if my intentions had been merely to return in order to fee my parents. The governor prefented me with a long letter, in which he communicated the moft flattering accounts of me to my father, and ftrongly recommended the project of eftablifhing me at Philadelphia, a plan which, according to his opinion, could not fail to make my fortune.

3   In

In defcending the river our veffel ftruck upon a fand bank, and fprung a leak; the weather was alfo ftormy, and the fea tempeftuous: in fhort we were obliged to make ufe of the pump without intermiffion, I myfelf working at it in my turn. We arrived, however, fafe and found at Bofton, at the end of fifteen days.

I had been abfent feven whole months, and during all that time, my parents had heard nothing of me, for my brother in law Holmes was not as yet returned, and had not written any thing to my friends concerning me. My unexpected appearance aftonifhed the whole family. All, however, except my brother, were charmed at my return, and came to bid me welcome. I went to fee him at his Printing-office; I was much better dreffed than I had ever been during the time I was in his fervice: I had on a complete new fuit of clothes, a watch and upwards of five guineas of ready money in my pocket. He did not receive me very kindly, for after examining me from head to foot, he applied himfelf again to his work.

The workmen afked me with great eagernefs, where I had been? what fort of a country it was? and how I liked it? I boafted much of Philadelphia, and the happy life that I led there, expreffing at the fame time my earneft intention of returning. One of them having enquired what kind of money was common there, I inftantly drew forth a whole handful of filver, and fpread it before them; this circumftance wonderfully gratified their curiofity, paper money alone

being

being in circulation at Bofton. I did not fail after this to produce my watch, but, at.length, perceiving my brother to be in a bad humour, I gave them a dollar to drink my health. and took my leave. This vifit on my part, piqued him exceedingly; for, when my mother, a fhort time afterwards, fpoke of a reconciliation, and of the defire fhe had to fee us live together for the future, as brothers, he informed her, that I had infulted him in fuch a grofs manner before his workmen, that he would not either forget or forgive it, during the whole courfe of his life; but in this he deceived himfelf greatly.

The governor's letter, appeared to occafion fome furprife to my father; he, however, fpoke to me, but little on that fubject. At the end of a few days, Captain Holmes being returned, he fhewed it to him, afked if he knew Sir William Keith? and enquired what fort of a man he was? adding, that, in his opinion, he had but very little difcernment to think of an eftablifhment for a boy, who ftill wanted three years of being arrived at that age, when he could be properly termed a man.

Holmes faid every thing in his power, in favour of the project; but my father infifted in the moft decifive manner on the incongruity of the plan, and at length pofitively refufed to countenance it.

After this, he wrote a civil letter to Sir William, in which he returned him many thanks for the patronage and protection he had fo obligingly offered to his fon, but refufed to affift me, at leaft for the prefent, in the plan. that had

E been

been pointed out, becaufe, according to his opinion,
I was yet too young to be entrufted with the management of fuch an important enterprife, more efpecially
as the neceffary preparations would require a confiderable capital.

My old friend Collins, who was a clerk in the Poft
Office, charmed with the accounts which I had given
him of Philadelphia, conceived a prodigious inclination to go and refide there alfo; and while I was
waiting for my father's determination, he fet off before me by land for Rhode Ifland, ordering his books,
which formed an excellent collection of tracts on
Natural Philofophy and the Mathematics, to be carried along with my baggage to New York, where he
propofed to wait for me.

Although my father did not relifh the propofition
made to him by Sir William, he was yet exceedingly
pleafed that I had obtained the patronage and recommendation of a perfon of his rank, and that my induftry and œconomy had enabled me to equip myfelf in fuch a refpectable manner, in fo fhort a time.

Seeing no probability of an agreement between
my brother and myfelf, after confenting to my return to Philadelphia, he advifed me to endeavour to
acquire the regard of all the world, to treat every
body with refpect, and above all things to avoid
fatire and farcafm, to which he thought that I had
but too great an inclination, adding, that with prudence, œconomy, and perfeverance, I might be able
to fave a fufficient quantity of money, before I was
twenty-one years of age, to eftablifh myfelf in bufinefs ;

nefs; and that if I then fhould be in want of a fmall fum, he would readily undertake to fupply me. This was all I was able to obtain, except a few trifling prefents which he and my mother gave me, in token of their affection.

I now embarked once more for New-York, au-thorifed, at length, with their approbation and be-nediction. The floop which I was on board, having touched at Newport, Rhode-Ifland, I paid a vifit to my brother John, who had been married and fettled there for fome years.

He had always loved, and now received me with great affection. One of his friends, of the name of Vernon, happening to have a debt of about thirty-fix pounds fterling due to him in Pennfylvania, re-quefted me to get payment of it and to keep the mo-ney till he fhould inform me how to employ it; he accordingly gave me an order for that purpofe. This affair occafioned me much uneafinefs in the fequel.

At Newport we took on board a number of paf-fengers, among whom were two young women, who were acquainted with each other, and a female Quaker, who was very grave, and very fenfible. I evinced an inclination to do her every fervice in my power; I fuppofe fhe was confcious of my good in-tentions, and in confequence took an intereft in every thing that concerned me. In fine, when fhe perceived that a familiarity had taken place, and feemed to increafe daily, between the two other female paffen-gers and me, which they endeavoured by all manner

of

of means to encourage, fhe took me apart, and one
afternoon fpoke to me as follows :

"Young man, I am quite unhappy about thee ;
"thou haft no relations to watch over thy conduct,
"and thou doft not feem to be much acquainted
"with the world, and with thofe fnares to which thy
"youth and inexperience render thee liable! Thou
"mayeft depend on what I am about to tell thee :
"Thefe young women lead a diforderly life; I per-
"ceive it in all their actions. If thou art not upon
"thy guard, they will draw thee into fome fcrape.
"They are ftrangers to thee. I advife thee; therefore,
"by the friendly intereft, which I take in thy pre-
"fervation; not to form any acquaintance with
"them."

As I did not at firft appear to think fo badly
of them, as fhe did; fhe recounted a number of circumftances to me, which fhe had either feen or heard,
and which, although they had efcaped my attention,
convinced me that fhe was entirely in the right. I
accordingly thanked her for her obliging advice, and
promifed to follow her counfels.

When we arrived at New-York, they told me
where they refided, and requefted me to go and fee
them. I did not, however, accept of their invitation,
and in this I was perfectly right ; for, on the next day,
the captain perceiving that he had loft a filver fpoon,
and fome other trifles, which were fcattered about in
the cabin, and knowing that thefe two women were
proftitutes, he obtained a fearch warrant, went to
their apartments, and having there difcovered the
ftolen

ſtolen goods, he delivered them over to the civil power, in order to be puniſhed according to law. Thus after having eſcaped a funken rock, on which the ſloop ſtruck in her paſſage, I alſo eſcaped in my own perſon from an infinitely more perilous ſhoal.

I found my old friend Collins at New-York; he had arrived there ſome time before me; we had been intimate ever ſince our infancy; we had read the fame books, and purſued the fame ſtudies together; but he had the advantage of being able to give up more of his time to thoſe purſuits, and to a paſſion for the mathematics, in which ſcience he left me far behind him.

When I reſided at Boſton, I was accuſtomed to ſpend moſt of my leiſure hours in company with him. He was at that time a ſober and induſtrious young man. His knowledge had conciliated general eſteem, both among the clergy and laity, and he ſeemed to promiſe to make a great figure in ſociety. But, during my abſence, he had unfortunately encouraged a paſſion for ſtrong liquors, brandy in particular, and I learned not only from the report of others, but from his own confeſſion, that he had got drunk every day ſince his arrival at New-York, and had conduct-ed himſelf in a very extravagant and diſorderly man-ner. He had alſo become fond of play, and loſt all his money, ſo that I was obliged to pay his bill for him at the inn in which he had reſided, and even to defray all his expences during the journey; this was a very great hardſhip upon me.

Mr.

Mr. Burnet, who was at that time Governor of New-York, having heard the captain obferve, that a young man, a paffenger on board his veffel, had a great number of books, requefted him to conduct me to his houfe. I accepted the invitation, and would have carried Collins along with me, if he had been fober. The governor received me with great polite-nefs, fhewed me his library, which was a very large one, and we talked a long time together about books and authors. This was the fecond governor who had honoured me with his attention; and to a poor boy, as I at that time was, thefe little adventures did not fail to be uncommonly agreeable.

We now fet off for Philadelphia: I procured the money that was due to Vernon, upon the road, and but for the aid of this fupply we fhould have been unable, without great difficulty, to have performed our journey.

Collins was defirous of being employed in fome merchant's counting-houfe; but although he had many excellent recommendations, either his breath or his countenance apparently betrayed the bad ha-bits that he had contracted, for he did not fucceed in any of his applications, fo that he continued to lodge and board along with me, and at my expence.

Knowing that I was in poffeffion of Vernon's mo-ney, he was continually begging a loan of part of it, always promifing to reimburfe me the moment he found employment. In fine, he prevailed upon me to give him fo much of it that I became exceedingly uneafy at the idea of what I fhould do, in cafe I fhould

be

be obliged to reftore the fum. His attachment for liquor did not in the leaft abate, and this circumftance contributed not a little to occafion a great coolnefs, and even difagreement between us; for when he had drank a little too much, he was exceedingly quarrelfome.

Happening one day to be in a boat on the Delaware, with fome other young men, he refufed to row in his turn.

" You fhall row me home," faid he, " to my " lodgings." " We fhall not row you an inch," replied I; " You fhall," added he, " or elfe re- " main all night upon the water!" " Come! come!" cried our companions, " what does it fignify whether " he rows or not?"

Being, however, exceedingly exafperated againft him, on account of his mean conduct, I continued to refufe to proceed any farther; on this, he fwore that if I did not row, he would throw me over-board. He accordingly proceeded towards me, walking at the fame time acrofs the benches.

As foon as he was within reach of me, I ftretched out my hand, feized hold of him by the breeches, and rifing up brifkly at the fame time, I threw him headforemoft into the river. I well knew that he was a good fwimmer, I was not therefore in the leaft apprehenfion for his life; in the mean while, before he was able to recover himfelf and board the boat, we got to a little diftance and entirely out of his reach, by means of our oars.

Every

Every time that he approached towards us, we afked him, if he would row ? and we gave him at the fame time a few ftrokes with our oars, in order to oblige him to defift from boarding us. He was nearly choaked with the excefs of his rage, and obftinately refufed to promife to affift us. Perceiving that his ftrength began to fail, we at length hauled him into the boat, and brought him home quite wet to his lodgings. After this adventure, our coolnefs augmented daily.

At length a captain of a veffel who traded to the Weft-Indies, and who was commiffioned to procure a tutor for the fon of a rich planter in Barbadoes, happening to fall in with him, propofed to carry him to that ifland, in order to fill that fituation. He accepted this offer and left me, with a promife to remit me part of his falary by way of repayment of the fum he ftood indebted to me, but I never afterwards received any intelligence whatever concerning him.

CHAP.

CHAP. IV.

Our Author spends a Sum of Money intrusted to his Care—
Curious Anecdote relative to Cod-Fish—Project for estab-
lishing a new Sect—Some Account of a Vegetable Diet—
A Poetical Contest—He is still patronised by the Governor—
Departs from Philadelphia—Is grossly deceived by his Pa-
tron—Arrives in London—Presents his Letters of Credit—
Is extremely uneasy relative to his future Conduct in Life
—Some Account of Governor Sir William Keith.

THE appropriation of the sum of money deposited
in my hands, and belonging to Mr. Vernon, was
one of the first grand errors in my life, and this cir-
cumstance fully proves that my father was not much
deceived in his judgment, when he supposed me to be
as yet too young to be entrusted with the management of any business of importance. Sir William
Keith, however, on reading his letter, observed that
he was by far too prudent, that there was a great
difference between individuals, and, that as discretion
did not always accompany maturity of years, so youth
on the contrary was not always deprived of it.

" Since he will not contribute to your establish-
" ment, (continues he,) I will undertake to do it my-
" self. Give me a list of the various articles which
" are necessary to be brought from England, and I
" will send for them directly; you may reim-
" burse me, whenever your situation permits you.

" I

" I am determined to have a good printer here, and " I am fure that you will fucceed."

He fpoke this with fuch an appearance of cordiality and friendfhip, that I did not doubt for a fingle moment of the fincerity of his profeffions. I had hitherto been filent in Philadelphia, relative to his promifes, and I ftill continued to keep them a fecret. If it had been known that I relied upon the governor's word, doubtlefs I fhould have found fome friend better acquainted with his character than myfelf, who would have advifed me not to have trufted to it ; for I learned in the end, that he was well known to be very liberal in promifes, but that he always forgot to fulfil them. Having never folicited any favour from him, how was it poffible for me to have divined that his profeffions were infincere? I actually looked upon him as the beft man in the whole world.

I foon after prefented him with a lift of the articles · neceffary for a fmall printing-houfe, the expence of which might amount, according to my calculation, to about £.100 fterling. He approved of every thing, but afked me at the fame time, if my prefence would not be neceffary in England, in order to fuperintend the completion of his order ; to infpect and choofe the letter-prefs, and to take care that every article fhould be excellent in its kind ? " You will alfo be " able, (adds he,) to form a connexion there, and " eftablifh a correfpondence in the book and paper " lines."

I acknowledged that fuch a fcheme would be exceedingly advantageous. " That being the cafe," fays he,

I

he, " be fure to get every thing ready, in order to " proceed with the Anna."

This was the annual veffel, and the only one at that time which made regular voyages between London and Philadelphia ; but as fome months would elapfe previous to the failing of the Anna, I continued to work with Keimer. I was not, however, without great uneafinefs in refpect to·the fums which Collins had borrowed of me ; indeed I experienced the moft violent and continual fears in regard to Vernon, who, however, very luckily for me, did not demand his money until fome years afterwards.

I believe that I have omitted a little incident in the recital of my firft voyage from Bofton to Philadelphia, which I fhall now relate, becaufe it will not be altogether mifplaced here.

During a calm, which ftopped us exactly oppofite Block-ifland, our failors made the neceffary preparations in order to catch fome cod. Until that moment, I had perfifted in my refolution of never eating any thing that had life in it, and upon this occafion, full of the ideas of my mafter Tryon, I looked upon the taking of every fifh, as a fpecies of wanton murder, committed without any manner of provocation whatever, becaufe not one of them had ever done, or could ever do, the leaft poffible evil to any perfon, which could juftify fo cruel a maffacre! This manner of reafoning feemed to me to be unanfwerable ; but I had formerly been a great lover of fifh ; and when it came out of the frying pan, it had a moft inviting fmell!

I balanced

I balanced for fome time between my principles and my appetite, until I began to recollect, that on cutting up thefe very cod, I had perceived a multitude of little fifh, taken out of their ftomachs. On this I inftantly faid to myfelf, " If you thus devour one " another, I fee no manner of reafon why we fhould " not eat you!"

In confequence of this, I inftantly fat down to the cod-fifh, with a moft excellent appetite, and have continued ever fince to eat like the reft of the world, returning however, from time to time, and by intervals, to a vegetable diet.

How commodious it is to be a *reafonable creature*, who knows either how to find, or to invent arguments for juftifying every thing, he is defirous of doing! . . . . ,

, ... , ...

I lived in great friendfhip with Keimer, and we agreed exceedingly, becaufe he never once dreamed of my project of fetting up in bufinefs for myfelf. He ftill preferved a great part of his enthufiafm, and was uncommonly fond of argument ; we accordingly had frequent difputations together. I was fo accuftomed to puzzle him with my Socratic method, and had confounded him fo often by my queftions, which at firft appeared to be very far diftant from the point in agitation, and yet led to it, infenfibly embarraffing him in difficulties, and contradiction, which he could not get rid of, that he at length became ridiculoufly circumfpect. He accordingly would never make any reply to the moft fimple and familiar queftion,

queſtion, without firſt aſking me, " What do you
" pretend to infer from that ?"

Notwithſtanding this, he had formed ſuch a high
idea of my ability in refuting the arguments of an
adverſary, that he ſeriouſly propoſed to me, to be his
colleague in a project he had formed of eſtabliſhing
a new ſect. He was to preach the doctrines, and it
was to be my buſineſs to confound all our opponents.
However, when he began to explain himſelf to me,
relative to his *dogmas*, I perceived a great number of
whimſical conceits, which I refuſed to allow, at leaſt,
unleſs my own opinions were permitted to be mixed
with them ; in ſhort, I would not conſent to any
thing if he did not agree to adopt ſome of my principles.

Keimer wore his beard long, becauſe it is ſaid in
the law of Moſes, " Thou ſhalt not cut the corners
" of thy beard." He alſo ſtrictly obſerved the ſab-
bath or the ſeventh-day ; and theſe, according to him,
were two eſſential points.

They both diſpleaſed me ; notwithſtanding this, I
conſented to admit them upon the expreſs condition,
that he would agree to eſtabliſh it as a precept, not to
uſe any food appertaining to the animal kingdom. He
doubted greatly whether his conſtitution would be
able to ſupport ſuch a *regimen*, but I aſſured him on
the contrary, that it would greatly contribute to the
eſtabliſhment of his health.

· He was naturally an epicure, and I was determined
to do every thing in my power in order to mortify
his appetites.

He

He confented at length to try the *regimen* propofed, and I agreed to keep him company. We accordingly fubmitted ourfelves to it, during three whole months.

A woman in the neighbourhood, purchafed, cooked, and brought us our victuals ; I gave her a lift of upwards of forty difhes, which fhe was to prepare for us at different times, and into the compofition of which, neither fifh nor flefh was admitted. This fantaftical mode of life was the more agreeable to me, at this time, becaufe it was extremely cheap, for the expences of our houfe-keeping did not exceed eighteen-pence a week.

I have fince kept *Lent* many times in the fame manner, and nearly with the utmoft poffible ftrictnefs, and I have for the moft part fuddenly fubftituted this *regimen* to my ordinary food, without experiencing the leaft inconvenience ; this circumftance makes me look upon the advice generally given of accuftoming one'sfelf by degrees to the change of diet, as a matter of very little importance.

I continued in good health and fpirits, but poor Keimer fuffered greatly. He became in a fhort time quite weary of the enterprize, and began to figh after the *flefh-pots* of Egypt.

At length he ordered a fucking pig to be roafted, and invited me, along with two females of our acquaintance, to dine with him ; but the pig having been brought home a little fooner than was expected, he could not refift the temptation arifing from fo delicious tious a morfel, and actually devoured the whole, before our arrival.

In the mean time I paid great attention to Mifs Read. I had much affection and esteem for her, and I had fome reafon to believe that fhe entertained fimilar fentiments in regard to me. But we were both very young, neither of us being much above eighteen years of age; and as I was upon the point of taking a long voyage; her mother thought that it would not be prudent to permit our attachment to go any farther lengths at prefent, becaufe if we were to be married, it would be much more convenient that this ceremony fhould take place after my return, when, as I had given out, I was to be eftablifhed in bufinefs for myfelf. Perhaps fhe alfo thought that my expectations were not fo well founded as I imagined.

My principal companions at this time, were Charles Ofborne, Jofeph Watfon, and James Ralph, all of them very fond of reading. The two firft were clerks to, and lived with Mr. Charles Brockden, one the principal attornies in the town; the other was a clerk in a merchant's counting-houfe.

Watfon was a young man of great integrity, very pious and fenfible: The others were a little more relaxed in regard to their religious principles, particularly Ralph, whofe faith as well as that of Collins, had been ftaggered by myfelf; they both made me fuffer fufficiently afterwards, by way of punifhment for this conduct. Ofborne poffeffed great fenfibility, was frank and open in his conduct, and exceedingly attached to his

his friends, but he affected too much to be a critic in regard to literature.

Ralph was witty, genteel in his manners, and extremely eloquent. I never, in the whole course of my life, met with a more agreeable speaker. Both of them were paffionately attached to poetry, and had begun to compofe little fonnets, &c.

We four were accustomed to take very agreeable walks every Sunday, in the woods bordering on the Schuylkill. We read in common, and then conferred on the subject before us. Ralph feemed determined to give himfelf entirely up to the ftudy of poetry. He flattered himfelf that he fhould be able to make great progrefs in this career, and even to acquire a fortune by means of it. He pretended that the greateft poets, on their firft attempting to write, had committed as many miftakes as he himfelf had done.

. Ofborne endeavoured to diffuade him from it, affuring him at the fame time, that he did not poffefs a poetical genius, and advifed him above all things, to ftick by the profeffion to which he had been brought up.

"In the mercantile line," faid he, "you will "be able by means of your diligence and affiduity; "even without a capital, to procure employment as a "factor, and you may thus, in time, acquire fufficient "ftock to begin trade with upon your own account."

As for me, I approved greatly that he fhould amufe himfelf from time to time with poetry, but thought that this fhould be done merely with a view to attain perfection in the language.

It .

It was one day propofed, that each of us, at the next interview, fhould produce a piece of his own compofition in verfe. Our object in this experiment was to improve each other, by means of our obferva- tions, our criticifms, and our mutual corrections, and as the language and expreffion was all we had in view, we excluded every idea of invention, agreeing that our common tafk fhould be a verfion of the eighteenth Pfalm, in which the defcent of the Divinity is defcribed.

The epoch of our interview was juft at hand, when Ralph called upon me, and told me that his tafk was prepared. I informed him that I had been too indo- lent to perform mine, becaufe, having but little incli- nation towards that fpecies of literature, I had neg- lected to do any thing. On this, he produced the verfes which he had compofed, and afked me what I thought of them. I approved of them highly, becaufe they appeared to me to poffefs great and extra- ordinary merit.

On this he addreffed me thus: "Ofborne will " never allow the leaft credit to any thing of my " compofition; his envy always dictates a thou- " fand ill-natured criticifms upon it. He is not fo " jealous of you; I defire therefore that you will " take this, and prefent it as your own. I fhall pre- " tend not to have had time, and confequently fhall " not produce any thing: We fhall then fee what he " fays on this fubject." I immediately confented to this little piece of roguery, and inftantly tranfcribed

Ralph's taſk, in order to avoid the poſſibility of detection.

The day at length arrives, and we repair to the place of rendezvous.

Watſon's work was the firſt that was read. It poſſeſſed ſome beauties, but many defects. We then peruſed Oſborne's, it was far ſuperior; Ralph did great juſtice to it, for while he animadverted upon a few faults, he applauded its numerous perfections. He had nothing to produce, and it was now my turn.

I made a number of difficulties, and ſeemed deſirous of being excuſed; I had not ſufficient time to make the proper corrections, to poliſh the ſtile, &c. &c. None of my apologies were, however, admitted; it was neceſſary that I ſhould produce my compoſition; I accordingly complied; it was read over and over again. Watſon and Oſborne immediately renounced every idea of competition, and joined in applauding it. Ralph alone made a few criticiſms, and propoſed ſome corrections, but I ſtrenuouſly defended my manuſcript. Oſborne was violent againſt Ralph, and told him, that he was no better calculated to criticiſe than to write verſes, and that he had equally failed in the corrections he had hazarded, and the poetry he had promiſed, but neglected to produce.

As ſoon as the others had left me in order to return home, Oſborne expreſſed himſelf ſtill more ſtrongly in favour of what he imagined to be my production. He pretended to have been hitherto reſtrained ftrained by fear, left I fhould think he meant to flatter me.

" But who would have imagined," added he, " that " Franklin was capable of fuch a compofition! What " painting! What ftrength! What fire! He has " actually furpaffed the original! In his ordinary " converfation he does not appear to give himfelf " any trouble about the choice of his words; he even " hefitates, and finds it difficult to exprefs his mean- " ing, and yet, good God! how he writes!"

At our next meeting, Ralph informed Ofborne of the trick we had played him, and he was rallied by us all on the occafion.

This adventure confirmed Ralph in his refolution of becoming a poet. I did every thing in my power in order to diffuade him from it; but he continued to make verfes, until he read Pope, and this entirely cured him of his paffion for the Mufes; he, however, became a moft excellent profe writer.

I fhall fpeak more about him by and by, but as I may not perhaps have occafion to fay any thing concerning the other two, I fhall only obferve here, that Watfon died in my arms a few years after. He was exceedingly regretted; for he was the moft amiable of all our fociety. Ofborne went to the Weft Indies, where he became a famous advocate, and acquired a great deal of money; but he was cut off at a very early period of his life. We ferioufly agreed together, that whichever of us two died firft, fhould, if poffible, return, and make an amicable vifit to the furvivor, in order to inform him fully in regard to a fu-

ture

ture ſtate :—But he has never as yet fulfilled his engagement.

The governor appeared to be much delighted with my company, and invited me frequently to his houſe. He ſtill continued to ſpeak of his intention of eſtabliſhing me in buſineſs, as a thing decided upon. I was to carry along with me letters of recommendation to ſeveral of his friends, and eſpecially a letter of credit, in order to procure me my printing-preſs, types, paper, &c. &c. He put off the delivery of theſe letters from time to time, and always promiſed me that they ſhould be ready when I called next; but on my appearance ſomething continually interfered ſo as to prevent their delivery.

Theſe reiterated delays always took place, until the veſſel, the departure of which had been often procraſtinated, was at length ready to ſail; on that occaſion I once more waited upon Sir William, in order to take my leave, and receive my diſpatches. His ſecretary, Dr. Bird, came to me, and informed me, that the governor was extremely buſy, at preſent, but that he would be at Newcaſtle, before the veſſel could poſſibly drop down there, and that then I might depend upon the letters being delivered to me.

Ralph was determined to accompany me in this voyage, although he was married and had a child. It was believed that he undertook it merely with a deſign of eſtabliſhing a correſpondence in England, and of procuring merchandize, in order to be ſold by commiſſion; but I afterwards diſcovered, that having

having fome occafion to complain of his wife's family, he was determined to leave her with them, and refolved never more to return to America.

After having taken leave of my friends and made an exchange of vows with Mifs Read, I left Philadelphia.

The veffel caft anchor at Newcaftle; the governor was there, and I repaired to his houfe. His fecretary, who received me with great politenefs, informed me from him, that I could not fee him then, being engaged in bufinefs of the utmoft importance, but that he would fend my letters on board, and that he wifhed me a good voyage, and fpeedy return, &c. &c.

I now repaired on board the veffel, exceedingly aftonifhed, but yet without conceiving the leaft doubt, as to his intentions.

Mr. Andrew Hamilton, a famous advocate of Philadelphia, had taken a paffage on board the fame fhip for himfelf and his fon, and in conjunction with Mr. Denham, a quaker merchant, and Meffrs. Oniam and Ruffel, the owners of an iron work in Maryland, had hired the great cabin; fo that Ralph and I were obliged to lie along with the failors, and as we were unknown to any perfon in the veffel, we were treated like the common men.

Mr. Hamilton and his fon James, who was afterwards governor, happened to return from Newcaftle to Philadelphia, being recalled at a great expence, in order to plead a caufe relative to a veffel that had been feized, fo that they did not proceed on the voyage.

A very

A very fhort time before we fet fail, Colonel French came on board, and fhewed me many civilities; from that moment a great deal more attention was paid to me; and the other paffengers having invited me and my friend Ralph to occupy the beds which the Meffrs. Hamiltons were to have flept in, we accepted of their offer without any difficulty, and found ourfelves in a far more commodious fituation than we had hitherto experienced.

Having learned that Colonel French had brought on board the governor's difpatches, I afked the captain for the letters which were to be intrufted to my care. He informed me they had been all put together in the letter bag, which he could not then untie, but added, that before their arrival in England, I fhould moft undoubtedly receive them. I was fatisfied for the moment with this anfwer, and we foon after proceeded on our voyage.

The paffengers in the great cabin were of a very fociable difpofition, and we were exceedingly lucky in regard to provifions, for we not only had our own, but a large quantity of poultry, &c. which Mr. Hamilton had left on board. In the courfe of the paffage, Mr. Denham contracted a friendfhip for me, which ended but with his life. In other refpects our voyage was not very pleafant, for we had exceedingly difagreeable weather.

When we arrived in the Channel, the captain kept his word with me, and gave me permiffion to fearch the bag for the governor's letters. I did not find a fingle one upon which my name was written, or on

which

which it was indicated that it was to be conveyed by my means. I picked out fix or feven however, which I judged by the directions to be thofe which had been promifed me, more efpecially as one of them was addreffed to Bafkerville, the King's printer, and another to a ftationer, who was the firft perfon whom I met with on my arrival. I accordingly prefented it to him as coming from Governor Keith.

" I am not acquainted with the man you mean," fays he, but on opening the letter, he exclaimed, " O " it is from Reddlefden ! I have known for fome " time paft that he is a great rafcal, and I neither " wifh to have any connection with, nor receive any " letters from him." Having faid this, he inftantly put the letter in queftion into my hand, turned round upon his heel, and left me in order to ferve fome of his cuftomers.

I was quite aftonifhed at difcovering that this letter was not written by the governor, and recalling now, for the firft time, a variety of circumftances to my memory, I began at length to doubt of his fincerity. I waited therefore upon my friend Denham, and explained the whole affair. He inftantly made me acquainted with governor Keith's character, and informed me that there was not the leaft probability that he had written a fingle line in my favour. He added, that no one who was acquainted with him ever trufted to his word, and he laughed heartily at my idea of receiving a letter of credit, from a perfon who could procure no credit for himfelf.

As

As I evinced fome uneafinefs relative to the part I
had now to take, he advifed me to endeavour to find
employment in my own profeffion, " You will here,
fays he, " be fure to add to your ftock of know-
" ledge, and this circumftance will enable you to
" eftablifh yourfelf more advantageoufly, on your
" return to America."

We were as much convinced as the ftationer was,
that lawyer Riddlefden was a great rogue. He had
nearly ruined Mifs Read's father, by prevailing upon
him to become furety for him. We alfo difcovered
by this letter, that he had entered into a fecret
intrigue againft Mr. Hamilton, who he fuppofed was
gone to Europe in the fame fhip with us, and that the
governor was privy to, and a party in the plot.

Denham, who was one of Hamilton's friends, was
of opinion, that he ought to be informed of this circumftance. In fine, as foon as he had arrived in England, which was but a few weeks after us, I went to
fee him ; and partly from regard to him, and partly
from refentment againft Keith, I delivered him up the
letter itfelf. He thanked me in the moft expreffive
manner, for the favour I did him, the information
contained in it being of the utmoft importance ; and
from that moment he conceived a friendfhip for me,
which was very advantageous, and ufeful on a variety
of occafions.

What is one to think of a governor like this, who
acted fuch a pitiful part, and impofed fo grofsly upon
a poor young man, deftitute of experience ?

It

It had actually become a *habit* with Sir William Keith. He wifhed to pleafe all the world, and having but little to give, he was prodigal of his promifes. Notwithftanding this he was a very fenfible and accomplifhed man, an excellent fcholar, and a good governor for the people over whom he prefided, although he was not efteemed by his conftituents the proprietors, whofe inftructions he often neglected.

Many of our beft laws were not only enacted under his adminiftration, but actually penned by himfelf.

CHAP. V.

The Author leads a diffipated Life in London—He lodges in the fame Houfe with Ralph—Makes Love to his Miftrefs— Becomes Author, and writes a Metaphyfical Work in An- fwer to Wollaston—Is introduced to Dr. Mandeville, Author of the Fable of the Bees—Some Account of that Gentleman —Removes to another Printing-Houfe—Drinks Water only, and is yet ftronger than fuch of his Companions as drink Beer—Enacts feveral wholefome Laws among his fellow Workmen—Ingenious Differtation on the folly of fwallowing Strong Beer—Anecdotes of a Nun—His excellence in the Art of Swimming—He is engaged as a Merchant's Clerk, and returns to Philadelphia.

RALPH and I were infeparable companions; we lodged together at the rate of three fhillings and a half per week; this was all that we were then in a fituation to afford. He difcovered feveral of his relations who refided in London, but they were all ex- ceedingly poor, and totally unable to affift him. He told me about this time, that it was his intention to remain in England, and that he was determined never more to return to Philadelphia. He was abfolutely deftitute of money, the little he had been able to procure, being fcarce fufficient to pay for his paffage.

I was ftill in poffeffion of fifteen *piftoles*, and he ap- plied to me from time to time, in order to affift him, until he fhould get fome employment.

Imagining

Imagining that he poffeffed the neceffary talents for becoming an actor, he had a prodigious inclination for a theatrical life; but Wilkes, to whom he addreffed himfelf, defired him to give over every idea of that profeffion, it being, as he frankly told him, totally impoffible for him to fucceed in it. He then applied to Roberts, a bookfeller in Paternofter-Row, to whom he propofed to write a weekly paper, after the manner of the Spectator, but the conditions not being agreeable, his propofition was rejected. He afterwards endeavoured to be employed as a copying-clerk for the law ftationers in the neighbourhood of the Temple; but he did not find any place vacant.

As to me, I was immediately admitted into the employment of Mr. Palmer, at that time a famous printer in St. Bartholomew's-Clofe, where I remained upwards of a twelve-month.

I was exceedingly affiduous at my bufinefs, but I fpent nearly every farthing I earned in company with Ralph. The play-houfes and other places of public entertainment which we frequented together, having exhaufted all my *piftoles*; we thenceforward were obliged to live from *hand to mouth*.

He appeared to have entirely forgotten his wife and child, and as for me, I had alfo nearly forgotten my engagements with Mifs Read, to whom I never wrote but one letter, and that merely to inform her, that I fhould not return fo foon as I had expected. This was another of the great errors of my life, which I fhould defire to correct, were I to begin it once more. In fhort, we led fuch a round of diffipation,

that

that it became utterly impoffible for me to pay my paffage.

I was employed by Palmer, to compofe the fecond edition of " Wollafton's Religion of Nature." Some of his reafoning not appearing to me to be well founded, I wrote a little metaphyfical effay, in which I made fome remarks upon thefe paffages. It was entitled, " a Differtation on Liberty and Neceffity, " Pleafure and Pain." I infcribed it to my friend Ralph, and having put it to prefs, threw off feveral copies of it.

This circumftance occafioned Mr. Palmer to en- tertain a greater refpect for me than before, and to look upon me as a young man of abilities, although he made me many ferious reproaches on the prin- ciples maintained in my work, which, according to him, was heathenifh and abominable. The im- preffion of this tract was another error in my life.

During the time that I lodged in Little Britain, I formed an acquaintance with a bookfeller of the name of Wilcox, whofe fhop adjoined the houfe in which I refided : He had an immenfe collection of books upon fale; circulating libraries were not then in fafhion. It was refolved in confequence of a rea- fonable allowance agreed upon between us, the amount of which I do not at prefent recollect, that I fhould enjoy the liberty of reading all the books I chofe, which were afterwards to be returned to him. I looked upon this bargain as very advantageous to me, and profited as much as poffible by it.

My

My pamphlet having fallen into the hands of a furgeon of the name of Lyons, author of a book entitled "The Infallability of Human Judgment," this circumftance occafioned an extraordinary intimacy between us. He teftified a great deal of efteem for me, came often to fee me, in order to converfe with me upon thefe matters, and introduced me to Doctor Mandeville, author of the "Fable of the Bees," who was prefident, and indeed the life and foul of a club, held at a tavern in Cheapfide.

He was a very facetious and amufing man. He prefented me at Batfon's coffee-houfe to Doctor Pemberton, who promifed to introduce me to Sir Ifaac Newton, an event which I was very eager to bring about: But he never kept his promife.

I had brought fome curiofities along with me from America, the principal of which was a purfe compofed of the filaments of the *Afbeftos*, which was cleaned by means of fire. Sir Hans Sloane having heard fome perfon mention this, came to fee me, and invited me to his houfe in Bloomfbury Square, where after having fhewn me all the rare productions of his collection, he perfuaded me to depofit this among the reft, paying me, however, a very liberal price for it.

A young woman who was a milliner, and had a fhop as I underftood, clofe to the Royal Exchange, happened to lodge in our houfe. She was at once lively and fenfible; fhe had received a fuperior education; her converfation was therefore very entertaining and agreeable.

Ralph

Ralph read comedies to her every evening, and this occafioned a great intimacy to take place between them. She removed to another lodging and he followed her. They lived fometime together, and he continued ftill deftitute of any employment whatever. Having a child, her income did not prove fufficient for the maintenance of all three, he therefore took the refolution to leave London, and refolved to keep a fchool in the country. He thought himfelf well calculated to fucceed in this fcheme, as he wrote a very fine hand, and was well acquainted with arithmetic and book-keeping.

He, however, regarded this fituation as infinitely below his abilities, and hoping for brighter profpects and happier days hereafter, during which he might be afhamed of having exercifed fuch a degrading profeffion, he changed his name, and did me the honour to adopt mine.

He actually fent me a letter a fhort time afterwards, in order to inform me that he was eftablifhed in a little day fchool in an obfcure village, where if I recollect right, he taught ten or a dozen children to read and write at fix-pence fterling a week each. He recommended Mrs. T——— to my care, and requefted me to addrefs my anfwer to Mr. Franklin, fchool mafter at N——— in Berkfhire.

He continued to write frequently, and to convey to me large fragments of an Epic poem, which he was at that time compofing, and upon which he demanded my remarks and my corrections. I accordingly tranfmitted them from time to time; but I conftantly
endeavoured

endeavoured to perfuade him to abandon this kind of purfuit.

Young happening much about this period to publifh one of his fatires; I copied, and tranfmitted that part of it to him in which the author points out the contempt into which the poets of the day had fallen, and demonftrates the folly of cultivating the Mufes, with the hope of rifing in the world by their means. Here follow the verfes I allude to:

" Th' abandon'd manners of our writing train
" May tempt mankind to think religion vain;
" But in their fate, their habit, and their mien,
" That Gods there are, is evidently feen:
" Heav'n ftands abfolv'd by vengeance on their pen,
" And marks the murderers of fame from men.
" Thro' meagre jaws they draw their venal breath,
" As ghaftly as their brothers in Macbeth:
" Their feet thro' faithlefs leather meets the dirt,
" And oftner chang'd their principles than fhirt:
" The tranfient veftments of thefe frugal men,
" Haften to paper for our mirth again:
" Too foon (O merry melancholy fate!)
" They beg in rhyme, and warble thro' a grate;
" The man lampoon'd, forgets it at the fight;
" The friend thro' pity gives, the foe thro' fpight;
" And tho' full confcious of his injur'd purfe,
" Lintot relents, nor Curll can wifh them worfe."

" An Author 'tis a venerable name!
" How few deferve it and what numbers claim?
" Unblefs'd with fenfe, above their peers refin'd,
" Who fhall ftand up, dictators to mankind?

" Nay,

" Nay, who dare fhine, if not in virtue's caufe?
" That fóle proprietor of juft applaufe.
" Ye reftlefs men ! who pant for letter'd praife,
" With whom would you confult to gain the bays?
" With thofe great authors whofe fam'd works you read?
__" 'Tis well; go, then, confult the laurell'd fhade,
" What anfwer will the laurell'd fhade return?
" Hear it and tremble, he commands you burn
" The nobleft works, his envy'd genius writ,
" That boafts of nought more excellent than wit,
" If this be true, as 'tis a truth moft dread,
" Wo to the page which has not that to plead !
" Fontaine and Chaucer dying, wifh'd unwrote
" The fprightlieft efforts of their wanton thought:
" Sidney and Waller, brigheft fons of fame,
" Condemn'd the charm of ages to the flame.

" Thus ends your courted fame—does lucre then,
" The facred thirft of gold, betray your pen ?
" In profe 'tis blameable, in verfe 'tis worfe,
" Provokes the Mufe, extorts Apollo's curfe ;
" His facred influence never fhould be fold ;
" 'Tis arrant fimony to fing for gold ;
" 'Tis immortality fhould fire your mind :
" Scorn a lefs paymafter than all mankind."
                              YOUNG, Vol. III. Epift. II. p. 70.

But all my efforts were ufelefs, and my labour entirely loft, for fheet upon fheet of the poem continued to arrive by every poft.

In the mean time Mrs. T———— having loft all
her friends, as well as her trade on his account, was
often reduced to the utmoft diftrefs. On thofe occafions fhe had recourfe to me, and I lent her
                                                    all

all the money in my power, in order to refcue her from her misfortunes.

I indeed began to conceive too great a regard for this young woman. Being at that time entirely deftitute of any curb from religion, and taking advantage of the neceffity fhe was under of applying to me, I endeavoured to take fome familiarities with her, (another error in my life,) which fhe repelled with a proper degree of fpirit and refentment. She even informed Ralph of my behaviour, and this adventure occafioned a quarrel between us.

Upon his return to London, he gave me to underftand, that he looked upon all the obligations which he was under to me, to be entirely annihilated by my conduct; from this I concluded that I could never hope to be reimburfed either the money which I had lent him, or advanced her upon his account. I was the lefs afflicted at this circumftance, as he was at prefent utterly unable to pay me; I confidered alfo, that although I had loft his friendfhip, I was eafed at the fame time of a very heavy burden.

I began from that moment to be more œconomical, and to fave a little money in order to fupply the wants of futurity.

The printing-houfe of Mr. Watts, near Lincoln's Inn Fields, being ftill more confiderable than that in which I was engaged, it was probable that I might find it turn out more to my account, to be employed there. I accordingly prefented myfelf and was inftantly admitted; I remained there all the reft of the time I ftaid in London.

G   Upon

Upon my firft entrance into this printing-houfe, I chofe to work at the prefs, becaufe I imagined that I ftood in need of that corporal exercife which I had been accuftomed to in America, where the workmen are preffmen and compofitors by turns.

I in the mean time drank nothing but water, while all the other workmen, to the number of fifty, were extremely fond of porter: Yet I was able to carry as great a weight with one hand, as any of them could do with two. They confeffed upon this, and a number of other occafions, that the *Aquatic American,* as they were pleafed to call me, was much ftronger than them, although they drank *ftrong beer.*

A boy from a neighbouring public-houfe, was conftantly employed during the whole day, in bringing porter to the workmen. My companion at the prefs drank a pint every morning before breakfaft, a pint at breakfaft with his bread and cheefe, another between breakfaft and dinner, one at dinner, another after dinner about fix o'clock in the afternoon, and one more after he had finifhed his day's work.

I looked upon this to be a moft deteftable cuftom; but it was abfolutely neceffary, according to him, to drink ftrong beer, in order to enable him to work.

I endeavoured to convince him, that the additional corporal ftrength produced by the beer, could only be in proportion to the quantity of grain, or barley diffolved in the water, out of which the beer was compofed; that there was much more in a half-penny worth of bread than in a pint of beer, and that
if

if he ate that quantity of bread with a pint of water, he would draw more nourifhment, and, confequently, more ftrength from it than from a pint of beer. This mode of reafoning did not prevent him however from continuing to drink, and to pay every Saturday night to the amount of four or five fhillings on account of this villainous liquor; an ex-pence from which I was entirely exempted. It is in this manner that thefe poor devils remain always in mifery.

After the lapfe of a few weeks, Watts having occa-fion for a compofitor, I quitted the prefs bufinefs. The other compofitors on this defired me to pay my *footing* once more, but I looked upon fuch a demand as an impofition, having paid it already to the prefs-men. The mafter was entirely of my way of think-ing, and ordered me not to comply with fo unreafon-able a requeft. I remained accordingly for two or three weeks without being admitted *a member of the fociety.* I was in confequence looked upon as an ex-communicated perfon, and if I happened to be abfent at any time, a few minutes from my bufinefs, I ex-perienced the effects of their malice in a thoufand trifles.

On my return I was fure to find my letter mixed together and confufed, my pages tranfpofed, my matter out of order, &c. &c. and all was attributed to the *Spirit of the Chapel* *, who according to

* This is the name given by the workmen to the Printing Houfe.

them always vexed thofe who were not regularly admitted.

I was at length obliged notwithftanding my mafter's protection, to fubmit myfelf fo far as to pay
their demand; being fully convinced, that it is a great
folly not to be on good terms with thofe among whom
one is obliged to live conftantly.

After this, I was well received by all of them, and
I foon acquired a confiderable influence over their
minds. I propofed fome alterations in the laws of
the *Chapel*, and I had interreft enough to get them
paffed in fpite of all oppofition.

My example had fuch an effect upon them that
many of them renounced their breakfaft of beer, and
bread and cheefe, and procured from a neighbouring
houfe in the fame manner as myfelf, a large porrin-
ger of water gruel with a lump of butter in the middle of it, and fome chippings of bread and a little
pepper ftrewed on the top. This was a much better
breakfaft, and did not coft more than the price of a
pint of beer ; that is to fay, three half-pence, while on
the other hand it kept the head infinitely more clear,
and enabled them to work better.

Thofe who continued to gorge themfelves with
beer all day long, by neglecting to pay their *fcore*
often loft all their credit at the ale-houfe. On fuch
occafions they had always recourfe to me, in order
that I might pafs my word for them ; " their light
" being out!" as they termed it. I placed myfelf at
the pay table every Saturday evening, in order to be
reimburfed

reimburfed the fmall fums that I had ftood furety for
during the preceding week.

This circumftance, added to my reputation of poffeffing a turn for fatire, contributed to fupport my
importance in the chapel. Befides this, I recommended myfelf to my mafter by my application and
affiduity, for I never kept St. Monday. My extraordinary quicknefs at compofition, was always fure to
procure me fuch works as were of a preffing nature,
which are generally the moft lucrative; I therefore
was enabled to live comfortably, and to pafs my time
very agreeably.

My apartment in Little Britain being too far diftant
from the printing-office, I removed to another in Duke
Street Lincoln's Inn Fields, exactly oppofite the
Roman Catholic chapel; it was at the back of an
Italian warehoufe. A widow kept the houfe; her
family confifted of a daughter, a female fervant, and
a fhopman, who lodged in an adjoining ftreet.

After having fent an order to make fome enquiries
relating to me, at the place in which I lived before,
fhe confented to let me an apartment at the fame
price (three fhillings and fix-pence, a week) content-
ing herfelf with fo little, fhe faid, on account of the
fafety that would accrue to fingle women, from the
circumftance of having a man to fleep in the fame
houfe with them.

She herfelf was a woman of a certain age, and the
daughter of a clergyman; fhe had been educated in
the Proteftant Religion, but her hufband, whofe memory fhe greatly revered, had converted her to the

Catholic

Catholic church. She had lived much among people of diſtinction, and had thouſands of anecdotes by heart, ſome of which extended as far back as the reign of Charles II.

She had loſt the uſe of her legs by means of the gout; and was often confined to her chamber, ſo that ſhe was frequently deſirous of having company to viſit her. Her converſation was ſo exceedingly amuſing to me, that I was eager to ſpend the evening with her, as often as ſhe requeſted me. Our ſupper conſiſted of nothing more than half an anchovy a piece, laid upon a ſlice of bread, with a little butter, and half a pint of. ale between us. This appears to be a ſcanty meal, but the regale conſiſted entirely in her converſation.

The care I took to return at an early hour, and the little trouble that I occaſioned to the family, made her dread the idea of a ſeparation, ſo that when I men‑ tioned a lodging that had been pointed out to me, much nearer the place where I worked, and which was to be let at two ſhillings a week, an offer which my deſire of ſaving money induced me to accept of, ſhe requeſted me to give up every idea of a change, as ſhe herſelf would take off two ſhillings from the ſum I then paid her. Thus my lodgings coſt me no more than eighteen-pence per week, during the reſt of the time I remained in London.

A maiden lady of 70 years of age lived in the moſt obſcure and retired manner in a garret in the ſame‑ houſe. The following particulars concerning her, were communicated to me, by my landlady:

She

She was a Roman Catholic, who in her early youth had been fent to the continent, where fhe entered into a convent with the intention of becoming a nun: but the climate difagreeing with her, fhe returned to England, and as there was not a nunnery in that country, fhe had made a vow to lead a monaftic life, as far, at leaft, as circumftances would permit her. In confequence of this, fhe had difpofed of moft of her property, in order to employ the produce of it in works of charity, and had only referved 12l. per annum to herfelf, part of which fmall fum fhe continued to diftribute among the poor. To enable her to do this, fhe lived entirely upon water gruel, and never lighted a fire but on purpofe to make it.

She had lodged for a great number of years in the fame garret, where fhe was permitted to remain *gratis*, by the Catholic families who had taken this houfe in fucceffion, and who looked upon her refidence with them as a bleffing from Heaven. A Prieft came daily in order to confefs her.

" I have afked her often, (faid my hoftefs,) confider-
" ing the manner in which fhe lived; how it was pof-
" fible for her to find fo much occupation for a Con-
" feffor ?" " O replied fhe, it is impoffible to avoid
" vain thoughts !"

I once received permiffion to pay her a vifit: fhe appeared gay, polite, and very agreeable in converfation. Her bed-chamber was neat, but fhe had not any other moveables in it befides a mattrafs, a table with a crucifix and a book upon it, a chair which

fhe

fhe prefented me to fit upon, and a picture·of St. Veronica over the chimney-piece, in which that holy female difplayed a handkerchief, with the face of Jefus Chrift miraculoufly imprinted upon it. The pious Catholic explained this circumftance to me, with a very ferious countenance.

Her face was pale, but fhe never had been fick, and I may give this as another example to prove how little money is neceffary, in order to fupport both life and health.

I got acquainted at the printing-office with a young man of the name of Wygate, whofe parents were opulent, and who, in confequence, had been better educated than the generality of printers. He was a very good Latin fcholar, fpoke French pretty well, and was very fond of reading. I taught him and feveral of his friends to fwim ; for this purpofe I carried them two or three times to the river Thames, and after a little practice they acquired a certain degree of facility and even perfection in this exercife. We one day made a party in order to go to Chelfea, to fee the College and the curiofities at Don Saltero's, with fome gentlemen in the neighbourhood of London, to whom they introduced me. On our return, at the requeft of the company whofe curiofity had been excited by Wygate, I undreffed myfelf, jumped into the river, and fwam nearly from Chelfea to Black-Friars, making a variety of evolutions and performing feveral feats of activity, as well on the top of the water, as below it.

· This

This afforded a great deal of pleafure, fatisfac-tion, and even aftonifhment, to thofe to whom fuch a fpeftacle was entirely new. I had been greatly ad-difted to, and had loved this delightful exercife from my early infancy. I was acquainted with, and prac-tifed all the motions and pofitions recommended by Thevenot, and had even invented fome new ones my-felf, in which I endeavoured to unite grace with utility. I took great care to do my utmoft to excel upon this occafion, and I was really flattered with the admiration I had excited by my fkill and aftivity.

Wygate who was exceedingly defirous of excell-ing in this art, attached himfelf fo much the more to me, as there was a great conformity between our ftudies, and our habits of life. In fhort he propofed to me to make the tour of Europe together, and to defray the expences of our journey, by working in our profeffion, in all the great cities which we might pafs through.

I was on the point of confenting to this fcheme. I even communicated it to my friend Mr. Den-ham, with whom I was always happy to pafs a leifure hour. He diffuaded me from this projeft, and advifed me to think ferioufly of returning to Philadelphia, where he himfelf was determined fhortly to repair. I fhall here recount a circumftance, which will ferve to give fome idea of the charafter of this worthy man.

He had been formerly a merchant in Briftol. Hav-ing failed in bufinefs there, he made a compofition with his creditors, and fet out for America, where by means

means of an affiduous application to trade, he acquired a confiderable fortune in a few years. On his return to England in the fame veffel with myfelf, as I have mentioned before, he invited all his former creditors to a feaft. When they were affembled, he returned them many thanks for the kind manner in which they had treated him, and while they expected nothing more than a good dinner, each of the guefts on changing his plate, found an order on a banker, for the payment of the remainder of the debt, befides intereft at 5 *per cent.*

He informed me, that he intended to return to America, and to carry out with him a large quantity of merchandize, with which he refolved to open a * ftore, and he moreover offered to take me out with him as a clerk in order to fuperintend his books, to copy his letters, &c. &c. &c. He added that as foon as I fhould become familiar with commercial matters, he would fend me as a fupercargo, with flour, pork, &c. &c. to the Weft Indies, and procure me a variety of lucrative commiffions; in fhort, he obferved, that with conduct and ability, I could not fail to eftablifh myfelf advantageoufly.

I was charmed with thefe propofitions. London began to be hateful to me; the agreeable moments I had fpent in Pennfylvania, were recalled to my memory, and I defired once more to enjoy fimilar fcenes.

I accordingly engaged with Mr. Denham at £.50 *per annum,* Pennfylvania money. This was indeed a

* This is the ufual appellation both in America and the Weft Indies, for a warehoufe.

lefs fum than what I might have gained as a Compofitor; but I had an infinitely more agreeable career opened to my ambition.

I now bid farewell, as I thought for the laft time, to the printing-houfe, and delivered myfelf entirely up to the ftudy of my new profeffion, paffing my whole time, either in vifiting the merchants with Mr. Denham in order to purchafe the different articles he ftood in need of, or running among the workmen, to haften them in their operations, &c. &c. When all was put on board, I had then a few days of leifure for myfelf.

During this fhort interval, I happened one morning to be fent for, by a perfon of diftinction, with whofe name only, I was acquainted: It was Sir William Wyndham; I repaired to him accordingly. He had heard a great deal, by what means I know not, about my fwimming from Chelfea to Black-friars, and alfo that I had taught this art, in a few hours, to Wygate and feveral of his companions. His two fons, he faid, were about to proceed upon their travels; he was defirous that they fhould firft learn to fwim, and he offered me a very liberal gratification, if I would undertake to teach them.

As they were not as yet arrived in town, and my ftay in the capital was wholly uncertain, I was of courfe unable to accept his propofition. I was, however, induced from this incident to believe, if I had chofen to have remained in England and opened a fchool for *Natation*, that I fhould in all human probability have gained a great deal of money. I was

6   fo

fo ftruck with the idea at the moment, that, if the fame propofition had been fuggefted a little fooner, I fhould never have thought of returning to America.

You and I, feveral years afterwards, had a matter of greater confequence to confer upon, with one of the fons of this very Sir William Wyndham, who was created Earl of Egremont.—But let us not anticipate events.

I had paffed in this manner eighteen months in London, working with great induftry at my trade, and incurring no other expence than that arifing from feeing a few plays, and purchafing a fmall collection of books.

My friend Ralph had, however, kept me in poverty; he owed me no lefs than £.27 which appeared to me to be fo much money loft; this was a great fum deducted from my little favings. Notwithftanding this, I loved him greatly, becaufe he poffeffed a number of very amiable qualities.

But although I had not improved my fortune, I had augmented my mafs of knowledge by reading many excellent books, and by converfing with men of letters, and feveral of thofe who excelled in the Arts and Sciences, with whom I found means to form an acquaintance, and even to become intimate.

We fet fail from Gravefend, on the . . . . of July, 1726. I refer you for the incidents of our voyage to my journal, where you will find every thing minutely detailed.

We landed at Philadelphia on the . . . . of October following.

CHAP.

C H A P. VI.

Our Author meets Governor Sir William Keith, on his re-
turn to Philidelphia—He hears that Mifs Read is mar-
ried—Sicknefs and Death of Mr. Denham—He changes
his Situation once more, and becomes a Printer again—Some
Account of an Oxford Scholar—Difpute with Keimer—Re-
conciliation—Paper Money—He removes to Burlington—
Hiftory of Ifaac Decon, Infpector General of New Jerfey—
Project of an Eftablifhment—A Differtation on Morality
and Religion—He begins to doubt his Metaphyfical Prin-
ciples—Refolves to act with Honefty in all his Dealings.

O N my return, Sir William Keith was no longer
governor of Pennfylvania, having been difpof-
feffed of his employment, and replaced by Major
Gordon. I met him walking in the ftreets as a fimple citizen; he appeared a little afhamed at feeing
me, but he paffed without taking any notice of me,
or even fpeaking a fingle word.

I myfelf fhould have been equally afhamed at feeing Mifs Read, if her family, defpairing with good
reafon of my return, after receiving the letter I had
fent her, had not perfuaded her to give up every idea
of me, and prevailed upon her to efpoufe a potter of
the name of Rogers, during my abfence. He, however,
did not make her a good hufband, and fhe feparated
from him foon after, refufing to cohabit with him,
and even to pafs by his name, becaufe it was rumoured that he had another wife ftill living. His
fkill

ſkill in his trade had induced Miſs Read's parents to conſent to this match, but he was an equally bad huſband and excellent workman. Having contracted ſeveral debts, he ran away, in 1727 or 1728, to the Weſt Indies, where he died.

During my abſence, Keimer had hired a more conſiderable houſe than the one which he occupied before, and he had opened a ſhop well furniſhed with paper and other goods of a ſimilar kind. He had alſo procured an abundance of new types, and a number of workmen, among whom there was not, however, a ſingle good one : He ſeemed to be in a thriving way, and to have great employment.

Mr. Denham hired a warehouſe in Water-Street, where we diſplayed our merchandize. I was aſſiduous in buſineſs ; I ſtudied book-keeping, and in a ſhort time I became exceedingly expert at it. We lodged and boarded together; he was ſincerely attached to me, and acted in every thing exactly the ſame as if he had been my father. On my ſide, I loved and reſpected him ; my ſituation indeed was extremely pleaſant, but this happineſs was of very ſhort duration.

About the beginning of February, 1727, the epoch at which I entered into the 22nd year of my age, we both fell ſick. I was attacked by a pleuriſy, which nearly carried me off; I ſuffered a great deal, and gave myſelf over for loſt. It was actually a ſort of diſappointment to me, when I found myſelf convaleſcent, and I regretted that I ſhould ſooner or later,

have

have the fame difagreeable career to run through hereafter.

I do not at prefent recollect what was the nature of the malady with which Mr. Denham was feized; but it was long in its continuance, and he at length funk beneath its preffure. He left me a fmall legacy in his will, as a teftimony of his affection, and thus I was once more delivered up to my own management, in the vaft ocean of the univerfe, for the ftore being confided to the care of the teftamentary legatee, I immediately received my difmiffion.

My brother-in-law, Captain Holmes, who happened at this time to be in Philadelphia, advifed me to return to my firft profeffion, and Keimer offered me a very large falary, provided I would undertake the management of his printing-houfe, in order to enable him to give up all his own time and attention to the fhop.

His wife, and her relations in London, had given me but a very indifferent idea of this man, and I did not care to have any thing to do with a perfon of his character. I accordingly fought for employment among the merchants, but not finding any immediate vacancy, I allowed myfelf to be prevailed upon by Keimer, to refide with him.

I found the following workmen in his printing-houfe :

Hugh Meredith, a Pennfylvanian about 35 years of age; he had been brought up as a farmer; he was honeft, fenfible, experienced, and was befides fond of books.

Stephen

Stephen Potts was a young man who poffeffed excellent natural qualifications, far fuperior indeed to
what is commonly met with among people in his fituation, and along with this he had much wit and
great gaiety of difpofition ; but he was rather lazy.

Keimer had hired thefe two by the week, at very
moderate wages, which were to be augmented at the
rate of one fhilling every three months, according to
their progrefs in their bufinefs. This future augmenta-
tion was the bait which he made ufe of in order to
gain them. Meredith was to be employed at prefs-
work, and Potts in book-binding, both of which
branches their honeft mafter undertook to teach
them, although he himfelf was entirely ignorant of
either of them.

The third was John Savage, he had not been educated to any trade whatever ; Keimer had purchafed
his fervice for four years from the captain of a veffel,
who had brought him over. He was deftined to
become a prefs-man.

George Webb was an Oxford fcholar, whofe fervice he had alfo purchafed for four years ; he was intended to be a compofitor. I fhall fpeak of him
hereafter.

The laft was David Harry, a country lad, whom
he had taken as an apprentice.

I foon perceived that Keimer's intention in engaging me at fuch high wages, and fo far beyond what
he was accuftomed to give, was in order that I might
educate and form as it were, all thofe new and unex-
penfive workmen, who were moft of them bound to

him

I alfo increafed the number of my acquaintance, at leaft among well-informed people, as much as poffible. Keimer himfelf treated me apparently with much civility and confideration, and nothing, at that period, gave me any uneafinefs except my debt to Vernon, which I was ftill incapable of paying, not having as yet been able to accumulate fo large a fum out of my little favings; but he was kind enough not to demand the reimburfement of it.

Our printing-houfe was often in want of different forts of *letter*, and there were no letter-founders in America. I, however, was able, with fome difficulty, to conftruct a mould; I made ufe of the letters which we had already, as *punches*; I caft the types in lead, by means of a clay matrix; and I thus made fhift ᴐ fupply the printing-houfe with whatever was n. ᴎting. True it is, that the letter was not good, to ᵢ was tolerable.

ber ᴄ ᴋ. upon occafion, engraved a variety of orna. had pᴜ ᴎᴈhade ink; I now and then put the fhop in in verfe ᴌᴤʃ ᴙ in fhort, I became, as-it were, Keimer's He foo.

mained for ᴦᴜᴛ ᴜfeful I might be, I foon perceived with a colleᵪ ᴈldᴤᴎcame daily of lefs importance, and to fee Londo, ᴦ ol ᴙactly in proportion as the other length happen ᴑ ᴌᴕ more expert at their bufinefs; payment of his qᴜ ᴢᴈᴎᴧy fecond quarter's wages, he of liquidating his ᴃᴡᴌᴈght them too high, and that concealed his gown ᴀ I ᴢᴜᴎᴐ make fome abatement. forward to London.. ᴎᴌᴕᴈᴦ oᴒ daily took upon him
                              ᴦʏ of a mafter. He
                                       often

Stephen Potts was a young man who poffeffed excellent natural qualifications, far fuperior indeed to
what is commonly met with among people in his fituation, and along with this he had much wit and
great gaiety of difpofition ; but he was rather lazy.

Keimer had hired thefe two by the week, at very
moderate wages, which were to be augmented at the
rate of one fhilling every three months, according to
their progrefs in their bufinefs. This future augmenta-
tion was the bait which he made ufe of in order to
gain them. Meredith was to be employed at prefs-
work, and Potts in book-binding, both of which
branches their honeft mafter undertook to teach
them, although he himfelf was entirely ignorant of
either of them.

The third was John Savage, he had not been ed·ᵓ
cated to any trade whatever; Keimer had purch ᶦⁿ⁻
his fervice for four years from the captain of ?
who had brought him over. He was dᵢ-red him
become a prefs-man.   ᶦent difpo-

George Webb was an Oxford fchol-ᶜ laft degree,
vice he had alfo purchafed for four y·
tended to be a compofitor. I fᵗˡ running away.
hereafter.   .able manner with

The laft was David Harry, a ·e fo much the more,
he had taken as an apprentice. of inftrufting them,

I foon perceived that Kˢ·new from me daily.
gaging me at fuch high wagᵃturday, becaufe it was.
he was accuftomed to gᵢ-ⁿus I had two days every
educate and form aˢ ᵃ to reading.

penfive workmen   I alfo

I alfo increafed the number of my acquaintance, at leaft among well-informed people, as much as poffible. Keimer himfelf treated me apparently with much civility and confideration, and nothing, at that period, gave me any uneafinefs except my debt to Vernon, which I was ftill incapable of paying, not having as yet been able to accumulate fo large a fum out of my little favings; but he was kind enough not to demand the reimburfement of it.

Our printing-houfe was often in want of different forts of *letter*, and there were no letter-founders in America. I, however, was able, with fome difficulty, to conftruct a mould; I made ufe of the letters which we had already, as *punches*; I caft the types in lead, by means of a clay matrix; and I thus made fhift to fupply the printing-houfe with whatever was wanting. True it is, that the letter was not good, but it was tolerable.

I alfo, upon occafion, engraved a variety of ornaments; I made ink; I now and then put the fhop in proper order; in fhort, I became, as it were, Keimer's *factotum*.

But, however ufeful I might be, I foon perceived that my fervices became daily of lefs importance, and that this happened exactly in proportion as the other workmen began to be more expert at their bufinefs; in fhort, on paying my fecond quarter's wages, he informed me, that he thought them too high, and that in his opinion, I ought to make fome abatement. He alfo became lefs civil, and daily took upon him more of the tone, and the authority of a mafter. He

often

often pretended to have occafion to find fault with me; he became more difficult to pleafe, and even feemed ready to come to an open rupture with me.

I continued, notwithftanding, to fupport his ill conduct with patience, thinking that the embarraff-ment of his affairs, was in part the occafion of his bad temper. At length a very flight incident diffolved our connection. Happening one day to hear a great noife in the neighbourhood of our houfe, I put my head out of the window in order to fee what had occafioned it. Keimer, who was in the ftreet, looked up, and having obferved me, told me in a loud and choleric tone of voice, to look to my bufinefs; he alfo added fome reproachful expreffions, which piqued me the more, becaufe they were delivered in public; all the neigh-bours, who, like myfelf, were attracted to the win-dow, having overheard the converfation, had been witneffes of the manner in which I was treated.

Not content with this, he came up ftairs into the printing-office, and continued to abufe me. Both of us waxed warm, and he gave me warning to quit his fervice at the approaching quarter, according to pre-vious ftipulation, teftifying at the fame time great un-eafinefs at being obliged to give me fo long a term.

In reply to this, I told him, that his regret was fu-perfluous, becaufe I was ready to leave him at that very moment. In fhort, I fnatched up my hat, and fallied out of the houfe, defiring Meredith, whom I faw below, to take fome of my effects which I had left behind me, and carry them at his leifure to my lodgings.

Meredith

Meredith accordingly called upon me that very evening, and we fpoke a great deal concerning what I had endured.

He had conceived a great veneration for me, and was extremely forry that I fhould leave the office while he refided there. He alfo diffuaded me from returning to my native province; for I actually began to form fuch an idea. He reminded me that Keimer owed a fum equal at leaft to the value of the property he was in poffeffion of; that his creditors began to be clamorous; that he carried on trade in a moft foolifh manner, often felling things without any profit, in order to procure ready money, and giving credit to any perfon from mere habit, and even without keeping an exact account of it. In confequence of this he argued, that in the end he muft fail in bufinefs, which would afford an opening, from which I might find means to profit greatly.

To this I objected my want of capital; but he informed me in reply, that his father had conceived the higheft opinion of me, and that in confequence of a converfation they had lately together, he was affured he would advance a fum of money to fet us up in bufinefs, if I would but admit him into partnerfhip with me.

" The time I am bound to Keimer," fays he, will " be out next fpring. By that period we may have " received our prefs and our types from London. " I know that I am not a good workman, but if you " will agree to my propofition, your knowledge in " bufinefs will be in fome meafure counterbalanced

" by

" by the capital advanced by me, and we fhall divide
" the profits equally between us."

His propofal was fo very reafonable, that we inftantly fhook hands upon it. His father too, who
happened to be in town at that very time, approved
of our fcheme. He knew that I had a great influence
over the mind of his fon, for I had prevailed upon
him, for fome months paft, to abftain from drinking
brandy, and he hoped that if we were more intimately
connected together, I fhould be able to make him
give over this unhappy cuftom altogether.

I gave his father a catalogue of the tools it would
be neceffary for us to receive from London. He
carried it immediately to a merchant's, and gave
him an order for procuring them. We had agreed
together to keep this matter a fecret, until their arrival, and I was in the mean time, to endeavour to
procure, if poffible, fome employment in another
printing-office; but there was no place vacant, and
fo I remained idle.

At the end of a few days, however, Keimer having
the expectation of being employed to print the paper
money for the State of New Jerfey, a job which required engravings, and different characters, which I
alone could furnifh, and fearing left Bradford fhould
engage me, and confequently procure this bufinefs,
fent me a very civil meffage. He faid that old friends
ought not to remain enemies, on account of a few
hafty words, fpoken in a moment of paffion, and that
he was exceedingly defirous that I fhould return to
him once more. Meredith perfuaded me to accept of

his

his invitation, and as an additional reafon, obferved, that it would be particularly advantageous to him, as he would thus have a better opportunity of improving himfelf in his profeffion, by means of my daily inftructions.

I accordingly returned, and we lived in greater harmony together than before our late feparation.

Keimer was lucky enough to be employed by the province of New Jerfey. In order to facilitate our operations, I conftructed a prefs for copper-plate printing: This was the firft that had ever been feen in America. I engraved a variety of *vignettes* and ornaments for the notes; Keimer and I then repaired to Burlington, where I executed the whole to the fatisfaction of every body, and he received a fum of money on this occafion, which helped him to *keep his head above water*, much longer than he would otherwife have been able to do.

At Burlington I got acquainted with the principal perfons of the province. Several of them had been nominated by the affembly, in order to fuperintend the prefs, and take care that there were no more *notes* printed than the number ordained by law. In confequence of this, they were by turns, conftantly with us, and whoever came according to rotation, commonly brought with him one or two friends to keep him company.

My mind was much more cultivated by reading than Keimer's ; it was probably on this account that they were better pleafed with my converfation than his. They invited me to their houfes, introduced me

to

to their friends, and treated me with the utmoſt atten‐
tion and politeneſs, while Keimer, although the maſ‐
ter, perceived himſelf a little neglected.

He was, in truth, a ſtrange animal ; entirely igno‐
rant of the common cuſtoms of life; ever ready to
oppoſe himſelf with bluntneſs to received opinions;
enthuſiaſtical in regard to ſome points of religion ;
diſguſting in his perſon ; and, in fine, in addition to
all this, a little bit of a rogue.

We remained near three months at Burlington,
and at the end of that period, I could reckon Judge
Allen, Samuel Butill, ſecretary of the province, Iſaac
Pearſon, Joſeph Cooper, ſeveral gentlemen of the
name of Smith, all members of the aſſembly, and
Iſaac Decon, the inſpector-general, among the num‐
ber of my friends.

This laſt was an able and intelligent man, who
told me, that in his early youth, be began the world
by digging clay for the brick-makers; he added, that
he was rather old when he learned to write ; that he
was at firſt employed in carrying the chain for the
ſurveyors, who taught him their trade, and that his
induſtry had at length procured him a genteel for‐
une.

" I foreſee," ſaid he to me one day, " that you
" will ſoon ſupplant this man (ſpeaking of Keimer)
" in his profeſſion, and that you will make your
" fortune by it hereafter in Philadelphia." He had
not, at that time, the leaſt poſſible knowledge of
my intention of ſetting up, either there, or elſe‐
where.

His

His friends were of great fervice to me in the end, 'as I alfo was, when ever opportunity ferved, to fome them, and they have all fince continued to teftify great regard towards me.

Before I relate the circumftances that attended my firft entrance into bufinefs, it may, perhaps be proper to inform you, what was, at that time, the ftate of my mind, relative to the principles of morality, that fo you may be enabled to judge, how far they have influenced the pofterior events of my life.

My parents at an early age, had given me religi- ous impreffions, and I received, in my infancy, a piòus education. I was brought up in the principles of the Prefbyterian religion; but fcarce had I attained the age of fifteen, when, after having doubted of dif- ferent points by turns, accordingly as I found them attacked in the different books that I perufed, I began actually to doubt of revelation itfelf.

Some tracts againft Deifm happened about this time to fall into my hands; they contained, as I was told in the preface, the fubftance of feveral fermons which had been preached in Boyle's laboratory. It fome how happened, that they operated a quite contrary effect, to that which had been propofed by the writer; for the arguments of the Deifts which had been cited in order to be refuted, appeared to me to be much ftronger than the refutation itfelf. In fhort, I became a complete Deift.

My mode of reafoning upon this fubject, alfo per- verted feveral other young men, particularly Collins and Ralph, but when I began afterwards to recollect;

that

that they had both of them done me a great deal of harm, without the leaft remorfe; when I confidered the proceedings of governor Keith, another *free thinker*, and my own conduct towards Vernon and Mifs Read, which, at times gave me great uneafinefs, I fufpected that this doctrine, although it might be true, was not very ufeful. I alfo began to have a worfe opinion than before of the pamphlet I had publifhed in London, which had the following quotation from Dryden, by way of motto :

" Whatever is is right;
" Tho' purblind man fees but a part of the chain ;
(" The neareft link ;)
" His eyes not carrying to the equal beam
" That poifes all above."

The conclufion I drew from this was, that in confequence of the goodnefs, the wifdom, and infinite power of the Deity, nothing could be wrong in this world, and that neither vice nor virtue exifted in reality, and were, in fhort, nothing more than vain diftinctions. I no longer looked upon this doctrine to be fo irreproachable, as I had at firft thought it, and I began to fufpect that fome imperceptible error had infinuated itfelf into my argument, which affected every thing that followed, as is commonly the cafe in metaphyfical reafonings.

I at length remained fully convinced, that truth, fincerity, and integrity, in the dealings of man with man, were of the utmoft importance to the happinefs of mankind, and from that moment I formed the re-

folution,

folution, and wrote it down in my journal, to practice them during the remainder of my life.

Revelation, *as fuch*, had not in truth, any influence upon my mind; but I was of opinion that although certain actions could not be bad, *becaufe it had prohibited them*, nor good, *becaufe it had commanded them*, that it was neverthelefs probable, that thefe actions were prohibited, becaufe *they were bad for us*, and commanded, *becaufe they were advantageous in their own nature*, all circumftances and things taken into confideration. And this perfuafion, aided by the fuccour of Divine Providence, or fome tutelary angel, and perhaps by circumftances and accidental fituations, which were favourable in themfelves, preferved me from all immorality, or at leaft from *grofs and voluntary* injuftice, which my want of religion tended to render me guilty of, during this dangerous period of youth, and amidft the difficult fituations which I fometimes found myfelf expofed to among ftrangers, and at a diftance from the eye and the counfels of my father.

I have thought fit to fay *voluntary*, becaufe the faults that I had hitherto committed, were in fome refpects *forced*, either by the inexperience of my youth or by the difhonefty of others.

I had confequently the principles, and I poffeffed the character of folid probity, before my entrance into the world on my own foundation. I was well aware of this advantage, and I was refolved to preferve it.

CHAP.

C H A P. VII.

Our Author fets up in Bufinefs—Some Account of the Cynic
Mickle—Eftablifhment of a Political and Philofophical Club
—He refolves to publifh a News-paper—His Scheme is
betrayed by a quondam Friend—He pays Vernon the Sum
of Money fo long due—Experiences new Embarraffments
—Generofity of two of his Friends—Diffolution of his
Partnerfhip with Meredith—Some Obfervations relative
to the Utility of Paper-Money—He opens a Stationer's Shop
—His extraordinary Prudence, Economy, and Affiduity—
He is at length united to Mifs Read—He plans a Public
Library.

WE had not returned but a few weeks to Philadelphia, when our types, prefs, &c. &c. arrived from London. I inftantly fettled my accounts
with Keimer, and left him with his own confent, before he had any knowledge of my defign.

We hired an empty houfe near the Market-Place;
in order to make the rent lefs inconvenient for us (it
was then let for £.24 fterling per annum, and I have
fince known it to be let for £.70) we received Thomas Godfrey, a glazier, and his family, as lodgers,
who fupported a confiderable portion of the expence,
and permitted us to board with them at a ftipulated
fum.

Scarce had we got our types in order, and fet up
our prefs, when George Houfe, an acquaintance of
mine, brought us a countryman, whom he had picked

up

up in the ftreets wandering about in fearch of a printer. Our money was at this time. nearly ex-haufted, on account of the variety of little fums we had been under the neceffity of expending, and the countryman's five fhillings, which were the firft pro-fits of our partnerfhip, came fo *a propos*, that I en-joyed more pleafure from the receipt of it, than from any fum I have ever gained fince. The gratitude which I felt in my heart, for the friendly conduct of George Houfe upon this occafion, rendered me in-finitely more ready than I fhould otherwife have been, to favour and encourage young men, in their firft outfet in life.

In every country, there are a number of morofe and cynical people, who are continually prognofti-cating the ruin of their neighbours. There was a perfon of this defcription, refiding at that very time at Philadelphia. He was a man of a certain age, he poffeffed a confiderable fortune, had an appearance of wifdom, and a very grave manner of fpeaking ; his name was Samuel Mickle.

This man, whom I was entirely unacquainted with, ftopped one day at my door, and afked me if I was the young man who had lately fet up a new printing houfe ; on my anfwering in the affirmative, he faid that he was very forry for me, becaufe it was an ha-zardous enterprize, the expence of which was entirely thrown away, as Philadelphia was then actually in a ftate of decay, all the inhabitants having either fhut up fhop, or being on the point of doing fo ; he added, that he was certain, from his own knowledge, that
every

every thing that might induce foolifh people to think otherwife, fuch as new buildings, and the increafed price paid for lodgings, were deceitful figns, which, in truth, only contributed to haften our ruin, and he gave me fuch a detailed account, both of the exifting misfortunes, and of fuch as were on the eve of taking place, that he left me almoft entirely difcouraged.

If I had actually known this man before my entrance into bufinefs, I fhould, beyond all doubt, never have attempted it.

He himfelf continued to live in this *ruined place*, and to declaim in the fame manner, refufing, for many years to purchafe a houfe, becaufe every thing was falling into *decay*; at length, however, I had the fatisfaction to fee him pay five times as much for one as if he had bought it, when he firft commenced his lamentations.

I ought to have obferved, that in the courfe of the preceding autumn, I had collected a number of the beft informed men of my acquaintance, in order to form a club, which we called the *Junto*, the intention of which inftitution was to improve our minds.

We met conftantly every Friday evening. The laws which I myfelf drew up, obliged every member in his turn, to propofe one or more queftions on fome point of morality, politics, or natural philofophy, in order to be difcuffed by the company prefent; and alfo to read once every three months, an effay of his own compofition, on any fubject that ftruck his fancy.

Our

Our debates were to be submitted to the regulation of a president, and were never to be excited but by the sincere desire of discovering the truth, without which the pleasure of disputation, or the vanity arising from victory, was to pass for nothing in our discussions. In short, in order to prevent bickerings and quarrels, all those expressions which might evince an obstinate, or head-strong opinion, and all direct contradictions, were prohibited under the penalty of little pecuniary fines.

The first members of our club were :

Joseph Brientnall, who was employed as a copying-clerk among the lawyers. He was a middle aged man, of a good natural disposition, greatly attached to his friends, very fond of poetry, reading all that he could meet with, and writing verses passably well; very ingenious, and exceedingly agreeable in conversation.

Thomas Godfrey, an able mathematician, who had studied this science without the assistance of a master, and who was afterwards the inventor of what is called Hadley's Quadrant; but he knew very little out of his own sphere, and was not supportable in company, always requiring, like most of the great mathematicians I have met with, an uncommon precision in every thing that was stated to them, and denying or distinguishing perpetually in regard to trifles ; the true means of troubling and disturbing all conversation.

He soon quitted us.

Nicholas

Nicholas Scull, a furveyor, who foon after became furveyor general. He was fond of books and made verfes.

William Parfons, brought up to the bufinefs of a fhoe-maker, but, who being fond of reading, had acquired a profound knowledge of the mathematicks. He ftudied this fcience at firft with an eye towards aftrology, at which he himfelf was afterwards the firft to laugh. He alfo became furveyor-general.

William Maugridge, a carpenter, and a moft excellent mechanic : In addition to this, he was a man, at once folid and fenfible.

Hugh Meredith, Stephen Potts, and George Webb; of whom I have before made mention.

Robert Grace, a young man of fortune, generous, lively, and witty ; he was fond of fatire, but he loved his friend ftill more than an epigram.

And laft of all, William Coleman, at that time clerk to a merchant, and much about my own age. He had the cooleft and cleareft head, the beft heart, and was the moft exact moralift, that I almoft ever happened to meet with. He afterwards became one of our moft refpectable merchants, and alfo one of the provincial judges. Our friendfhip exifted without any interruption, for more than forty years, to the very day of his death ; the club lafted nearly as long.

It was actually the beft fchool in the province for philofophy and politics ; for our queftions, which were given out a whole week previous to their being difcuffed, put us under the neceffity of making diligent

gent

gent inquiries concerning the different objects propofed to be canvaffed, in order to enable us to fpeak
more pertinently upon the fubjects under debate.

We thus alfo acquired the habit of a more agreeable
kind of converfation than we had been before accuftomed to, every queftion being debated according to
the exprefs laws of the fociety, and in fuch a manner
as to prevent all difguft.

It is to this circumftance that we may attribute the
duration of our club, of which I fhall often have occafion to fpeak hereafter.

I fhall now only mention it as one of the means on
which I reckoned for the increafe of our bufinefs, each
of the members endeavouring, as much as poffible,
to get us employment. Brentnall, in particular, prevailed upon the Quakers to employ us, to print part
of their hiftory ; the remainder was to be completed
under the infpection of Keimer. It was impoffible
to take much pains with the work, as we had contracted to finifh it at a very low price. It was a folio
volume printed on *pro patria* paper, with a *Cicero*
character ; the notes, which were exceedingly long,
were in a fmaller type. I compofed half a fheet per
day of it, and Meredith immediately put it to prefs. It
was often eleven o'clock at night, and fometimes later,
before I had finifhed my diftribution for next day's
work ; the little trifles which we did from time
to time, for our friends, kept us behind-hand, but I
was refolutely determined to finifh my tafk. Having
one night impofed my *form*, and, as I thought,
finifhed my labour, an accident occurred which

I   intirely

intirely difplaced my two folio pages of *Cicero*; on this I inftantly diftributed them again, and recom-pofed the whole, previous to my retiring to reft.

This vigilance and induftry, which our neighbours did not fail to perceive, began to acquire us both credit and reputation. I learned, among other things, that the merchants' club, which aflembled every night, happening accidentally to talk about the new printing-houfe, it was the general opinion that it would not fucceed, there being two printers (Keimer and Bradford) already eftablifhed in the town. But Doctor Baird, whom you and I had occafion to fee a great number of years after, in the place of his na-tivity, at St. Andrew's in Scotland, was of a contrary opinion.

" The induftry of that Franklin (faid he) is in-
" finitely beyond any thing of the kind I ever knew
" in my life before. I fee him ftill at work every
" night when I go home from the club, and he is
" again up and at bufinefs, before his neighbours are
" out of their beds."

This circumftance made a great impreffion upon the reft of the aflembly, and in a fhort time afterwards one of the members came and offered to furnifh us with articles in the paper line; but we were de-termined not as yet to embarrafs ourfelves by open-ing a fhop.

It is not in order to offer up incenfe to myfelf, that I here enter fo fully into details relative to my in-duftry; it is done merely with the idea that fuch of my defcendants as read thefe Memoirs, may appreciate

ciate the advantage of this virtue, by perceiving, in the recital of my life, the happy effects which it produced in my favour.

George Webb, having found a friend who lent him money to re-purchase his indentures from Keimer, came one day in order to offer himself to us as a workman. We could not immediately give him employment; but I foolishly told him, by way of secret, that we intended speedily to publish a newspaper, and that we should then take him into our service. My hopes of success, which I freely communicated to him, were founded on the consideration, that the only paper which we had at that time in Philadelphia, and which was printed by Bradford, was a paltry publication, which although miserably conducted, and destitute of amusement, yet produced him a considerable profit.

Webb betrayed my confidence, and instantly communicated my project to Keimer, who, in order to anticipate me, published the *prospectus* of a paper, which he himself intended to print, and upon which Webb was to be employed.

I was provoked partly at my own indiscretion, and partly at the unfair advantage which had been taken of it: by way of opposition therefore, being as yet unable to begin our intended paper, I wrote several diverting little essays, for Bradford's journal, under the name of the " Busy Body," which Brentall continued for several months. I thus fixed the attention of the public upon it, and Keimer's *prospectus*, which we turned into ridicule, was despised.

Notwithſtanding this, he actually publiſhed his paper, and after continuing it nine months, having at that time no more than ninety ſubſcribers, he offered to ſell it to me for a mere trifle. I was then at full liberty to conduct it; I therefore purchaſed the copy-right, and began to print it immediately upon my own account: In a few years afterwards it afforded me a handſome profit.

I perceive that I am now talking in the *ſingular* number, although our partnerſhip ſtill exiſted. It is, perhaps, becauſe in fact the whole enterpriſe depended entirely upon my exertion. Meredith was not a compoſitor, he was nothing more than a poor preſſman, and he but rarely abſtained from drinking ſpirits. My friends were ſorry to ſee me connected with him, but I managed matters as well as poſſible.

The firſt numbers of our paper made a far different ſenſation than any publication of the ſame kind that had yet appeared in the province, as well on account of the ſtyle, as the manner of printing. Some keen remarks which I made after my own manner, concerning the diſpute which a little before that time had taken place between governor Burnet and the aſſembly of Maſſachuſets, ſtruck perſons as ſomething above what is common, and occaſioned a great deal to be ſaid relative to the paper and its editor, ſo that in a few weeks we had a multitude of ſubſcribers. Their example was ſoon followed by many others, and our ſubſcription increaſed daily. This was one of the firſt good effects produced by my endeavours to communicate my ideas to paper. I alſo drew another

advantage

advantage from it, for the principal people in the province, perceiving me to be a man well calculated for my fituation, thought it advantageous to themfelves to do me every fervice, and encourage me by all means in their power.

Bradford ftill publifhed the motions made in the affembly, the laws paffed there, and all the other public proceedings. He had printed an addrefs from the houfe of reprefentatives to the governor, in a negligent and incorrect manner. We reprinted it with accuracy and elegance, and fent a copy of it to every member. They inftantly perceived the difference, and this circumftance feconded the influence of our well-wifhers in fuch a manner, that we were nominated printers to the affembly for the fucceeding year.

Among my friends in that houfe, I ought not to forget one of the members, Mr. Hamilton, of whom I have made mention before, and who by this time had returned from England. He interefted himfelf warmly on my account upon the prefent occafion, as he did on many others afterwards, having continued his kindnefs to me to the day of his death.

Mr. Vernon about this time reminded me of my debt to him, but without preffing me for the payment of it : I wrote a complimentary letter full of thanks in return, and befought him to wait a little longer, which he readily complied with, and as foon as it was in my power I paid him the whole, both principal and intereft, at the fame time teftifying the great ob-

ligations

ligations I lay under to him ; fo that this error of my life was in fome refpeft correfted.

But another embarraffment occurred, which I never expefted to have experienced.

Meredith's father, who, according to agreement, was to have advanced the whole fum of money neceffary for the payment of our types, prefs, &c. &c. had only given £100 fterling. There was as much more ftill due to the merchant, who became impatient for his money, and dunned us continually. We indeed gave him fecurity, but we had the melancholy profpeft before us, that if the money was not ready by the time agreed upon, a writ would be fued out, the judgment would be put in execution, all our fine projefts would evaporate, and we fhould be intirely ruined, as the prefs and types would be fold, perhaps at one half of the original price, by way of liquidating the debt!

In the midft of this diftrefs, two true friends, whofe generous proceedings I never have, nor ever fhall forget, while I am able to recollect any thing, came to me feparately, and unknown to each other, and without my having fpoken to them on the fubjeft, each of them offered to advance all the money neceffary, in order to enable me to take the bufinefs entirely into my own hands, if it fhould be practicable fo to do, becaufe they did not choofe that I fhould remain in partnerfhip with Meredith, whom, they faid, they had often feen drunk in the ftreets, and playing at games of chance in the ale-houfes, cir-

cumftances

cumſtances which could not fail to be extremely diſ-
advantageous to our credit.

Theſe two friends were William Coleman and
Robert Grace. I replied to them, that while any
probability remained that the Merediths would perform that part of our agreement which they had un-
dertaken to fulfil, I could not think of propoſing a ſeparation, as I was under a great obligation to them,
for what they had already done, and what they would,
doubtleſs, ſtill do for me, provided, it were in their
power.

While things remained in this ſtate, I ſaid one day
to my partner :

" Your father is perhaps diſcontented at your en-
" tering into trade along with me, and does not
" chooſe to do for two, what he would do for one.
" If this be the caſe, tell me ſo honeſtly, and I will
" repay you the whole ſum advanced, and take the
" buſineſs into my own hands."

" No, (replies he,) my father has actually been
" diſappointed in his hopes ; he is unable to
" pay the remainder of the money, and I wiſh not
" to make him uneaſy on the ſubject. I perceive
" at length, that I myſelf am not in the leaſt quali-
" fied for being a printer : I was brought up as a
" farmer, and it was a fooliſh thing in me to come to
" town, and bind myſelf, at thirty years of age, as an
" apprentice to a new buſineſs. Several of my old
" acquaintances are about to form an eſtabliſhment
" in North Carolina, where the land is extremely
" fertile and productive. I am tempted to go with

I 4   " them,

" them, and refume my former occupation. You,
" doubtlefs, may find friends to affift you : If you
" will, therefore, undertake to pay the debts con-
" tracted by the partnerfhip, reftore to my father the
" hundred pounds he has advanced, liquidate my own
" little trifling debts, and give me thirty pounds and a
" new faddle, I will refign up my claim to every thing,
" and leave the whole bufinefs intirely to yourfelf."

I inftantly accepted this propofition without the
leaft hefitation. The terms were immediately committed to writing, and figned and fealed without any
delay. I agreed to every thing he required, and he
foon after fet off for South Carolina, from whence in
the courfe of the next year he fent me two long letters, containing the beft accounts that had hitherto
appeared, relative to that country, in regard to the
climate, foil, agriculture, &c. &c.; for he was exceedingly expert in all thofe matters. I publifhed this
correfpondence in my newfpaper, and it was read
with the utmoft fatisfaction.

As foon as he was gone, I addreffed myfelf to my
two friends, and not wifhing to give one a difobliging
preference over the other, I accepted of each of them
one half the fum he had offered me; this was abfolutely neceffary for the fettlement of my affairs.

I then paid the debts due by the partnerfhip, and
continued to carry on bufinefs in my own name,
taking care to inform the public, by means of an advertifement, that the connexion was diffolved. I
think that this was either in or about the year
1729.

About

About the fame epoch, the people began to be clamorous for a new emiffion of paper money, which had never been iffued in the province to a greater amount than £15,000 fterling, and the notes were become exceedingly fcarce.

The rich inhabitants, prepoffeffed againft all paper of this kind, for fear left the value of money fhould be lowered, as had been done in New-England, to the prejudice of all thofe who were creditors, oppofed themfelves to this demand.

We had often difcuffed the queftion in our *Junta*, where I had been always on the fide that patronifed the new emiffion, being fully perfuaded that the firft fmall fum, iffued in 1723, had done much good in the province, by favouring commerce, induftry, and population, as I perceived all the houfes inhabited, and many more were then building; whereas I recollected very well, when I wandered, for the firft time, along the ftreets of Philadelphia, eating my loaf, and looking around me, that I had feen moft of the houfes in Wallnut-Street, and Second-Street, and Fourth-Street, as well as a great number of others in Chefnut-Street, and elfewhere, with bills upon them; a circumftance which made me then think that the inhabitants of Philadelphia would abandon it, one after the other.

Our frequent debates had put me fo fully in pof-feffion of this fubject, that I wrote and publifhed an anonymous pamphlet, on "The Nature and Neceffity "of Paper Money." It was well received by the public in general, but it greatly difpleafed the rich, becaufe

becaufe it increafed and fortified the clamours of thofe who were in favour of a new creation of paper money. But being utterly deftitute of a writer capable of making any reply, their oppofition began to be mollified, and the majority of the affembly being in favour of the project, a law foon after paffed for this purpofe.

My numerous friends in that houfe, fully perfuaded that I had been very ferviceable upon this occafion, refolved to make me fome little recompenfe by employing me to print the paper money: It was a lucrative job, and was of prodigious fervice to me. This was another advantage that I derived from a facility in managing my pen.

Time and experience fo evidently demonftrated the utility and advantage of paper money, that it never afterwards experienced much oppofition, fo that it foon amounted to £55,000 fterling, and in 1739 to £80,000 fterling. Since that epoch it increafed, during the late war, to £350,000 fterling; commerce, new buildings, and inhabitants continually increafing in the interval: I am however perfuaded, that there are certain limits, beyond which the emiffion of paper money may become prejudicial.

I obtained foon after, by means of my friend Hamilton, the impreffion of the paper money belonging to Newcaftle, another profitable piece of bufinefs, as I then thought it, little things always appearing great to thofe whofe fortunes are moderate ; and this was really uncommonly advantageous, becaufe it was very encouraging to me. He alfo procured me the privilege

vilege of printing the laws and proceedings of that affembly, and this bufinefs conftantly continued to be
done by me, while I exercifed the profeffion of a printer.

I afterwards opened a little fhop for the fale of
paper and ftationary. I kept *blanks* of all kinds, and
they were by far the moft correct that had ever appeared among us ; I was affifted in this operation by
my friend Brentnall. I alfo fold parchment, pafte-
board, books, &c. &c.

A perfon of the name of Witemach, whom I had
known in London, and who was a moft excellent
compofitor, offered himfelf to me about this time;
I immediately employed him, and he worked conftantly and diligently with me. I alfo took the fon
of Aquila Rofe, as an apprentice.

I then began little by little to pay off the debt
which I had contracted for my utenfils, and on purpofe to fubftantiate my credit as a tradefman, I took
care not only to be *really* induftrious and frugal, but
even to avoid the appearance of the contrary..;

I was clothed with great fimplicity, and was never
feen in any place of public amufement. I never went
with parties of pleafure either to fifh or to hunt.
True indeed, a favourite book would now and then
debauch me from my bufinefs, but this was but feldom
the cafe; and when it fo occurred, it was in *private*,
and *without giving fcandal.* In order alfo to fhew
that I was not above my profeffion, I fometimes carried home the paper which I had bought from the
merchants, in a wheel-barrow, which I rolled through
the ftreets before me.

I thus

· I thus begun to be generally known as an induftri-ous young man, and one very exact in all his pay-ments ; the merchants who imported paper, folicited my cuftom ; others came and made me the firft offer of books, fo that my little bufinefs went on increafing wonderfully.

In the mean time, Keimer's trade and credit began daily to decline, and he was at length obliged to fell off his goods in order to fatisfy his creditors. After this he repaired to Barbadoes, where he lived for fome time in great poverty.

His former apprentice, David Harry, whom I had inftructed during my refidence with Keimer, having purchafed his materials, fet up in his place. I was at firft afraid that I fhould find a powerful rival in David, becaufe he belonged to an opulent and refpectable fa-mily. In confequence of this idea, I propofed to him to enter into partnerfhip together ; this, very luckily for me, he rejected with great haughtinefs.

He was very proud and lofty in his manners, and talked and acted as if he had been a lord; he lived alfo at a confiderable expence, and took a great deal of pleafure abroad. At length he began to run in debt and to neglect his bufinefs, and in confequence of this, *his bufinefs left him.* Perceiving in a fhort time, that he could procure no more employment in this country, he followed Keimer to Barbadoes, carrying his printing tools along with him. On his arrival in that ifland, the apprentice employed his *quondam* mafter as a journeyman. They often difputed and quarrelled with each other, and Harry, who once

more

more fell behind-hand, was at length obliged to fell
his printing prefs and types, and return to his former
occupation as a farmer, in Pennfylvania. The perfon
who purchafed them from him, employed Keimer to
work for him, but he died a few years after.

I had now no other competitor except Bradford,
who being very opulent, contented himfelf with a
fmall fhare of bufinefs, and was not in the leaft defirous of extending his trade. However, as he had
the poft-office, it was imagined that he was in a better
fituation to procure intelligence than I. His newfpaper alfo poffeffed the reputation of enjoying a more
extenfive circulation than mine, and in confequence of
this, he received a far greater number of advertife-
ments ; this circumftance was equally profitable for
him and difadvantageous to me.

I diftributed my newfpapers regularly by means of
the poft ; but the public was of a contrary opinion,
becaufe they knew that I could not accomplifh this by
any other means than that of corrupting the poft-boys,
who confequently could not take charge of them but
by ftealth, Bradford being envious enough to prohibit them. This mode of proceeding made me exceedingly angry, and I looked upon it to be fo scan-
dalous, that when in the courfe of a few years I found
myfelf in his place, I was exceedingly cautious not to
imitate him.

I had continued until now to board with Godfrey,
who, with his wife and children, ftill occupied a part
of my houfe, and half my fhop, which was very ferviceable to him in his bufinefs as a glazier ; it muft
be

be obferved, however, that he worked but very feldom, being conftantly abforbed in his mathematical
purfuits.

Mrs. Godfrey about this time took it into her head
to marry me to the daughter of one of her relations.
She was ftudious to find out opportunities of leaving
us together, until fhe perceived that I was really
fmitten with her coufin, a circumftance not very difficult to be atchieved, as fhe had great perfonal
merit.

The parents encouraged my addreffes, by inviting
me frequently to fupper, until they at length thought
that it was time to come to an explanation. Mrs.
Godfrey undertook to negotiate this bufinefs, and to
bring the match between us to a conclufion.

I informed her that I expected to receive a fum of
money along with the young woman, fufficient to enable me to liquidate the remainder of my debt for
my printing tools. I believe that it did not then exceed the fum of £100 fterling. She returned me for
anfwer, that her parents had not fuch a large fum
at their command. I obferved in reply, that they
might borrow it any where upon the fecurity of their
houfe. At the end of a few days a meffage was
brought me, that they did not approve of the alliance,
and that having confulted Bradford, they had learned
from him that the trade of a printer was far from being lucrative; that his types would be foon worn
out, and that he would then be in want of others;
that Keimer and David Harry had failed one after

the

the other, and that I fhould, in all human probability, follow their example.

In confequence of this, they forbad me the houfe, and fhut up their daughter. I know not rightly, whether this proceeded from a change of opinion, or folely from an artifice, arifing from the fuppofition that we were too far engaged with each other to defift, and that, in confequence, we fhould endeavour to be united together by means of a clandeftine marriage, which would fet them entirely at liberty, either to give or refufe their confent, as they fhould judge neceffary.

Sufpecting this to be their motive, I became piqued at their conduct, and never afterwards went near them.

Mrs. Godfrey told me fome time after, that they entertained the moft favourable difpofitions in regard to me, and that they would enter anew into a treaty of marriage, but I declared that I was abfolutely determined to have nothing more to do with the family.

The Godfreys having teftified much refentment againft me upon this occafion, we began to difagree, and at length found it inconvenient to live in the fame houfe together; they therefore changed the place of their abode, leaving me the premifes entirely to myfelf.

I refolved from that moment never more to let lodgings.

This affair having turned my thoughts towards marriage, I began to look around me, and make

I   overtures

overtures in other places, but I foon found that as a
printer's was in general thought to be a very poor
trade, I muft not expect to get any money with a
wife, at leaft if I wifhed her to poffefs any of the
good qualities that could alone make a helpmate
defirable.

In the mean time, that paffion of youth, which is
fo very difficult to govern, often drew me into intrigues with low and loofe women, who happened
to fall in my way, fo that this kind of life was not
without inconvenience and expence, befides the perpetual rifk of ruining my health, by acquiring fome
terrible diforder, which I dreaded above all other
things in the world. I was however happy enough
to efcape from this calamity.

I had alway kept up a friendly connection and
intercourfe with Mifs Read's family, both as neighbours and old acquaintances. Her parents had entertained a regard for me, from the moment that I
firft lodged in their houfe. I was often invited to
vifit them, they confulted me upon all their affairs,
and I was happy enough to be fometimes ferviceable
to them.

I was affected with the unfortunate fituation of
their daughter, who had become melancholy, was
feldom feen to fmile, and was attached to folitude.

I looked upon my wildnefs and inconftancy during
my ftay in London, as the principal caufe of her mif-
fortunes, although her mother had candour enough
to attribute the fault to herfelf rather than to me, becaufe fhe had not only prevented our marriage before

my

my departure, but had alſo prevailed upon: her daughter to marry another perſon in my abſence. -

Our former mutual affection began once more to revive in our hearts; but there were many obſtacles to our union. Her marriage indeed was looked upon as illegal and invalid, her huſband, as it was rumoured, having a former wife, ſtill living in England; but it was extremely difficult to have legal proof of this at ſo great a diſtance; and although it was reported every where that he himſelf was dead, yet we had not the leaſt certainty of the fact, and even if it had been certified to us, he had left a great number of debts, for the payment of which his ſucceſſor might have been troubled.

Notwithſtanding all theſe difficulties, we were determined to be united to each other, and I accordingly eſpouſed her on the firſt of September 1730.

None of the inconveniences which we had foreſeen ever occurred; ſhe proved a good and faithful companion to me, and aſſiſted me greatly in the management of my ſhop.

We were exceedingly proſperous together, and we always endeavoured to render one another happy; thus I corrected, as well as I was able, this great error of my youth.

Our club did not as yet meet at a tavern. We aſſembled at Mr. Grace's, who had fitted up part of his houſe expreſsly for this purpoſe.

One of the members happened to obſerve, that as our books were often quoted as authorities relative to the queſtions propoſed, it would be the

K beſt

beft mode to colleĉt them in the place where we were accuftomed to meet, in order that they might be oc. cafionally confulted, and that in thus forming one common library out of our private colleĉtions, each of us might enjoy the advantage of making ufe of the books of the other members, which would be nearly as convenient as if one perfon poffeffed the whole.

This idea was inftantly adopted and carried into execution, and we all depofited what books we could readily fpare at the bottom of the hall. They were not, however, fo numerous as we expeĉted ; and although we made great ufe of them from time to time, fome inconveniencies having at length arifen from want of care and attention, it was determined that each perfon fhould take home his own books again.

About this period I formed a plan for eftablifhing a circulating library. I drew up the *profpeĉtus*, and put the conditions into a regular and legal form by the affiftance of our famous lawyer Brockden, and my projeĉt fucceeded to admiration, as will be feen hereafter.

[Here ends that Part of the Life of the late BEN-JAMIN FRANKLIN, *LL. D. originally written by himfelf.]*

THE

L I F E

OF

BENJAMIN FRANKLIN, LL.D.

PART II.

CHAP. I.

Franklin begins to distinguish himself as Conductor of the Pennsylvania Gazette—He becomes acquainted with Mr. Whitefield—Establishment of the Philosophical Society of America—Experiments in Electricity—Discovery tending to demonstrate the Identity of Lightning and the Electric Fluid—Electric Kite—Metallic Conductors—Mode of preserving Houses from the destructive Effects of Lightning —Advice to those unacquainted with the Nature of the Electric Fluid.

WE have already beheld the author of these memoirs, rising from obscurity in spite of every obstacle, and by means of his own prudence and industry, struggling into wealth and reputation.

Hitherto he was only known as an active and intelligent young man, and was conspicuous for little else except his diligence and punctuality. But soon after his marriage with Miss Read he became proprietor of the "Pennsylvania Gazette," and in a short

time

time exhibited fuch an extent of capacity, as the editor of it, that he acquired a confiderable portion of celebrity. This circumftance procured him a number of valuable friends, among whom was the Rev. George Whitefield, who, although then a very young man, difplayed a wonderful degree of eloquehce in his difcourfes, and poffeffed the rare and extraordinary talent of influencing the paffions, captivating the hearts, and amending the morals of the multitude.

At that very period he was occupied in preaching his doctrines throughout North-America, and his fuccefs in fo important a miffion was unexampled. Having compofed a volume of fermons, for the ufe of the fectarifts of his own perfuafion, who were exceedingly numerous, he employed his friend Mr. Franklin to print them for him; and the extraordinary fuccefs of this work tended not a little to extend the trade and connexions of the latter.

Although our author was uncommonly affiduous, both in his profeffion as a printer and in his bufinefs as a bookfeller, yet he found means to confecrate a few hours of his time to the purfuit of his favourite ftudy, which was natural philofophy.

A number of perfons, eminent for their abilities, having determined, in 1743, to form themfelves into a fociety for the propagation of knowledge, he was unanimoufly appointed to draw up the plan of the inftitution. This affociation, afterwards fo celebrated under the name of the " Philofophical Society of
" America,"

" America," is ftill in exiftence, and reckons among its members a number of celebrated men.

Within a few years after the eftablifhment of this fociety, the number of its members increafed fo con-fiderably, that it was judged proper to divide them into the following fix committees : *

I. Natural Philofophy, Mathematics, Optics, Aftro-nomy, and Geography.

II. Medicine, Chemiftry, and Anatomy.

III. Natural Hiftory and Botany.

IV. Commerce and Navigation.

V. Mechanics and Architecture; and,

VI. Rural Œconomy, and the Amelioration of Wafte Lands.

A profpectus of the plan was circulated over the continent, and the learned of all countries were invited to an amicable correfpondence.

Thefe meafures were attended with the moft ample fuccefs, and this inftitution began in a fhort time to affume a very refpectable appearance.

Accuftomed to fee and examine every thing with his own eyes, to deduct confequences from the *phe-nomena* which he obferved, and never blindly to fol-low the opinions of other men ; Franklin foon ac-quired a vigorous judgment, a prodigious fund of knowledge, and a manner of reafoning at once pre-cife, clear, and convincing.

Amidft a variety of commercial concerns, he found leifure occafionally to indulge his genius in philofo-phical fpeculations. Among thefe, electricity, the leaft cultivated of all the branches of natural know-

K 3 ledge,

ledge, more efpecially engaged his attention ; and he communicated his difcoveries in that fcience between the years 1747 and 1754, to Peter Collinfon, Efq. of London, a fellow of the Royal Society.

Thefe letters were afterwards publifhed, and nothing written on the fubject of electricity was ever more generally read and admired, not in Great-Britain and America only, but in all parts of Europe.

The Englifh were rather tardy in acknowledging the merits of this great man, but foreign countries did ample juftice to his genius, and even gave the name of the Franklinian Syftem to his difcoveries. In a word, his experiments and obfervations on this fubject bid fair to be handed down to pofterity, as the true principles of electricity, in the fame manner as the Newtonian Philofophy is acknowledged to be the true fyftem of nature in general.

The greateft difcovery which Dr. Franklin made concerning electricity, and which has been of the moft practical ufe to mankind, is that of the perfect fimilarity or rather *famenefs* between electrical fire and lightning. He begins his account of this fimilarity, by cautioning his readers againft being ftaggered at the great difference of the effects, in point of *degree*, fince that can be no argument of any difparity in their nature. " It is no wonder," fays he, " if the effects of the " one fhould be much greater than thofe of the " other; for if two electrified gun-barrels will ftrike at " two inches diftance, and make a loud report, at " how great a diftance will 10,000 acres of electric " cloud

" cloud ſtrike and give its fire, and how loud muſt
" be that report !"

Having diſcovered that metallic bars pointed towards the end, poſſeſſed the power of attraĉting the
eleĉtric matter, at a great diſtance, and became in
their turn eleĉtrified by their communication with the
clouds, he communicated his ideas on this ſubjeĉt to
the public, and a number of theſe inſulated and
pointed rods were ereĉted in different parts of England and France. The firſt of theſe machines viſited
by the celeſtial fluid, was an iron bar forty feet in
length, placed at the top of his ſummer-houſe, at
Merly-la-ville, by M. Dalibard; this was eleĉtrified
during the ſpace of a whole hour, on the 10th of
May 1752.

After having publiſhed the mode of verifying his
hypotheſis concerning the identity of eleĉtricity and
lightning, Franklin determined to ereĉt a pyramid
at Philadelphia, in order to perform his experiments.

Recolleĉting at length, that a kite would have a
more ſpeedy and eaſy acceſs to the regions of thunder, than any building elevated by human induſtry,
he determined to carry this idea into praĉtice. He
accordingly adjuſted a ſilk handkerchief to two ſticks
placed croſs-wiſe. At the approach of the firſt ſtorm
he repaired to a field where there was an out-houſe
conveniently ſituated for his experiment; and in order
to obviate the ridicule that but too commonly ac-
companies unſucceſsful attempts for the promotion
of the ſciences, he took care to communicate his in-

K 4   tentions

tentions to no one but his fon, whofe affiftance was abfolutely neceffary upon this occafion.

Having launched his kite into the air, with a pointed wire fixed to the end of it, he foon fucceeded fo far as to elevate it to the proper height. It was a long time before he difcovered the leaft appearance of electricity. A denfe black cloud had already paffed over his head without any effect whatever, and he began actually to defpair of fuccefs, when happening to look with more than ordinary attention, he at length perceived a lambent flame to ftream along the hempen cord. The lightning (for it was actually fuch!) defcended along the ftring, and was received by an iron key tied to the extremity of it, while this was connected with his hand by means of apiece of filken cord.

What muft have been his joy, when prefenting his knuckles to the key at the end of the hempen ftring, he felt an electric fhock, and found out that his difcovery was complete!

He now clearly perceived the electric fparks; more followed in fucceffion, and when the ftring became humid by means of the rain, it conducted the electric fluid with ftill greater freedom, fo that it would ftream out plentifully from the key, at the approach of a perfon's finger. At this key he charged phials, and from electric fire thus obtained, kindled fpirits, and performed all other electrical experiments which are ufually exhibited by means of an excited globe or tube.

This memorable and indeed wonderful experiment took place in June 1752, one month after his theory had been actually verified in France, but before

he

* as a note from J. A. M S
line 6 read Profeffor —

he could have poffibly received any notice of its fuccefs.

Having fucceeded fo completely with his electrical
kite, Mr. Franklin determined to perfevere in his·
difcoveries.' He accordingly erected an· infulated
iron rod, on purpofe to draw the lightning·into his·
houfe, to make experiments whenever there fhould be
a confiderable quantity of it in the-atmofphere; and,'
that he might not lofe any· opportunity of that nature, he connected two bells with his apparatus,
which gave him notice by their ringing, whenever his
rod was electrified,

But this difcovery, although it feemed to the ignorant and fuperficial to be only a matter of curiofity
and furprife, was attended with confequences highly
beneficial to the human race. The grand practical
ufe which our author converted it to, was, to prevent
buildings from being damaged by lightning. This
he accomplifhed by fixing a metallic rod higher
than any part of the edifice, and contriving it in fuch
a manner·as to communicate with the earth, or ra-·
ther with the neareft·water. The lightning was
fure to feize·upon the rod, preferably to any other'·
part of the building, and that dangerous element, in-·
ftead of committing its ufual deftruction, was harm-
lefsly brought in contact with the ground, without
doing any harm whatever. .

His letters on electricity having been publifhed in
the philofophical tranfactions of the Royal Society,'
his fame continued to augment daily, and the uni-'
verfity of Oxford foon after paid a juft tribute to his·
talents,

talents, by conferring upon him the honorary title of
Doctor of Laws, in the month of April 1762. At
this period he had arrived at the zenith of his philofophical glory. The moft diftinguifhed men of the age
began now to cultivate his friendfhip and to revere
his name.

The letters of Dr. Franklin abound with a variety
of mifcellaneous obfervations, highly important in
their nature, as they tend to preferve the lives of
men from the ravages of an element that has heretofore been confidered as one of the fcourges of humanity. The following paffage will ferve as a leffon
to thofe perfons unacquainted with the nature of
the electrical fluid, who are accuftomed, whenever
they hear thunder, to take refuge either beneath
trees, or under the fhelter of lofty buildings :

" When a tempeft," fays the Doctor, " paffes over
" a country, high mountains, tall trees, elevated
" towers, pyramids, mafts of fhips, chimnies, and
" in general all kinds of eminences, attract the
" electric matter, and it is upon fuch objects as
" thefe that the clouds difcharge themfelves. It is
" extremely dangerous for any perfon to fhelter
" himfelf under a tree during a ftorm ; a great num-
" ber of men and animals have been killed in this
" manner. It is much more fafe to remain in the
" open field ; and this for another reafon : While the
" clothes are drenched with rain, if a flafh of light-
" ning, darting downwards towards the earth, fhould
" happen to come in contact with the head of the
" paffenger, the fluid would be conducted all along the

" furface of the body, by means of the wet. Thus
" we have often feen, that a half-drowned rat cannot
" be killed by the explofion of a bottle of electric
" matter, whereas a rat whofe fkin is perfectly dry,
" is inftantly put to death.

" Thefe facts are proved by a multitude of ex-
" amples : I fhall only mention two. The firft oc-
" curred fome years fince at Lancafter, in the pro-
" vince of Pennfylvania, in the manner I am now
" about to recount.

" Three children of that town, all of whom were
" nearly thirteen years of age, went into the country
" in the morning of the 24th of July, in order to
" gather cherries. As they returned, about four
" o'clock in the afternoon, they were overtaken by
" a fhower of rain, and although already wet, they
" took refuge beneath a large oak, which they per-
" ceived in the midft of the highway, and which was
" about forty yards diftant from any other tree
" whatever.

" One of the children leaned againft this oak, in
" fuch a manner that his head and part of his left
" fide touched the trunk. The other two fat them-
" felves down at a certain diftance, beneath the
" fhelter of one of its long and bufhy branches. Se-
" veral fucceffive claps of thunder were now heard
" in a wefterly direction ; the explofions become
" louder and more frequent ; at length the lightning
" envelopes the tree, inftantly kills the boy who was
" fitting againft its trunk, and alfo a dog that lay
" between his feet, and overturns the two others,
" who

" who remain for fome minutes entirely motion-
" lefs, and without the ufe of their fpeech. At length
" one of them acquires fufficient ftrength to rife,
" but he feems ftunned and enfeebled, and reels
" backwards and forwards like a drunken perfon.

" As foon as he was able to reflect on the caufe
" of this accident, he fearches after his companions,
" and perceiving that the one near him ftill evinced
" fome fymptoms of life, he attempts to raife him
" up ; not fucceeding in this, he proceeds towards
" the other, whom he finds exactly in the fame pofture
" as when alive, except that his body was incurv-
" ated by means of the electrical fhock which had
" firft ftruck him on the head. His eyes alfo were
" open and immoveable, and all his joints ftiff, as if
" they had been intirely deprived of articulation.

" Scarcely recovered from his own fright, and
" ftill more alarmed at this fpectacle, the child ran
" as faft as poffible to the houfe of a perfon of the
" name of John Stonner, to whom he recounted this
" unlucky accident.

" The two furviving children were immediately
" put to bed, and recovered foon afterwards. I my-
" felf, accompanied by fome friends, went to fee
" them. They were extremely fenfible for their
" years, and replied to all our queftions in a very
" fatisfactory manner. Having afked them if they
" heard any noife at the moment they felt themfelves
" ftruck, ' we heard a noife,' faid they, ' as if
" a number of cannon had been fired all at once ;'
" as to the fenfation, they obferved, ' that it ap-
6   " peared

" peared as if a large bundle of lighted wood had
" fallen upon them, and enveloped them in its flame.'
" After examining the bodies and clothes of thefe
" poor children, and confidering what an enormous
" volume of the fluid they had been expofed to, we
" were not able to conceive how it had been poffible
" for them to efcape. The only manner of account-
" ing for this *phenomenon*, (Divine Providence apart,)
" is to fuppofe, that having been wet by the rain,
" previous to their fitting under the tree, their
" clothes had ferved as conductors to a great part of
" the electric fluid.
" The fecond inftance took place at Savannah, in
" Georgia, in the month of July 1773. In a veffel
" deftined for the Bahamas, and moored along-fide of
" the Key were twelve horfes. The captain had cleared
" out at the cuftom-houfe, and was about to fet fail,
" when all of a fudden a terrible ftorm came on, as is
" often the cafe there at that feafon of the year.
" The lightning ftruck the maft of the fhip, and the
" maft conducted it to the horfes, of whom ten were
" inftantly killed. The two which efcaped had juft
" come on board, and had but a few minutes before
" been bathed in the river Savannah, a circumftance
" which had probably faved their lives."

Notwithftanding the accidents occafioned by lightning were very common, and generally very alarming,
in America, and the utility of the metallic conductors
was univerfally acknowledged, yet but few houfes
were furnifhed with them on the new continent; nay,
feveral fectarifts in Pennfylvania condemned the ufe

of them, faying, that it was "rafhnefs, and a want "of confidence in the firft great Caufe." Notwith-ftanding this, thefe people, fo very full of *confidence*, never rejected the affiftance of medicine, and were not afraid of being let blood, or of applying reme-dies to the various diforders with which they might happen to be afflicted.

It was thus that Franklin employed the leifure part of his life, in philofophical refearches; in founding foci-eties; propagating knowledge; and in communicating a multitude of inventions ufeful to mankind. We fhall foon behold him attaching himfelf to political inveftigation, bending his great and comprehenfive talents to the ftudy of government, repreffing the tyranny of one nation, and teaching another to foar at liberty and independence!

CHAP.

LETTERS

FROM

DR. FRANKLIN TO GOVERNOR SHIRLEY.

LETTER I.

SIR,   *Tuefday Morning.*

I RETURN you the loofe fheets of the plan, with thanks to your Excellency for communicating them.

I apprehend, that excluding the people of the co-lonies from all fhare in the choice of the grand coun-cil, will give extreme diffatisfaction, as well as the taxing them by act of parliament, where they have no reprefentation.

It is very poffible that this general government might be as well and faithfully adminiftered without the people as with them; but when heavy burdens are to be laid upon them, it has been found ufeful to make it, as much as poffible, their own act; for they bear better, when they have, or think they have, fome fhare in the direction; and when any public meafures are generally grievous, or even diftafteful to the peo-ple, the wheels of government move more heavily.

I am, Sir, &c.

B. FRANKLIN.

L

LETTER II.

SIR, *Wednesday Morning.*

I MENTIONED it yefterday to your Excellency as. my opinion, that excluding the people of the colonies from all fhare in the choice of the grand council, would probably give extreme diffatisfaction, as well as the taxing them by act of parliament, where they have no reprefentation. In matters of general con-- cern to the people, and efpecially where burdens are to be laid upon them, it is of ufe to confider, as well what they will be apt to think and fay, as what they ought to think : I fhall therefore, as your Excellency requires it of me, briefly mention what of either kind occurs to me on this occafion.

Firft, They will fay, and perhaps with juftice, the body of the people in the colonies are as loyal, and as firmly attached to the prefent conftitution and reigning family, as any fubjects in the king's dominions.

That there is no reafon to doubt the readinefs and willingnefs of the reprefentatives they may chufe, to grant fuch fums for the defence of the country, as fhall be judged neceffary, fo far as their abilities will allow.

That the people in the colonies who are to feel the immediate mifchiefs of invafion and conqueft by an enemy, in the lofs of their eftates, lives, and liberties, are likely to be better judges of the quantity of forces

neceffary

heceffary to be raifed and maintained, forts to be built and fupported, and of their own abilities to bear the expence, than the parliament of England at fo great a diftance.

That governors often come to colonies merely to make fortunes, with which they intend to return to Britain ; are not always men of the beft abili- ties or integrity; have many of them no eftates here, nor any natural connections with us that fhould make them heartily concerned for our welfare ; and might poffibly be fond of raifing and keeping up more forces than neceffary, from the profits accruing to them- felves, and to make provifion for their friends and dependents.

That the counfellors in moft of the colonies, being appointed by the crown, on the recommendation of governors, are often (N. B.) of fmall eftates, fre- quently dependent on the governors for offices, and therefore too much under influence.

That there is therefore great reafon to be jealous of a power in fuch governors and councils to raife fuch fums as they fhall judge neceffary, by drafts on the lords of the treafury, to be afterwards laid on the colonies by act of parliament, and paid by the people here ; fince they might abufe it, by projecting ufelefs expeditions, haraffing the people, and taking them from their labour to execute fuch projects, merely to create offices and employments, gratify their dependents, and divide the profits.

That the parliament of England is at a great dif- tance, fubject to be mifinformed and mifled by fuch

governors

governors and councils, whofe united intereft might probably fecure them againft the effect of any complaint from hence.

That it is fuppofed an undoubted right of Englifhmen, not to be taxed but by their own confent, given through their reprefentatives.

That the colonies have no reprefentatives in parliament.

That to propofe taxing them by parliament, and refufe them the liberty of chufing a reprefentative council, to meet in the colonies, and confider and judge of the neceffity of any general tax, and the *quantum,* fhews a fufpicion of their loyalty to the crown, or of their regard for their country, or of their common fenfe and underftanding, which they have not deferved.

That compelling the colonies to pay money without their confent, would be rather like raifing contributions in an enemy's country, than taxing of Englifhmen for their own public benefit.

That it would be treating them as a conquered people, and not as true Britifh fubjects.

That a tax laid by the reprefentatives of the colonies might be eafily leffened; but being once laid by parliament under the influence of the reprefentations made by governors, would probably be kept up, and continued for the benefit of the governors, to the grievous burthen and difcontent of the colonies, and prevention of their growth and increafe.

That a power in governors, to march the inhabitants from one end of the Britifh and French colonies to the other, being a country at leaft 1500 miles long, without the approbation or confent of the reprefentatives firft obtained to fuch expeditions, might be grievous and ruinous to the people, and would put them upon a footing with the fubjects of France in Canada, that now groans under fuch oppreffion from their governors, who, for two years paft, have haraffed them with long and deftructive marches to the Ohio.

That if the colonies in a body, may be well governed by the governors and councils appointed by the crown, without reprefentatives, particular colonies may be as well, or better, fo governed; a tax may be laid upon them all by act of parliament for fupport of government; and their affemblies may be difmiffed as an ufelefs part of the conftitution.

That the powers propofed by the Albany plan of union to be vefted in a grand council reprefentative of the people, even with regard to military matters, are not fo great as thofe of the colonies of Rhode-Ifland and Connecticut are entrufted with by their charters, and have never abufed; for, by this plan, the prefident general is appointed by the crown, and controuls all by his negative; but in thofe governments the people chufe the governor, and yet allow him no negative.

That the Britifh colonies bordering on the French are properly frontiers of the Britifh empire; and the frontiers of an empire are properly defended at the joint expence of the body of the people in fuch empire: It would now be thought hard, by act of parlia-

ment

ment to oblige the cinque-ports or fea-coaft of Britain to maintain the whole navy, becaufe they are more immediately defended by it, not allowing them at the fame time a vote in chufing members of parliament ; and as the frontiers of America bear the expences of their own defence, it feems hard to allow them no fhare in voting the money, judging of the neceffity and fum, or advifing the meafures.

That, befides the taxes neceffary for the defence of the frontiers, the colonies pay yearly great fums to the mother-country unnoticed : For taxes paid in Britain by the land-holder or artificer, muft enter into and increafe the price of the produce of land and manufactures made of it, and great part of this is paid by confumers in the colonies, who thereby pay a confiderable part of the Britifh taxes.

We are reftrained in our trade with foreign nations, notwithftanding we could be fupplied with many manufactures cheaper from them, but muft buy the fame dearer from Britain. The difference of price is a clear tax to Britain. We are obliged to carry a great part of our produce directly to Britain; and where the duties laid upon it leffen its price to the planter, or it fells for lefs than it would in foreign markets, the difference is a tax paid to Britain.

Some manufactures we could make, but are forbidden, and muft take them of Britifh merchants : The whole price is a tax paid to Britain.

By our greatly increafing the demand and confumption of Britifh manufactures, their price is confiderably raifed of late years ; the advantage is clear

profit

profit to Britain, and enables its people better to pay
great taxes, and much of it being paid by us, is a
clear tax to Britain.

In fhort, as we are not fuffered to regulate our
trade, and reftrain the importation and confumption
of Britifh fuperfluities (as Britain can the confumption of foreign fuperfluities), our whole wealth cen-
ters finally amongft the merchants and inhabitants of
Britain; and if we make them richer, and enable
them better to pay their taxes, it is nearly the fame
as being taxed ourfelves, and equally beneficial to the
crown.

This kind of fecondary taxes, however, we do not
complain of; though we have no fhare in the laying
or difpofing of them; but to pay immediate heavy
taxes, in the laying on, appropriation, and difpofition
of which, we have no part, and which perhaps we
may know to be grievous, muft feem hard meafure
to Englifhmen, who cannot conceive that, by ha-
zarding their lives and fortunes in fubduing and fet-
tling new countries, and extending and increafing the
commerce of the mother nation, they have forfeited
the native right of Britons, which they think ought
rather to be given to them, as due to fuch merit, if
they had been before in a ftate of flavery.

Thefe, and fuch kind of things as thefe, I apprehend, will be thought and faid by the people, if the
propofed alteration of the Albany plan fhould take
place. Then the adminiftration of the board of governors and council fo appointed, not having the reprefentative body of the people to approve and unite

in

in its meafures, and conciliate the minds of the people to them, will probably become fufpeded and
odious; dangerous animofities and feuds will arife
between the governors and governed, and every thing
go into confufion,

Perhaps I am too apprehenfive in this matter;
but, having freely given my opinion and reafons,
your Excellency can judge better than I, whether
there can be any weight in them; and the fhortnefs of
the time allowed me, will, I hope, in fome degree,
excufe the imperfedions of this fcrawl.

With the greateft refped and fidelity, I have the
honour to be your Excellency's moft obedient and
moft humble fervant,

B. FRANKLIN,

LETTER III.

SIR,

SINCE the converfation your Excellency was pleafed
to honour me with, on the fubjed of a more intimate connexion between the colonies and Great-Britain, by allowing them reprefentatives in Parliament;
I have fomething further confidered that matter, and
am of opinion, that fuch an union would be very
acceptable to the colonies, provided they had a reafonable number of reprefentatives allowed them; and
that all the old ads of parliament, reftraining the
trade or cramping the manufadures of the colonies,
be at the fame time repealed, and the Britifh fubjeds
on

on this fide of the water put, in thofe refpects, on' the fame footing with thofe in Great-Britain, till the new parliament reprefenting the whole, fhall think it for the intereft of the whole to enact fome or all' of them: It is not that I imagine fo many reprefent-atives will be allowed the colonies, as to have any great weight by their numbers; but I think there might be fufficient to occafion thofe laws to be better and more impartially confidered, and perhaps to over-come the intereft of a petty corporation, or of any particular fet of artificers or traders in England, who heretofore feem, in fome inftances, to have been more regarded than all the colonies, or than was confiftent with the general intereft or national good.

I think too, that the government of the colonies, by a parliament, in which they are fairly reprefented, would be vaftly more agreeable to the people than the method lately attempted to be introduced by royal inftructions, as well as more agreeable to the nature of the Englifh conftitution, and to Eng-lifh liberty; and that fuch laws as now feem to bear hard on the colonies, would (when judged by fuch parliament, for the beft intereft of the whole) be more cheerfully fubmitted to, and more eafily ex-ecuted.

I fhould hope too, that by fuch an union the peo-ple of Great-Britain, and the people of the colonies, would learn to confider themfelves, as not belonging to different communities with different interefts, but to one community with one intereft; which I ima-gine

gine would contribute to ftrengthen the whole, and greatly leffen the danger of future feparations.

It is, I fuppofe, agreed to be the general intereft of any ftate, that its people fhould be numerous and rich ; men enow to fight in its defence, and enow to pay fufficient taxes to defray the charges ; for thefe circumftances tend to the fecurity of the ftate, and its protection from foreign powers. But it feems not of fo much importance, whether the fighting be done by John or Thomas, or the tax paid by William or Charles.

The iron manufacture employs and enriches Britifh fubjects, but is it of any importance to the ftate whether the manufacturers live at Birmingham or Sheffield, or both, fince they are ftill within its bounds, and their wealth and perfons are ftill at its command?

Could the Goodwin fands be laid dry by banks, and land equal to a large country thereby gained to England, and prefently filled with Englifh inhabitants; would it be right to deprive fuch inhabitants of the common privileges enjoyed by other Englifhmen, the right of vending their produce in the fame ports, or of making their own fhoes, becaufe a merchant or a fhoe-maker, living on the old land, might fancy it more for his own advantage to trade or make fhoes for them? Would this be right, even if the land were gained at the expence of the ftate ? And would it not feem lefs right, if the charge and labour of gaining the additional territory to Britain, had been borne by the fettlers themfelves? And would not the

the hardſhip appear yet greater, if the people of the
new country ſhould be allowed no repreſentatives in
a parliament, enacting ſuch impoſitions? Now I look
on the colonies as ſo many countries gained to Great-
Britain, and more advantageous to it than if they
had been gained out of the ſea around our coaſt, and
joined to its land; for, being in different climates,
they afford greater variety of produce, and materials
for more manufactures; and being ſeparated by the
ocean, they increaſe much more its ſhipping and ſea-
men; and ſince they are all included in the Britiſh
empire, which has only extended itſelf by their
means, and the ſtrength and wealth of the whole;
what imports it to the general ſtate, whether a merchant, a ſmith, or a hatter, grow rich in Old or New
England? And if, through increaſe of people, two
ſmiths are wanted for one employed before, why may
not the new ſmith be allowed to live and thrive in
the new country, as well as the old one in the old?
In fine, why ſhould the countenance of a ſtate be par-
tially afforded to its people, unleſs it be moſt in favour of thoſe who have moſt merit? And, if there
be any difference, thoſe who have moſt contributed
to enlarge Britain's empire and commerce, increaſe
her ſtrength, her wealth, and the numbers of her people, at the riſque of their own lives and private fortunes, in new and ſtrange countries, methinks ought
rather to expect ſome preference.—With the greateſt
reſpect and eſteem, I have the honour to be your
Excellency's moſt obedient and humble ſervant,

                                    B. FRANKLIN.

THE idea fuggefted in Letter III. of forming a
more intimate union between Great-Britain and the
colonies, by allowing them reprefentatives in parliament, would, in all human probability, have been attended with the happieft confequences to both ; for,
in the firft place, it would have entirely precluded a
civil war, and in the next, by infufing a certain quantity of found and untainted blood into the body-po-
litic, it might have repreffed the grofs degeneracy of
latter times, and ftemmed that torrent of corruption,
which at prefent bids fair to fweep public virtue
away from the face of the land.

During the war before the laft, Dr. Franklin was
eminently ferviceable to the Britifh government, by
encouraging his countrymen to repel with vigour the
common enemy ; on this occafion he commanded a
company of artillery, and more than once headed the
militia in feveral hazardous and fuccefsful enterprifes.

When Canada was reduced, he came over to England, and endeavoured, both by writing and converfation, to demonftrate to the then miniftry, the fuperior
importance of that province to all our acquifitions in
the Weft-Indies ; and as the peace of Paris was concluded upon this principle, our author's arguments and
information may be fuppofed to have influenced, in
fome degree, a meafure fo obnoxious at that time to
the greater part of the nation, and which, as far as

regards

regards the intereſt of Great-Britain alone, muſt be allowed to have proved highly impolitic.

There is every reaſon to believe that Dr. Franklin was ſtimulated upon that occaſion, by a ſincere deſire for the ſecurity and proſperity of Britiſh America, as connected with the parent ſtate, and that although he might have contemplated the future independency of the colonies, as an abſtract queſtion, he never could have been prevailed upon to make the experiment until he was forced, along with his countrymen, into a juſtifiable and meritorious oppoſition to a ſcheme, big with the moſt ruinous conſequences to the inhabitants of America, and perhaps, had it proved ſuccefsful, to the liberties of .Great-Britain.

CHAP.

C H A P. III.

He becomes a Member of the Affembly of Pennfylvania—Is appointed Agent to feveral of the American States—Sails for England—Is examined before a Committee of the Privy Council—Infulted by the Attorney General—Departs privately for America.

IT was not until after he had paffed the meridian of his life, that Dr. Franklin difplayed to the world, that his talents were no lefs adapted to politics than the fciences. His objeftions to the Albany plan, which we have already mentioned, his oppofition to the *proprietary*, and his efforts in order to introduce the royal form of government into America in its ftead, foon made him known to his fellow-citizens, and even to the Englifh miniftry, to whom he communicated a new plan for regulating the poft-office in America. By way of recompenfe for this, he was appointed poft-mafter general for the fouthern department.

Being furnifhed with all the qualities neceffary for conciliating popular favour, he alfo obtained a feat in the affembly of Pennfylvania.

He was foon after appointed agent from that province, in order to fuperintend its interefts in England, and was at that period held in fuch high and general eftimation by his countrymen, that he was alfo nominated agent for the provinces of New Jerfey, Virginia, and Georgia.

1   When

When the ftamp-act, laying a certain tax upon bonds, notes, &c. was attempted to be impofed in 1766 by the Britifh parliament, on the inhabitants of North America, it experienced the warmeft and moft decided oppofition on the part of the Doctor; and this impolitic bill was at length repealed. He himfelf is accufed of having been the original projector of this very act; but let it be recollected that it was not the duty, but the *mode*, that he then objected to ; a mode which eftablifhed the principle of levying imposts upon a people, without, and even contrary to, their exprefs-confent, and thus bereaved them of the right of reprefentation. His examination before the houfe of commons in 1767, did him great honour, and the queftions afked by the then adminiftration, and his replies, which were extremely forcible, were circulated and applauded throughout all the colonies.

The Americans now began to be fenfible of their own confequence, and the inhabitants of Bofton, at a public meeting on the 27th of October 1767, entered into a variety of refolutions for encouraging manufactures, promoting economy, and reftraining the ufe of foreign fuperfluities. Thefe refolutions, all of which were highly prejudicial to the trade of the mother-country, contained a long lift of articles, which it was either determined not to ufe at all, or at leaft in the fmalleft poffible quantities.

A fubfcription was opened at the fame time, and a committee appointed, for the increafe of their old manufactures, and the eftablifhment of new ones. Among other things, it was determined to give particular

ticular encouragement to the making of paper, glaſs, and the other commodities that were liable to the payment of the new duties upon importation. It was alſo reſolved to reſtrain the expences of funerals, to reduce dreſs to a degree of primitive ſimplicity and plainneſs, and in general not to purchaſe any commodities from the mother-country, that could be procured in any of the colonies.

All theſe reſolutions were either adopted, or ſimilar ones entered into, by all the old colonies on the continent.

The Americans being well acquainted with their own rights, were determined to maintain them, and they accordingly oppoſed to the acts of a venal court, reſolved to ſubjugate them to its authority, that calm and ſteady perſeverance worthy of men who were determined to be free.

The Engliſh miniſtry having once more evinced a deſign to tax the *unrepreſented* colonies, Dr. Franklin, who happened to be then in London, was examined before the privy-council, on the 11th and 19th of January 1774, reſpecting the ſtate of America. On that occaſion he diſplayed his uſual firmneſs and capacity, although he was treated in a very unpolite manner by the then attorney-general, who at this day preſides as chief - juſtice in one of the courts of law.

This unworthy conduct was borne by the philoſopher with a calm and dignified ſerenity. It is aſſerted, however, that, after his examination, he

. paſſed

paſſed by the " pert, prim prater *," in his way out,
and took occaſion to whiſper the following truth in
his ear: " *I will make your maſter a little king*
" *for this !*"

Soon after this examination, the Doctor was removed from his employment as poſt-maſter general
of the ſouthern provinces of America, and was
looked upon by the Britiſh government with ſuch a
jealous eye, that ſome thoughts were entertained of
arreſting him, under pretence of his having fomented a
rebellion in the colonies. Having received intimation
of their intentions, he left England in the beginning of
the year 1775, and took his meaſures with ſuch pri-
vacy, that he had actually arrived in America before
he was ſuſpected of entertaining any deſign of re-
moving from the kingdom.

The act for impoſing a duty upon tea had now
put the whole continent in commotion. The flame
of liberty ſpread with the rapidity of lightning, from
New Hampſhire to Georgia ; councils of ſafety were
formed in all the provinces ; and every thing indicated a ſpeedy determination of that queſtion, whether America was henceforth to be peopled by freemen or by ſlaves ?

* See Churchill's Works.

M CHAP.

C H A P. IV.

The Doctor, soon after the Battle of Lexington, writes circular Letters to all the Colonies—Copy of a Letter to Mr. Strahan, a Printer and Member of Parliament—The Americans are in want of Money, Arms, and Ammunition—Emission of Paper Money—The Views of the People and their Leaders—General Lee a staunch Republican—The Congress declares the United States independent—The Doctor, at the Age of Seventy, repairs to France—The Success of his Mission—His great and important Services to America—His Return to his native Country.

IN the spring of 1775, the Doctor *electrified* the whole continent by means of circular letters, written soon after the battle of Lexington. His bold and pathetic description of this engagement aroused the spirit of liberty in every bosom, and in some measure rendered a reconciliation impracticable between the mother-country and her colonies. Much about the same time, the following laconic epistle, addressed by him to Mr. Strahan, an eminent printer, at that time member for Malmsbury, and formerly one of his most intimate friends, appeared in the public papers:

" Mr. Strahan,   *Philadelphia, July* 5, 1775.
" You are a member of that parliament, and
" have formed part of that majority, which has con-
" demned my native country to destruction.
" You

" You have begun to burn our towns, and to
" deftroy their inhabitants!

" Look at your hands—they are ftained with the
" blood of your relations and your acquaintances.

" You and I were long friends; you are at pre-
" fent my enemy, and I am your's.

" BENJAMIN FRANKLIN."

The difputes between Great-Britain and her colonies began now to affume the moft ferious afpect.
Determined to perfift in their oppofition to the impofts attempted to be levied by means of Englifh acts
of parliament, it was neceffary for the Americans to
bethink themfelves of adopting proper and efficacious
means of refiftance. They poffeffed little or no coin,
and even arms and ammunition were wanting. In this
fituation, the adoption of paper money became indif-
penfably neceffary, and Dr. Franklin was one
of the firft to demonftrate the propriety of that
meafure: Without this, it would have been impoffible to have made any other than a very feeble
and a very fhort refiftance againft the mother-
country.

The firft emiffion, to the amount of three millions of
dollars, accordingly took place on the 25th of July
1775, under a promife of exchanging the notes againft
gold or filver in the fpace of three years; and towards
the end of 1776, more than twenty-one millions additional were put in circulation. The Congrefs at
length began to be uneafy, not knowing how it would
be poffible to redeem fo large a fum; and fome of its

M 2   members

members having waited upon our author, in order to confult him upon this occafion, he fpoke to them as follows : " Do not make yourfelves unhappy ; con- " tinue to iffue your paper money as long as it " will pay for the paper, ink, and printing, and we " fhall be enabled by its means to liquidate all the " expences of the war."

It is a certain fact, that, at the beginning of the difturbances, the bulk of the people acted from no fixed and determined plan whatever, and had not even an idea of independence ; for all the addreffes from the different colonies were filled with profeffions of loyalty towards their fovereign, and breathed the moft ardent wifhes for an immediate reconciliation. It is probable, however, that the principal leaders looked up to this as an ultimate, and perhaps neceffary object.

The late General Lee in particular, inflamed with a republican zeal, travelled from colony to colony, ftirred up a fpirit of liberty in the breaft of every American, and fcorning to make ufe of diffimulation, with all the candour and opennefs of a foldier, pub-- licly preached up the doctrine of independence.

At length this important queftion was agitated in Congrefs ; the debate lafted for feveral days, and the fcheme encountered the moft violent oppofition. It was combated by feveral diftinguifhed orators, and in particular by Mr. Dickinfon, author of the " Farmer's " Letters," Mr. Wilfon, a celebrated lawyer, and Mr. Galloway, who afterwards attached himfelf to the Englifh government.

Doctor

Doctor Franklin, however, was firm as a rock, and remained inviolably attached to his darling fcheme. No arguments adopted by them could make him abandon a fyftem, the adoption of which he felt to be abfolutely neceffary ; and moft of his opponents at length feeing his unalterable determination, were induced to join with him in his plan.

After having gained this great and effential point, he perceived the immediate neceffity of atchieving fomething more. The continental paper money began to fall into difcredit ; arms, ammunition, and officers, were wanting ; and without thefe, it would be in vain to combat the armies and the refources of Great-Britain. He therefore turned his eyes towards Europe, and fixed them upon the fole kingdom, whence he could draw the fupplies neceffary for the defence of his native country, and the prefervation of her independence. He accordingly obtained a commiffion from Congrefs, and, in the 71ft year of his age, repaired to France as their ambaffador, perfuaded that this was the proper theatre for the exertion of his talents, and that his reputation as a philofopher would conciliate the affection of a nation, whofe interefts were eminently connected with thofe of America.

He was right in his conjectures. He landed at Nantz on the 17th of December 1776, and the moment he arrived there, all ranks of men were eager to pay their refpects to him.

Soon

Soon after his appearance at the court of Verfailles, where he was received with every mark of diftin&ion and efteem, he and Mr. Silas Deane, his colleague, tranfmitted feveral memorials to Lord Stormont, the Englifh ambaffador there, relative to the exchange of prifoners; but that nobleman, with an ariftocratic pride, worthy of the caufe in which he was engaged, replied haughtily, " that he would not receive any " letters from rebels, unlefs they contained a petition " for pardon ! ! !"

In conjunction with Mr. Deane, he now granted letters of marque to a number of French-American privateers, which haraffed the Englifh coafts, and intercepted an immenfe number of merchantmen.

Lord Stormont immediately prefented a memorial to the minifter, and demanded a categorical anfwer relative to the conduct of France.

On this, Count de Vergennes affected to obferve a greater degree of referve in regard to the American plenipotentiaries, who were now but very rarely honoured with an audience.

At length the news of the furrender of the Britifh army commanded by General Burgoyne, to that of the Americans under General Gates, at Saratoga, on the 17th of October 1777, arrived in France, at the very moment when the cabinet council was as yet undecided in regard to the fteps to be adopted relative to the United States. This memorable event immediately inclined the balance, and fixed the French nation in their attachment to the infant republic.

The

The news of the defeat and the capture of this Britifh general, was received in France with as great demonftrations of joy, as if it had been a victory gained over their own enemies.

Franklin, with his ufual addrefs, took advantage of this circumftance, and hinted to the Count de Maure-pas, " that there was not a fingle moment to be loft, " if he wifhed to fecure the friendfhip of America, " and detach her entirely from the mother-country."

Fearful left a reconciliation fhould take place between Great-Britain and her colonies, the court of France inftantly determined to declare its intentions, and accordingly, on the 16th of December 1777, M. Gerard, fecretary to the council, repaired to the hotel of the American ambaffadors, and informed them, by order of the King : " that after a long and " mature deliberation upon their propofitions, his " Majefty had refolved to recognize the independence " of, and to enter into a treaty of commerce and alli- " ance with, the United States of America; and that he " would not only acknowledge their independence, " but actually fupport it with all the means in his " power ; that perhaps he was about to find himfelf " engaged in an expenfive war upon their ac- " count, but that he did not expect to be reimburfed " by them; that, in fine, the Americans were not " to think that he had entered into this refolution " folely with a view of ferving them, fince, independ- " ently of his real attachment to them and their " caufe, it was evidently the intereft of France to

M 4 " diminifh

" diminifh the power of England, by diffevering her
" colonies from her."

On the 30th of January 1778, a treaty was accordingly figned and concluded at Paris, between
France and America. This will ever form a memorable epoch in the hiftory of mankind, becaufe it was in
confequence of this alliance that the infurgent colonies were able to refift the mother-country, and that
the French nation, 'in the fhort fpace of ten years,
acquired a fondnefs and attachment to the caufe of
liberty, that impelled them to vindicate their own
rights, and put an end to a defpotifm at once difgraceful and humiliating to humanity.

The Englifh ambaffador about this time thought
proper to leave Paris ; and it has been affirmed, that
the day on which Lord Stormont quitted the French
capital, formed the happieft one in the whole courfe
of Dr. Franklin's life.

. Hoftilities commenced foon after this, between
Great-Britain and France, and M. Gerard was nominated by his moft Chriftian Majefty, ambaffador to
the new States of America.

Before his departure, our author communicated a
plan to him, for furprifing the Britifh fleet and army
then in the Delaware; and Count d'Eftaing was employed to execute this important enterprife; which
would certainly have proved fuccefsful, had it not
been for a feries of bad weather and contrary winds.
In confequence of thefe unforefeen obftacles, the
French admiral arrived too late upon the American
coaft;

coaft ; for the Englifh army had evacuated Philadelphia, and the fleet was then riding in perfect fafety at
Sandy-Hook.

The affection of the French for the Americans
feemed to rife to a degree little fhort of enthufiafm.
The portraits of the principal perfons engaged in the
revolution, occupied the pencils and the gravers of
their moft famous artifts, while their lives employed
the pens of their moft celebrated writers. But among
all thefe great characters, our philofopher was diftinguifhed in a particular manner, and feveral of the
provinces of France actually difputed the honour of
having given birth to his anceftors, and endeavoured
to prove, by the fimilitude of the name, that he
was of French defcent! The following is an extract from the Gazette of Amiens, the capital of
Picardy :

" The painter to his moft Chriftian Majefty" (fays
the editor) " has exhaufted all his talents upon a pic-
" ture dedicated to the genius of Franklin. One be-
" holds the philofopher holding in one hand the
" Ægis of Minerva, which he oppofes to a thunder-
" bolt, and with the other ordering the god of war
" to combat avarice and tyranny, while America, re-
" pofing upon his breaft in a noble attitude, and
" holding in her hand a bundle of rods, the faithful
" emblem of the United States, furveys her con-
" quered enemies with a look of tranquillity. In
" this compofition, the painter has very faithfully co-
" pied the idea prefented by the Latin hemiftich, fo
" frequently applied to him.

" The

" The name of Franklin is fo celebrated, that it
" ought to render every one vain who bears it. It
" may be even permitted to a nation to claim the re-
" putation of having originally produced the family
" of a man fo renowned; and we think that we have
" a right to difpute with the Englifh that honour, of
" which they have rendered themfelves fo un-
" worthy.

" Franklin, as the very name implies, appears at
" firft fight to belong to the French rather than to
" their neighbours. It is certain that the name of
" Franklin, or *Franquelin*, is very common in Pi-
" cardy, more efpecially in the diftricts of Virneu and
" Ponthieu.

" It is very probable that one of the Doctor's
" anceftors inhabited this country, whence he
" paffed into England either with the fleet under the
" command of *Jean de Biencourt*, or that which was
" fitted out by the nobility of the fame province. In
" genealogical conjectures there are far more bold
" and hardy fuppofitions than this.

" There alfo lived at Abbeville, during the fif-
" teenth and fixteenth centuries, a family of the
" name of Franklin. We find in the public regifters
" of that city, that in 1521 a perfon of the name of
" John, and another of Thomas Franklin, were
" woollen-drapers at Abbeville. This family re-
" mained there until the year 1600. It then dif-
" perfed into the country, and fome of its defcendants
" are to be found at this very day at *Aix le-Chateau.*

" Thefe

" Thefe obfervations are a new homage which we
" offer to the genius of Franklin."

All thofe devoted to letters and to fcience were ambitious to pay their refpects to the philofopher of
Philadelphia. Louis XVI. having inftituted the Royal
Society of Medicine, by letters patent, in 1778, Dr.
Franklin was appointed one of the fixty correfponding
members, his name having been put at the head of
the lift, by *the King's own hand*.

Thus our author enjoyed the fatisfaction of feeing
himfelf generally honoured and efteemed in France.
His influence even extended to Spain and feveral
other countries; where he kept up a correfpondence
that proved highly ferviceable to the American
caufe.

" All Europe," fays he, in a letter to a friend at
Philadelphia, " is united in our favour. They
" have tranflated and publifhed here, the infti-
" tutes of the United States, a circumftance which
" affords ample matter for reflection and fpeculation
" to our politicians. The opinion of the beft im-
" formed men is, that if you fucceed in eftablifhing
" your liberty, the moment that peace is declared,
" you will receive an immenfe addition of riches,
" by means of the families who will be eager to leave
" this hemifphere, in order to partake of your pri-
" vileges. Tyranny is fo generally eftablifhed in
" Europe, that the profpect of *an afylum* in America
" caufes an univerfal joy to all thofe who love free-
" dom;

" dom; and your caufe is already efteemed that
" of the human race."

The Doctor was foon enabled to draw confiderable
fuccour and affiftance from his new allies, and in
matters of finance the Congrefs more than once had
recourfe to his talents.

Out of the fums furnifhed by the court of France
for the pay and fupport of the American armies, he
found means to honour an immenfe number of bills
drawn upon him from America, to advance the fa-
laries of all the minifters employed in Europe,
and to relieve the diftreffes of fuch of his unfortunate
countrymen as had fallen into the hands of the
Englifh.

It is evident that the addrefs, patriotifm, and abilities of this philofophical ftatefman, were eminently
ferviceable to his countrymen, and it is more than
probable that, without his aid, Congrefs would
never have been able to have 'fupported their
armies at home, or acquired alliances and affiftance
abroad.

During the fpace of nine whole years, Dr.
Franklin was engaged in the moft important and
active fcenes, as minifter plenipotentiary from
America at the court of France. Having at length
beheld the accomplifhment of all his wifhes, by
the conclufion of a general peace in 1783, in confequence of which the independence of the United
States was fully acknowledged and recognifed, he
became defirous of revifiting his native country.

He

He accordingly requefted to be recalled, and, after repeated folicitations, Mr. Jefferfon was appointed his fucceffor. On the arrival of that gentleman in Paris, Dr. Franklin repaired to Havre de Grace, and croffing the Englifh Channel, landed in the Ifle of Wight. At this place he again embarked on board of the London Packet, Captain Truxton, and arrived in Philadelphia in September 1785.

CHAP.

CHAP. V.

*Dr. Franklin arrives in Philadelphia amidst the Acclama-
tions of his Fellow-citizens—Is elected Governor of Pennsylvania—Assists at the General Convention—Speech on the
Conclusion of the New Constitution—The Effect of early
Habits and Attachments.*

ON his arrival in Philadelphia, Dr. Franklin was
received amidst the acclamations of an immense
number of the inhabitants, who flocked from all
parts in order to see him, and conducted him in triumph to his own house. In the mean time, the cannon and the bells of the city announced the glad
tidings to the neighbouring country, and he was
waited upon by the Congress, the university, and all
the principal citizens, who were eager to testify their
esteem and veneration for his character.

In the month of October following, he was elected
Governor of Pennsylvania, and he occupied that honourable office until October 1788.

The Americans, on the return of peace, did not enjoy all the advantages arising from their emancipation
so suddenly as had been predicted. The credit of
many of the States was at a very low ebb; some of
them were torn with the intrigues of contending
parties; the government was without either force
or dignity; their commerce was circumscribed
within very narrow bounds; and their merchants
in general were not far removed from a state

of

of bankruptcy. In this pofture of affairs, it was
thought proper to affemble a general convention, in
order to form a more energetic conftitution.

The convention accordingly affembled at Philadelphia in 1788, and Dr. Franklin fat in it as the reprefentative of Pennfylvania. At the conclufion of
their deliberations, he rofe and fpoke as follows :

" Mr. President,

" I muft frankly avow, that I do not approve the
" whole of the prefent conftitution, but I dare not
" affirm that I fhall never approve of it. I have
" lived a great many years, and I have been obliged
" twenty times, after more ample information, and
" more mature deliberations, to alter my opinions,
" even in matters of the utmoft importance.

" The more I have advanced in years, the more I
" have learned to diftruft my own judgment, and to
" refpect that of others. The majority of mankind,
" like the majority of religious fects, think that they,
" and they only, poffefs the knowledge of falvation,
" and term every thing error and untruth, which
" contradicts, or even differs from, their fyftem.

" A great Englifh writer, in a dedication to the
" Pope, fays, ' the only difference that exifts between
" your church and ours, relative to the certainty of
" their doctrines, is, that the church of Rome is in-
" fallible, and that the church of England is never
" in the wrong.'

" Although moft individuals have nearly as high
" an opinion of their own infallibility, as that of
" their fect, no perfon perhaps ever expreffed this
" opinion

" opinion fo naturally as a young French woman,
" in a trifling difpute with her brother : ' I do not
" know how it comes about,' fays fhe, ' but I can
" never find any perfon always in the right, like
" myfelf !'

" It is in confequence of thefe fentiments, Mr. Pre-
" fident, that I adhere to the new conftitution, and I
" adopt it with all its faults, if it has any, becaufe I
" know we are abfolutely in want of a *general go-*
" *vernment*, and that there is not any government,
" whatever may be its form, which cannot be made
" a good one, provided it be well adminiftered.

" I know alfo, that this which we have adopted
" may be well adminiftered, during a number of
" years, and that if it at length fhould degenerate
" into defpotifm (an inconvenience which until
" this day no government has been able to avoid),
" this at leaft will not happen until the people
" become fo corrupt, as not to be ruled by any other
" than a defpot.

" I know not neither, whether any fimilar affem-
" bly could make a better conftitution; for whenever
" many men affemble together in order to communi-
" cate their knowledge and their fentiments, it is im-
" poffible to prevent their prejudices, their paffions,
" their errors, their local and perfonal interefts, from
" *affembling* along with them.

" From an affociation of men fo compofed, is a
" perfect work to be expected ?

" I am indeed aftonifhed to fee that the fyftem
" eftablifhed by us, approaches fo near to perfection;

5   " I alfo

" I alfo think, that it is admirably calculated to fur-
" prife our enemies, who expected to hear that we
" were in a ftate of tumult and confufion; that the
" different States were on the point of difuniting,
" and that the Americans would never meet but in
" order to cut each others throats.

" I adhere, Mr. Prefident, to this conftitution, be-
" caufe I could not expect a better; and becaufe I
" am not fure that it is not the beft which we could
" have.

" I facrifice my private opinion to the general
" good; if I have thought that I difcovered errors in
" it, I have not faid a fingle word on that fubject out
" of this houfe. Thefe errors (if they really exift)
" have originated within thefe walls; they ought alfo
" to perifh here: But if any of us, on our return
" home among our conftituents, permit ourfelves to
" repeat the objections we have heard urged in this
" place againft any part of the new conftitution; and
" if, in order to fupport our objections, we endea-
" vour to make partifans, we fhall, in confequence
" of this, lofe the effects and advantages that ought
" naturally to refult from our unanimity, whether
" real or apparent, as well in our own country, as
" among foreign nations.

" The force and efficacy of a government, as far
" as it concerns the creating and infuring the happi-
" nefs of a people, depends greatly on opinion; I
" fay upon the opinion generally eftablifhed of the
" goodnefs of that government, as well as of the
" fagacity and integrity of thofe who govern.

N   " I hope

" I hope, therefore, for our own good, for that
" of the people, and for that of our posterity, that we
" shall reunite every heart and every will upon this
" occasion; that all our efforts henceforth shall tend
" to make the constitution be beloved, cherished, and
" respected, wherever our influence may extend, and
" that henceforth we shall only occupy our minds with
" the best means of administering and enforcing it.

" I desire, above all things, Mr. President, that
" every member of the Assembly who may have any
" objections to make against the constitution, would,
" upon this occasion, doubt a little with me of his
" own *absolute infallibility*; and in order to manifest
" our unanimity, subscribe his name to this public
" act.—I now, therefore, move, that the conclusion
" of this bill shall run as follows :—" Enacted in Ge-
" neral Assembly, by the unanimous consent of all
" the, &c. &c."

The above motion was instantly adopted.

This amiable and conciliatory discourse, which
fully demonstrates, that an obstinate and pertinacious
self-sufficiency formed no part of the character of this
great and amiable man, was the last pronounced by
him in public. As long, however, as his faculties
remained in full vigour, he continued to publish political admonitions to his countrymen.

It is with difficulty that any one abandons the
studies and occupations he has been accustomed to
during his youth. Thus we have seen the Rev.
John Wesley, while nearly in his ninetieth year, travelling through the kingdom, and propagating his
religious tenets. Thus, also, the great Franklin, in

an

an age nearly as advanced, continued to occupy his mind with his favourite ideas; to inftruct the people by means of his writings; to excite their ambition by his example, and to improve their morals by his fage and benevolent converfation.

CHAP.

CHAP. VI.

*Effects of Temperance—Dr Franklin's Health becomes infirm—
He is seized with a Fever—Dies in consequence of an Impost-
hume—Character—Opinions concerning Death—Legacies—
—Testimonies of Foreigners respecting his Philosophical La-
bours—Burial—Account of the Honours paid to his Memory
—List of his Works—Epitaph.*

DURING the greatest part of his life, Dr.
Franklin had enjoyed an almost uninterrupted
state of good health, and this he entirely attributed
to his exemplary temperance.

In the year 1735, indeed, he was seized with a
pleurisy, which ended in a suppuration of the left
lobe of the lungs, so that he was almost suffocated
by the quantity of matter thrown up. But from
this, as well as from another attack of the same
kind, he recovered so completely, that his breath
was not in the least affected.

As he advanced in years, however, he became
subject to fits of the gout, to which, in 1782, a
nephritic cholic was superadded. From this time, he
was also affected with the stone, as well as the
gout; and for the last twelve months of his life, these
complaints almost intirely confined him to his bed.

Notwithstanding his distressed situation, neither his
mental faculties nor his natural cheerfulness ever
forsook

forfook him. His memory was tenacious to the very laft; and he feemed to be an exception to the general rule, that, at a certain period of life, the organs which are fubfervient to this faculty become callous; a remarkable inftance of which is, that he learned to fpeak French after he had attained the age of feventy.

In the beginning of April 1790, about fixteen days before his death, he was feized with a feverifh diforder, which at firft did not exhibit any particular fymptoms; but upon the third or fourth day was attended with a pain in the left breaft. This at length became very acute, and was accompanied with a cough and a difficulty of breathing. He continued in this fituation for five days, when the painful fymptoms ceafed at once, and his family began to flatter themfelves with hopes of his recovery. But a new impofthume had now taken place in the lungs, which breaking fuddenly as the others had done, he was unable to expectorate the matter fully. In confequence of this, an oppreffion of the organs of refpiration, and a lethargic difpofition, came on, which gradually increafing, he expired foon after.

Thus died, on the 17th of April 1790, in the eighty-fifth year of his age, Dr. Benjamin Franklin, one of the moft celebrated and extraordinary men of which the prefent age can boaft.

His life affords one of the fineft moral leffons that can be offered up to the admiration, the applaufe, or the imitation of mankind.

As

As a man, we have beheld him practifing and in‑ culcating the virtues of frugality, temperance, and induftry.

As a citizen, we have feen him repelling the ef‑ forts of tyranny, and afcertaining the liberty of his countrymen.

As a legiflator, he affords a bright example of a genius foaring above corruption, and continually aiming at the happinefs of his conftituents.

As a politician, we furvey him, on one hand, ac‑ quiring the aid of a powerful nation, by means of his fkilful negotiations ; and on the other, calling forth the common ftrength of a congrefs of republics, by fixing a central point to which they could all look up, and concentrating their common force, for the purpofes of union, harmony, legiflation, and defence.

As a philofopher, his labours and his difcoveries are calculated to advance the interefts of humanity : He might, indeed, have been juftly termed the friend of man, the benefactor of the univerfe !

The purfuits and occupations of his early youth afford a moft excellent and inftructive example to the young ; his middle life, to the adult ; his advanced years, to the aged. From him the poor may learn to acquire wealth, and the rich to adapt it to the purpofes of beneficence.

In regard to his character, he was rather fenten‑ tious than fluent ; more difpofed to liften, than to talk ; a judicious, rather than an engaging companion. He was what, perhaps, every able man is, impatient of interruption ; for he ufed to mention the cuftom

of

of the Indians with great applaufe, who, after liften-ing with a profound attention to the obfervations of each other, preferve a refpectful filence for fome minutes, before they begin their own reply.

He was polite in his manners, and never gave a pointed contradiction to the affertions of his friends or his antagonifts, but treated every argument with great calmnefs, and conquered his adverfaries rather by the force of reafon, than affertion. His fenti-ments refpecting death may be gathered from the following extract of a letter, written near forty years ago, to Mifs Hubbard, on the deceafe of her father-in-law, Mr. John Franklin :

" We are fpirits. That bodies fhould be lent us,
" while they can afford us pleafure, and affift us in
" acquiring knowledge, or doing good to our fel-
" low-creatures, is a kind and benevolent act of God.

" When they are unfit for thefe purpofes, and af-
" ford us pain, in the place of pleafure ; inftead of
" an aid they become an incumbrance, and anfwer
" none of the intentions for which they were given ;
" it is then equally kind and benevolent to provide
" us a way, by which we may get rid of them.

" Death is that way.

" Our friend and we are invited abroad on a
" party of pleafure, that is to laft for ever. His car-
" riage was firft ready, and he is gone before us ;
" we could not all conveniently ftart together ; why
" fhould you and I, my dear madam, be grieved at
" this, fince we are foon to follow, and know where
" to find him ?"

Dr.

Dr. Franklin left one fon, Governor William Franklin, a zealous loyalift during the unfortunate American war, and a daughter married to Mr. William Bache, a merchant in Philadelphia.

This lady, who was a great favourite, attended him during his laft illnefs. Three days previous to his deceafe, he begged that his bed might be made, " in " order that he might die in a decent manner ;" an idea evidently fuggefted by an acquaintance with the cuftoms of the ancients. Mrs. Bache having replied, that fhe hoped he would recover, and live many years longer, he inftantly rejoined, " I hope not."

He bequeathed the greateft part of his fortune to Mr. and Mrs. Bache for their joint lives, and ordered that it fhould be equally divided afterwards, among their children. To the Governor's fon, William Temple Franklin, he left fome lands in Georgia, the greateft part of his library, and all his manufcripts, befides fomething additional in cafe of marriage. He alfo left feveral public legacies; to the library of Philadelphia 3000 volumes ; to Judge Hopkins, his philofophical apparatus ; and to the Prefident of the United States, his gold-headed cane.

The teftamentary devife of the latter is as follows :

" My gold-headed cane, curioufly wrought in the " form of a cap of liberty, I leave to my friend, and " the friend of mankind, General Wafhington ; if it " were a fceptre, he has merited it, and would be " come it."

The moft illuftrious foreigners have teftified their admiration of his philofophical labours. Beccaria, fo celebrated for his Effay on " Crimes and Punifh, " ments,"

" ments," to his curious treatife, intitled, " Elettrico
" Artificiale," has prefixed a complimentary letter to
Dr. Franklin, in which he confiders him as " the
" father of electricity," and fpeaks of his difcoveries
with enthufiafm.

" To you," fays he, addreffing himfelf to the
American philofopher, " it was given to enlighten
" the mind of man in this new fcience. It is you
" who have difarmed the thunder of all its terrors,
" and your daring genius has even taught the fire of
" Heaven, that was looked upon as the weapon of
" Omnipotence, to obey your voice !"

" Newton," adds the Chevalier de Chatelleux,
in his difcourfe *De la Felicité Publique*, " has dif-
" covered the laws of optics, and Defcartes, of
" dioptrics. A great and magnificent difcovery was
" referved for thefe times—and this is electricity,
" the terrible effects of which have placed mankind
" on an equality with the gods of antiquity ; for
" Franklin, like another Prometheus, has acquired
" the art of ftealing celeftial fire, and rendering it
" ductile to his laws."

M. D'Alembert, upon his reception as a member
of the French Academy, alluding to the fuccefs of
his philofophical and political labours, welcomed
him with the well-known line, which rivals the bold-
nefs and fublimity of Lucan :

" Eripuit coelo fulmen, fceptrumque tyrannis."

And M. Dubourg, the firft Frenchman who openly
efpoufed the caufe of America, placed the following
infcription under his buft :

" Il

" Il a ravi le feu des cieux :
" Il fait fleurir les arts en des climats fauvages :
" L'Amerique le place à la tête de fes fages;
" La Grece l'auroit mis au nombre de fes dieux."

All that was mortal of this great man, was interred
on the 21ft of April, in the cemetery of Chrift's
Church, Philadelphia, in that part adjoining to
Arch-ftreet, in order that, if a monument fhould be
erected over his grave, it might be feen to more advantage.

Never was any funeral fo. numeroufly and fo re-
fpectably attended in any part of the States of America. The concourfe of people affembled upon this
occafion was immenfe. All the bells in the city were
muffled, and the very newfpapers were publifhed
with black edges. The body was interred amidft
peals of artillery ; and nothing was omitted that
could difplay the veneration of the citizens for fuch
an illuftrious character.

The Congrefs ordered a general mourning for
one month, throughout America ; the National Affembly * of France paid the fame compliment for three.
days ;

* *National Affembly*, 11th *June* 1790.
M. Mirabeau the elder, having demanded and obtained leave
to fpeak, addreffed the Affembly as follows :
" FRANKLIN IS DEAD !" . . . .
[*A profound filence reigns throughout the hall.*]
" The genius, which gave freedom to America, and fcattered
" torrents of light upon Europe, is returned to the bofom of the
< Divinity.
" The

days; and the commons of Paris, as an extraordinary tribute of honour to his memory, aſſiſted in a body at

" The ſage, whom two worlds claim ; the man, diſputed by the " hiſtory of the ſciences and the hiſtory of empires, holds, moſt " undoubtedly, an elevated rank in the human ſpecies.

" Political cabinets have but too long notified the death of " thoſe who were never great but in their funeral orations ; the " etiquette of courts has but too long ſanctioned hypocritical " grief.—Nations ought only to mourn for their benefactors ; " the repreſentatives of free men ought never to recommend any " other than the heroes of humanity to their homage.

" The Congreſs hath ordered a general mourning for one " month throughout the fourteen confederated States, on account " of the death of Franklin: And America hath thus acquitted her " tribute of admiration in behalf of one of the fathers of her " conſtitution.

" Would it not be worthy of you, fellow-legiſlators, to unite " yourſelves in this religious act, to participate in this homage " rendered in the face of the univerſe to the rights of man, and " to the philoſopher who has ſo eminently propagated the con- " queſt of them throughout the world ?

" Antiquity would have elevated altars to that mortal, who, " for the advantage of the human race, embracing both heaven " and earth in his vaſt and extenſive mind, knew how to ſubdue " thunder and tyranny.

" Enlightened and free, Europe at leaſt owes its remembrance " and its regret to one of the greateſt men who has ever ſerved " the cauſe of philoſophy and of liberty.

" I propoſe, that a decree do now paſs, enacting, that the Na- " tional Aſſembly ſhall wear mourning during three days for " Benjamin Franklin."

M. M. de Rochefoucault and La Fayette immediately roſe, in order to ſecond this motion.

The Aſſembly adopted it, at firſt by acclamation ; and after- wards decreed, by a large majority, amidſt the plaudits of all the ſpectators, at the funeral oration *, delivered by the Abbé Fauchet (now conſtitutional biſhop of Calvados), in the Rotunda, which was hung with black, illuminated with chandeliers, and decorated with devices analogous to the occaſion.

Dr. Smith, Provoſt of the College of Philadelphia, and Mr. Rittenhouſe, one of its members, were ſelected by the Philoſophical Society to prepare an eulogium to the memory of its founder ; and the ſubſcribers to the city library, who had juſt erected a handſome building for containing their books, left a vacant niche for a ſtatue of their benefactor.

This was accordingly placed there a few months ſince. It was imported from Italy ; the name of the artiſt is Francis Lazzarini ; it is compoſed of Carara marble, and coſt 500 guineas.

It is the firſt piece of ſculpture of that ſize, which has ever been ſeen in America. The following inſcription, which perhaps ſays too much concerning the donor, and too little about the philoſopher, is engraven on the pedeſtal :

THIS STATUE

O F

DR. BENJAMIN FRANKLIN,

WAS PRESENTED BY

WILLIAM BINGHAM, Eſq.

1792.

ſpectators, that on Monday the 14th of June it ſhould go into mourning for three days ; that the diſcourſe of M. Mirabeau ſhould be printed ; and that the Preſident ſhould write a letter of condolence, upon the occaſion, to the Congreſs of America.

* See a tranſlation of this at the end of this volume.

Dr.

Dr. Franklin is reprefented in a ftanding pofture; one arm is fupported by means of fome books, in his right hand he wields an inverted fceptre, an emblem of his antimonarchical principles; and in his left, a fcroll of paper. He is dreffed in a Roman toga. The refemblance is faid to be correct; the head is a copy from the famous buft produced by the chiffel of Houdon.

The works of Dr. Franklin are numerous, and fully difplay the verfatility of his genius, for which nothing appears to have been too little or too great.

I. Some Letters, which he addreffed to Sir Hans Sloane, in the year 1726, when he was only 21 years of age.

II. Experiments and Obfervations.in. Electricity, &c. made at Philadelphia ; in two parts. 4to, 1753.

III. New Experiments, &c. on the fame, fubject. 1754.

N. B. Thefe two laft were publifhed in one volume, in 1769; and contain, befides his experiments in natural philofophy, a defcription of his "new-invent-" ed Pennfylvania fire-ftoves" for the better warming of rooms with a fmall expence of fuel ; obferva-tions concerning the increafe of mankind, and the peopling of countries ; aphorifms on the nature and caufe of evaporation; obfervations on the nature of fire ; the production of animal heat; the phenomena and probable caufes of whirlwinds ; a comparifon between the old Scotch and the modern Italian mufic, &c. &c.

IV. An Hiftorical Review of the Conftitution and Government of Pennfylvania, 1759. Anonymous.

5   V. The

V. The Intereſt of Great Britain conſidered with regard to her Colonies, and the Acquiſition of Canada and Guadeloupe. 1760. Anon.

VI. Political, Miſcellaneous, and Philoſophical Pieces, never before collected. 1779. 4to and 8vo.

N. B. The papers in this collection are arranged in five different diviſions.

The 1ſt contains eſſays on general politics.

The 2d, upon ſubjects relative to America before the breaking out of the civil war. Theſe breathe throughout the ſpirit of peace and conciliation. They expreſs the moſt anxious deſire to unite and blend the intereſts of the parent country and her colonies in one common maſs of public felicity; and to prevent every meaſure that had a tendency to eſtrange and alienate the two countries from each other.

The 3d contains papers written during the conteſt.

The 4th, papers on provincial and local politics.

And the 5th, all his philoſophical and miſcellaneous pieces not printed.

Among the papers in this diviſion, we ought not to omit mentioning a production read by his country-men with much avidity. It is called " The Way to " Wealth, as clearly ſhewn in the Preface of an old " Pennſylvania Almanack, intitled, " Poor Richard " improved." Dr. Franklin, who had for many years publiſhed " Poor Richard's Almanack," in Phila-delphia, furniſhed it with a variety of ſentences and proverbs relative to induſtry, attention to buſineſs, frugality, &c. The greater part of theſe he at laſt collected, and digeſted in the above general preface.

VII. Phy-

VII. Phyfical and Meteorological Obfervations, Conjectures, and Suppofitions. N. B. This appeared firft in the Philof. Tranf. vol. lv. for 1765; and in vol. lxiv. part i. for 1774, appeared his curious paper, " on the ftilling " of Waves by means of Oil."

In fhort, the aim of this great man was to be generally ufeful.

His Advice to Servants—to Settlers in America; his Rules for Clubs and Converfation; his Directions for the Cure of Smoky Chimnies, &c. &c. abundantly evince that he deemed no fubject too humble for his pen, provided it might be ferviceable to his fellow-creatures *.

The

* The following circumftance will evince how much and how generally this great man was beloved in France:

On the 14th of June 1790, the citizens of Paris, imitating the example of the National Affembly, appeared alfo in mourning.— On the fame day, the friends of the Revolution, and of humanity, affembled at the *Café Procope*, and wifhing to render all the honors to the memory of the celebrated Franklin, which are fo juftly due to it, ordered all the glaffes to be covered with crape, and the inner apartment to be hung with black. On the door towards the ftreet, was the following infcription :

FRANKLIN EST MORT!

(*Franklin is dead!*)

At one end of the apartment, was placed his buft crowned with oak-leaves; and at the foot of the pedeftal, was engraven the word

V I R.

Two cypreffes elevated their melancholy branches above it; on the two fides of it, were the celeftial and terreftrial globes, charts, &c.; and under it, a ferpent biting his tail, as an emblem of immortality.

An

The following epitaph, written by himfelf, fome years before his death, conveys at once a true idea of the fimplicity of his manners, and of the ingenioufnefs with which he could make ufe of the terms of his original profeffion, as a medium for conveying his thoughts :

THE BODY

O F

BENJAMIN FRANKLIN, Printer,

(LIKE THE COVER OF AN OLD BOOK,
ITS CONTENTS TORN OUT,
AND STRIPPED OF ITS LETTERING AND GILDING,)
LIES HERE, FOOD FOR THE WORMS ;
YET THE WORK ITSELF SHALL NOT BE LOST,
FOR IT SHALL, AS HE BELIEVES,
APPEAR, ONCE MORE,
IN A NEW
AND MOST BEAUTIFUL EDITION,
CORRECTED AND REVISED

B Y

THE AUTHOR.

An orator read a fimple but pathetic difcourfe, in which he recounted the benefits this illuftrious Philofopher had conferred upon mankind ; and in order to honour his *manes* in a manner ftill more worthy of him, on the preceding day, a quantity of bread bought by fubfcription, in which every one was eager to concur, was diftributed among the people.

PART III.

COLLECTION

OF

FRAGMENTS, ANECDOTES, &c, &c.

RELATING TO

BENJAMIN FRANKLIN, LL.D.

* THE American Revolution has produced a multitude of virtuous citizens, intrepid warriors, and enlightened politicians ; but we have feen no one poffefs, in fo high a degree, the character of a true philofopher, as Dr. Benjamin Franklin. His love of mankind occupied every inftant of his life ; and he difplayed the moft indefatigable zeal in their fervice. His knowledge was great and extenfive, his manners were fimple, his morals were pure.

This portrait will not afford a line of feparation fufficiently marked between him and other patriot politicians, if I do not add a characteriftic feature to

* Tranflated from the *Patriote François* of M. Briffot de Warville, a member of the National Affembly and National Convention of France.

o   it ;

it; this is, that Franklin, in the midft of the vaft
fcene in which he acted fuch a brilliant and confpi-
cuous character, kept his eyes conftantly fixed on a
theatre infinitely more vaft and extenfive,—on
Heaven, and a future life! This is the fole circumftance that can fupport and aggrandize man upon
earth, and make of him a true philofopher.

The different anecdotes recounted in the firft part
of his private life, might afford, to an attentive ob-
ferver, fome idea of his character; and it indeed
appears to me to be impoffible to read it, without a
certain degree of tendernefs, mingled with refpect.—
It exhibits Franklin ftrolling about the ftreets of
Philadelphia with about four-and-fixpence in his
pocket, unknown to any of the inhabitants, eating one
loaf with avidity, holding another under each arm,
and quenching his thirft with the water of the Delaware!

Who could have dreamed that this miferable wan-
derer fhould become one of the future legiflators of
America; the ornament of the new world; the
pride of modern philofophy, and an ambaffador to
a nation the moft rich, the moft powerful, and the
moft enlightened in the univerfe?

Who could have believed that France, that Europe,
fhould one day elevate ftatues to a man, who had
nowhere to repofe his head?

This circumftance recalls to my memory J. J.
Rouffeau, with three halfpence (his whole fortune)
in his purfe, and tormented by famine, balancing
in his own mind whether he ought to facrifice his all,

in

in order to procure a fupper, or a bed! After putting
an end to this combat between reft and hunger, he
lies down, and falls afleep in the open air; and thus,
feemingly abandoned by nature and by men, he en-
joys the protection of the one, and defpifes. that of the
other. The citizen of Lyons, who difdained Rouffeau
becaufe he was ill clothed, has died unknown; and
the man in rags, has now altars erected to his memory.

Thefe examples ought to confole men of genius,
who have been reduced by fortune to a fimilar condition, and who are obliged to ftruggle againft want.

Adverfity is calculated to form them; let them
perfevere, and the fame recompenfe awaits them.

Puritanifm, with all its hideous aufterity, at one
time reigned in the colony of Maffachuffet. It appears, from many circumftances, however, that Franklin, even while a boy, knew how to appreciate this
religious grimace.

As his father was accuftomed to precede all his
meals with long prayers, and even to fay grace over
every particular difh, he was defirous to correct this
folly by means of the following fally of wit:

Old Franklin, one day, at the beginning of winter,
being bufied in falting provifions; "Father," fays
his fon, " you ought to afk a bleffing, once for all,
" upon the whole cafk of provifions, *as it would be*
" *a wonderful faving of time!*"

Young Benjamin fully difplayed his future character in the concluding obfervation, the principle of
which formed the bafis of all his politics.

Franklin

Franklin being perfuaded that knowledge could never fpread, unlefs it had been firft collected in a central point, as it were, was always extremely de-firous to encourage literary, and political clubs. In one of thefe clubs, founded by him, the following were the queftions put to the candidate :

" Do you believe, that a man ought to be defpifed
" or perfecuted for opinions merely fpeculative, on
" account of any particular faith that he may hap-
" pen to profefs ?"

" Do you love truth, for its own fake ?"

" Will you employ all your efforts, in order to
" know it yourfelf, and to inftill it into others ?"

---

* Having, during his refidence in England, remark-ed the advantages refulting from newfpapers, and affo-ciations, known under the denomination of *Clubs,* and focieties formed on the bafis of a voluntary fub-fcription, Franklin propofed to make them adopted by his native country.

He accordingly began by publifhing a Gazette, the columns of which he filled up, during a fcarcity of news, by means of effays of his own compofition, in which the moral was generally prefented under the form of an apologue; in which reafon was animated by gay but amiable pleafantries ; and in which phi-lofophy, without ceafing to be within the comprehen-fion of the fimple colonifts for whom it was deftined, was on a level with the ideas of an European.

* Tranflated from the " Eloge de Franklin," by the cele-brated Condorcet.

It

It was a new Spectator, as it were, that he produced, but with much more nature, fimplicity, and
grace; with an aim more extended, and, above all,
more ufeful.

Inftead of the uncertain hope of correcting fome
few of the vices of a nation, corrupted by riches
and inequality, he conceived a reafonable expectation
of rectifying the ideas, of depurating and polifhing
the virtues of a nafcent people.

Several of the fugitive pieces printed at that period
by Franklin, have been preferved; and there are
fome of them, which Voltaire and Montefquieu would
not have difavowed.

He would never permit his journal to be difgraced
by *perfonalities*. This fpecies of malice, which prefents the ready means of drawing down the popular
vengeance upon thofe whom an editor is inclined
to hate, appeared to him to be equally hurtful and
dangerous. It feemed to furnifh a perfidious kind of
arms, which the hypocritical and the factious might ufe
with addrefs, in order to provoke fufpicion againft
virtues and talents the moft eminent; to render
all reputations uncertain; to deftroy character, and
the authority of a good name, a circumftance fo neceffary in an infant republic, and then deliver up the
public confidence to thofe obfcure and intriguing
men who know how to furprife it.

The Americans were not then that enlightened
people, who have fince aftonifhed us by the wifdom of
their conftitutions. Religion, and the inceffant labour neceffary to form eftablifhments in a wild and

favage

favage country, had alone occupied the minds and the bodies of the firft generations of Europeans.

Franklin perceived how much they ftood in need of the light of philofophy; but it was neceffary to make them feel this, without announcing an intention, which would have but too plainly dif-covered his own fuperiority.

He accordingly formed a club, compofed of feveral of the inhabitants of Philadelphia, whofe fortunes were on a level with his own. It confifted of only twelve perfons, and the number was never augmented. But in confequence of his advice, the majority of the members eftablifhed fimilar affociations; by this means, they all became animated with the fame fpirit; but he was careful not to connect them by a folemn confederation, and ftill lefs by a dependence upon the mother fociety.

It was his intention to form a more liberal com-munication of knowledge, and of fentiments, among the citizens; to habituate them to the cuftom of act-ing together in behalf of their common interefts; and to enable them to propagate and difperfe their opi-nions, without forming a party.

He thought that if a private affociation ought never to conceal itfelf, it ought ftill lefs to exhibit itfelf to public view; that ufeful, while it acts by the fepa-rate interefts of its members, by the concert of their intentions, by the weight which their virtues or their talents give to their opinions, it might become dan-gerous, if, operating in a mafs, and forming in fome refpects a nation within a nation, it fhould be at

length

length able to oppose its own will to that of the people, and to place between individuals and the national power, a foreign force, which, directed by an ambitious man, might equally menace liberty and the laws *.

It is customary, in the English clubs, to subject all those to a slight fine, who transgress their laws. In that of Philadelphia, a slight fine was levied every time an improper expression was made use of.— Those most obstinate in the belief of their own *infallibility*, were obliged to make use of a certain diffidence in their assertions, and to adopt a degree of modest circumlocution, that prevented the self-love of the company from being shocked by the powerful influence of words upon ideas,—this at length extended even to opinions †.

---

* This idea is perhaps adapted only to an established commonwealth. What could France have opposed to the treachery of the Executive Power, save and except a club, to which (however unpopular it may now be) the empire is indebted for its liberties ?

† " 1mo, To declare that the candidate had no animosity " against any of the members of the assembly.

" 2do, To profess an equal degree of love for all men, whatever might be their faith.

" 3tio, To look upon every attempt against the independence " of religion, and of opinion, to be tyranny.

" 4to, To love the truth for its own sake—to take pleasure in " extending and propagating it.

" This," says M. Condorcet, " was the profession of faith " of a society which rendered great service to the Assembly of " Pennsylvania, without ever pretending to govern it."

In

In the mean time, Franklin began, in an adroit manner, to declare war againſt fanaticiſm, which of courſe muſt have taken deep root in a country peopled by perſecution. Thoſe ſentiments of univerſal bene-volence, which ſo eaſily enter into mild and gentle minds; thoſe maxims of ſimple truth which good ſenſe never rejeĉts, conduĉt, by little and little, to indulgence, and to reaſon; and at leaſt reduce to a ſtate incapable of doing them hurt, that enemy to mankind, which it would have been imprudent to have attacked in front.

Thus, at the very ſame epoch, in two different parts of the globe, philoſophy avenged humanity of the tyranny which had a long while oppreſſed and diſhonoured it; but it combated her with different weapons.

In the one, fanaticiſm was an error of individuals, and the unhappy conſequence of their education and their ſtudies; to enlighten them, it was ſufficient to diſſipate the phantoms of a wandering imagination. In fine, it was only the fanatics themſelves that it was neceſſary to cure.

In the other, where fanaticiſm, guided by poli-tics, had founded upon error a ſyſtem of domination, and where, leagued with every ſpecies of tyranny, it had promiſed to blind mankind, provided it was permitted to oppreſs them, it became neceſſary to rear up againſt it the whole force of public opinion, and to oppoſe, to ſo dangerous a power, all the ef-forts of the friends of reaſon and of liberty. The buſineſs there, was not to enlighten the fanatics, but

to

to unmafk and difarm them. One might add to this parallel, new in the hiftory of philofophy, that Voltaire and Franklin, the two men who had feparately, but at one and the fame time, conceived this falutary projeƈt, had the happinefs to meet, in their old age, at Paris—to enjoy their glory together, and congratulate each other upon their triumph.

The philofopher, who prepared the felicity of his country by enlightening men, and forming them into citizens, was deftined to render it fervices ftill more direƈt, and no lefs ufeful. The times were no longer fuch, as when the poverty of the Englifh colonies was fufficient to prevent the wars of Europe from extending to them. They had already become fufficiently flourifhing to tempt the avidity of an enemy; and it was equally dangerous for their repofe and their liberty, to be either abandoned by Great-Britain, or defended by its armies.

Dr. Franklin, who, ever fince the year 1736, had aƈted as Secretary to the Affembly of Pennfylvania, thought that it would be proper to profit by a war in which England was fo nearly interefted, in order to teach the Pennfylvanians to affume, for the defence of the mother country, thofe arms which would be one day neceffary againft herf. lf, for the maintenance of their own rights; and accordingly, in 1744, he formed the plan of a national militia.

The people relifhed the propofal; Philadelphia alone furnifhed a thoufand men. The command was offered to Franklin; he refufed it, and ferved as a common foldier under Mr. Laurence, whom he

himfelf

himfelf had propofed as the fitteft perfon to act as General.

It was neceffary to build forts, and money was wanting ; he provided the neceffary fums by means of a lottery, of which he himfelf formed the plan.

The fuccefs of this meafure was retarded for fome time, by a very fingular difficulty.

The Quakers form a very numerous body in Penn-fylvania ; and fuch is the purity of the principles of that fect, that they look upon it as criminal, to contribute money even in behalf of a defenfive war. The natural effect of an exaggerated morality, adopt-ed by enthufiafm, is to place its fectarifts under the neceffity of either violating its precepts, or of facri-ficing the counfels of reafon, and the dictates of judgment. At length they endeavour to elude their own laws ; they diffemble the violation of them by means of fubtile diftinctions, and by adroit and equi-vocal modes of reafoning. By thefe means, they pre-vent the fanatics and hypocrites of their own fect from rifing againft them, and do not wound the feelings of the people, who, in all religions, attach their ideas of morality to certain confecrated words *.

The

* It is thus that the Quakers, on being folicited for money in order to purchafe gunpowder, prefented the fum demanded, *under the pretence* of its being intended for corn. The Dunkars, more wife perhaps than the Quakers, have never committed their *dog-mas* nor their precepts to writing. They were afraid, as one of their principal men told Dr. Franklin, of either expofing them-felves to the danger of profeffing that which they did not any longer believe, or to the fhame of having changed their opinions.

CONDORCET.

The philofophical indulgence of Dr. Franklin, and the addrefs which he made ufe of upon more than one occafion, often enabled him to conciliate the patriotifm of the Quakers with the principles of their fect.

Never was any man more anxious to exhibit the moft fcrupulous refpect for the religious weakneffes and follies of other men; towards feeble and fickly minds, he ever evinced the fame delicate attentions, which worthy men generally make ufe of in regard to the infirmities of infancy.

The education of Dr. Franklin had not opened to him the career of the fciences, but nature had given him a genius capable of comprehending, and even of embellifhing them.

His firft effays on electricity fully prove, that he was but very little acquainted with this part of natural philofophy. Being at an immenfe diftance from Europe, he poffeffed but imperfect machines. Notwithftanding this difadvantage, he foon difcovered the immediate caufe of electrical *phenomena*. He explained it, by demonftrating the exiftence of a fluid, infenfible while it remains in a ftate of equilibrium, and which inftantly manifefts itfelf, either when this equilibrium is deftroyed, or while it endeavours to re-eftablifh it. His Analyfis of the grand Leyden experiment, is a *chef-d'œuvre* at once, of fagacity, of perfpicacity, and of art.

Soon after this, he perceived an analogy between the effects of thunder and electricity, which ftruck him prodigioufly. He conceived the idea of an apparatus,

paratus, by means of which, he propofed to interro-
gate the heavens; he makes the experiment, and the
anfwer fully confirms his conjectures. Thus the
caufe of lightning is now known. Its effects, fo
ruinous, fo irregular in appearance, are not only explained, but imitated.

We at length know why the lightning filently and
peaceably follows certain bodies, and difperfes others
with a loud noife; why it melts metals, fometimes fhivers to atoms, and fometimes feems to refpect, thofe fubftances which furround it.

But it was but little to imitate the thunder:
Dr. Franklin conceived the audacious idea of averting its vengeance.

He imagined, that a bar of iron, pointed at the
end, and connected with the ground, or rather with
the water, would eftablifh a communication between
a cloud and the earth, and thus guarantee or protect the objects in the immediate neighbourhood of
fuch a conductor.

The fuccefs of this idea was fully commenfurate
to all his wifhes; and thus man was enabled to wield
a power fufficient to difarm the wrath of Heaven.

This great difcovery was by far too brilliant, and
too fingular, not to conjure up a numerous hoft of
enemies againft it. Notwithftanding this, the cuftom
of ufing conductors was adopted in America and in
Great Britain; but at the commencement of war
with the mother-country, the Englifh philofophers
endeavoured, by unfair experiments, to throw doubts
upon the utility of his fcheme, and feemed to indi-

cate

cate a wifh to ravifh this difcovery from Benjamin Franklin, by way of punifhing him for the lofs of thirteen colonies.

It is unfortunately more eafy to miflead a nation in regard to its proper interefts, than to impofe upon men of fcience relative to an experiment;· thus thofe prejudices, which were able to draw England into an unjuft and fatal conteft, could not make the learned of Europe, change the form of the electrical conductors. They multiplied in France, after France had become allied to America; in truth, the fentence of the police has been oppofed to it in fome of our towns, as it has been oppofed in Italy by the decifions of cafuifts, and with juft as little fuccefs!

In a free country, the law follows the public opinion; in defpotic governments, the public opinion often contradicts the laws, but always concludes at length by fubmitting itfelf to their influence.— At this day, the ufe of this prefervative has become common among almoft all nations, but without being univerfally adopted. A long courfe of experiments does not permit us any longer to doubt of its efficacy.

If the edifices provided with it, have ftill fome dangers to dread, this happens, becaufe, between the bounded efforts of man, and the boundlefs force of nature, there can never be eftablifhed any other, but an unequal conteft.

But what an immenfe career has this fuccefsful experiment opened to our hopes?

Why may we not one day hope to fee the baneful activity of all the fcourges of mankind melt away,

2   a₂

as that of thunder has done, before the powers of genius, exercifed through immenfity of ages; when all the regions of nature are difarmed by the happy ufe of her gifts, we fhall experience nothing but her benefits ?

In 1754, the King of England, who had formed the project of attacking France, convoked a general congrefs of the deputies of the different colonies, in order to concert a fyftem of common defence.   Dr. Franklin was fent thither, and propofed a plan, which was accepted by the Congrefs; but it was neither agreeable to the affemblies of the particular States, nor to the Britifh miniftry.   No menace had as yet made the colonies perceive the neceffity of this union, which was about to take away. from each a part of its independence ; and the Englifh government was at one and the fame time too cunning not to forefee that this new inftitution prepared a refiftance to its tyrannical enterprifes, and was too little enlightened to know, that nothing remained for it but to direct a revolution, which was an inevitable confequence of the increafing profperity of the colonies.   Indolence or pride on one fide, and perfidy on the other, occafioned the rejection of a fcheme formed by forefight and traced by wifdom.

Twenty-four years afterwards, it ferved as a bafis to that Congrefs which declared the independence of the United States ; and perhaps it would have been a *defideratum* in the new conftitution, to have imitated more its fage fimplicity.

It has been urged as a reproach to Franklin, that he had given a *negative* to the governor appointed by

2   the

the King of Great Britain; but circumftances required
this facrifice; it was the band that would have connected a fucker, at that time young and tender, to
the parent tree, from which it had fprouted forth;
and which ought not to have been cut until the moment that the young plant, after having extended its
roots, and developed its branches, had acquired fufficient vigour to nourifh it by means of its own proper ftrength.

While he remained in England, in quality of agent
for the American provinces, the minifters fometimes
deigned to confult him. They affected, however, to
regard all thofe who happened not to be of their way
of thinking, as enemies to Great Britain. This
was no other than announcing, that they wifhed to
be deceived; and the governors of the colonies underftood this but too well.

Notwithftanding this, Franklin, faithful to his
principles, continued alone to tell the truth. Therefore, not content with taking away from him a place
which he held in America *, and to which they had
no longer the power to appoint a fucceffor, they ftopped the arrears of his falary, and at laft commenced
a profecution againft him.

Thefe proceffes, in a free country, are the *lettres de
cachet* of its minifters; and it is in this manner that, a
few years before, they found means to be avenged of

* The office of Poft Mafter General for the Southern Department. TRANS.

Mr.

Mr. Wilkes *. The prefent, however, was not attended with any difagreeable circumftances ; they could not find a pretext in any exifting law for condemning him; and the minifterial vengeance was obliged to be content with the outrages of a lawyer, whofe complaifance has fince been recompenfed by a peerage †.

At the epoch when Franklin was fent to France, this country did not poffefs a free conftitution ; but the French could not be properly termed flaves. If the people groaned beneath an arbitrary government, and ftill more under the yoke of bad laws, *their fouls were not fubjugated*, for their minds ftill preferved their independence.

It did not refemble a nation where there does not exift but a defpot, a treafury, and an army ; it was not indifferent that a war was conformable or contrary to the national will, for the French were already thought worthy of being confulted; their mi-

* The intereft which minifters have in preferving the means of indirect oppreffion, is one of the principal obftacles to the perfection of the laws of England.

Criminal laws, which are vague, or which enact penalties againft actions innocent in themfelves, civil laws, obfcure in their nature, and explained by tribunals which either by their conftitution, or their want of independence, are not altogether unexpofed to influence, are fo many inftruments, which either indolence or corruption, leave too often in the hands of defpotifm. Every nation that wifhes to remain free, ought to haften to fnatch that odious power from the hands that wield it. CONDORCET.

† M. Condorcet feems to be miftaken in this particular ; a procefs was indeed threatened, but it was never commenced. TRANS.

nifters

nifters following the policy adopted among free nations, before they commenced a war, waited until it
was folicited by the voice of the people.

As a negotiator, Franklin obferved much, but did
little.

He wifely left to the minifters of the allied powers,
to decide on the manner of attacking England and
fuccouring America, for fear left the bad fuccefs of
any meafure imputed to his counfels, or to his de-
mands, fhould cool their zeal.

It was in order to maintain in France an idea of
the conftancy and refources of America, and to fupport that enthufiafm created by himfelf, that he employed all his pains and attention, until, perceiving the
approaching difgrace of the Englifh miniftry, who had
commenced and carried on the war, he forefaw that his
native country was about to be declared independent.

He beheld the aufpicious moment at length arrive ;
and figned, with a tranquil hand, that treaty which
affured the freedom and the glory of America ;
he had ever contemplated, with a firm eye, her dangers
and her fufferings.

This calmnefs of mind did not proceed from indifference ; it was the refult of a fincere conviction,
that the independence of America was to be bought
at a larger or a fmaller price, and recognifed fome
years fooner or later—but that it could never be in
danger of being loft.

Thefe were the reflections of a man, who knew
that the moral is fubjected, like the natural world, to
certain laws ; and who anticipated, in thefe immu-

P   table

table decrees, the triumph of his country. They also proceeded from the abfence of every perfonal confi- deration; for this corrupting influence often fullies the love of liberty, by thofe anxieties, thofe fears, thofe furious impulfes which degrade, by rendering it but too fimilar to the bafe paffions arifing from intereft and vanity. The patriotifm of Franklin was, as it ought to be, calm, like that of Socrates and of Phocion, whom the orators fold to the purpofes of a faction, or paid by tyrants, accufed of not loving their coun- try enough.

France, during the progrefs of this war, had pre- fented him with a fpectacle worthy of interefting his prying genius.

He had beheld the opinions which had been con- demned in the works of philofophers, adopted and eftablifhed in manifeftoes; a people tranquil amidft its ancient chains, intoxicated with the pleafure of breaking thofe of another hemifphere; republican principles openly profeffed under an arbitrary govern- ment; the rights of men violated by the laws, and by authority of the magiftrates, but proved and eftablifhed in books; political knowledge, worthy of the moft enlightened age, and the wifeft nation, fhining amidft a crowd of abfurd and barbarous in- ftitutions; a people applauding the maxims of liberty in the theatres, but yet obedient to the maxims of flavery; free in their fentiments, in their opinions, in their converfation, and appearing to behold, with extreme indifference, actions obliged to fubmit to the very laws which they defpifed.

It

· It was eafy for him to forefee, that a nation, already fo worthy of liberty, would foon be able to reconquer it; and that the revolution of France, like that of America, was one of the events which human knowledge might fubtract from the empire of reafon, and of the paffions *.

---

† On his arrival in France, Franklin announced himfelf as a philofopher, who, afflicted with the troubles of his country, and averting his eyes from fo many objects of defolation, had come to Europe on purpofe to find an afylum.

He at firft lodged in a village at the gates of Paris, and on the road to Verfailles. He foon after hired a houfe at Paffy; in this retreat, he faw but little company, and remained conftantly upon his guard.

He ufed to whifper, that the hatred of the Englifh miniftry conftantly expofed him to the greateft dangers—and this idea alone rendered him more interefting.

Franklin never entered the metropolis, unlefs accompanied by a numerous train, among whom were many men of genius, who, although neglected or perfecuted by their countrymen, neverthelefs reflected a luftre upon this foreigner, whom they honoured with their efteem.

---

* Dr. Franklin, while in France, faid one day, in a public company, " you perceive liberty eftablifh herfelf, and flourifh al-
" moft under your very eyes ; I dare to predict that, by and by,
" you will be anxious to tafte her bleffings." Condorcet.

† From Helliard d'Auberteuil.

Every

· Every thing about him announced that fimplicity, of manners, which the authors and philofophers of antiquity have fo well defcribed, and which unfor‑ tunately have perhaps never been fo perfect as in their defcriptions.

He had thrown away the wig which in Eng‑ land had concealed the baldnefs of his forehead ; and banifhed all that ufelefs parade of drefs, which could only have placed him upon a level with the reft of his countrymen.

He exhibited, to the aftonifhed multitude, a head worthy of the pencil of Guido, who excelled in the portraits of old men ; his body was ftraight and vigor‑ ous, and covered with the moft fimple drapery.— His eyes were fhaded by a large pair of fpectacles, and in his hand he wielded a white wand.

He fpoke but little; he knew how to be unpolite, without being rude ; and his pride feemed to be that of nature.

Such a perfonage was admirably calculated to ex‑ cite the curiofity of Paris. The people affembled wherever he intended to pafs; they demanded of each other " Who is that aged peafant, with fo, " noble an afpect ?"—and replied, with emulation, " It is the celebrated Franklin !"

He repaired to all the places where men ufually affociate for amiable, or ufeful, or humane purpofes ; and his arrival was always announced with plaudits.

He was to be feen at the public meetings of the Academy of Sciences, and the French Academy ; at the audiences of the Parliament, at the exhibition of the

the pictures in the academy of painting and fculp-
ture; at the free fociety of emulation for the encouragement to ufeful arts; and in thofe haunts, guard-
ed with fecrecy, where Peace and Liberty affembled,
which had been frequented by Helvetius and Voltaire, and where he was worthy of prefiding along
with them.

Never was any man fo much honoured, without ex-
citing envy; for every time that his name happened
to be quoted, it was always the cuftom to add, " He
" is a moft refpectable gentleman." In three months
after his arrival at Paris, his portrait was engraved,
and to be feen every-where.

In the mean time, the cabinet of London could not
be perfuaded that France and Spain were about to intereft themfelves in favour of America. " The
" French colonies," faid Lord George Germaine in
the Houfe of Commons, " are perhaps ftill more
" difcontented than our own :—Is it then to be
" believed, that the Court of Verfailles would dare
" to encourage a rebellion in their neighbourhood?
" Will it not be afraid, left its own iflands, in the
" Weft-Indies, fhould be tempted to participate in
" the unlimited rights of liberty?

" Will not thofe of Spain find a commerce with all
" nations infinitely more advantageous than with the
" Bifcay company; and the exclufive enjoyment of
" their own treafures, infinitely more agreeable, than,
" as now, to be obliged to dig their mines for an
" European monarch?

P 3   " he

" The neighbourhood of a large independent ftate,
" would always afford a perpetual fubject of uneafi_
" nefs to France and Spain ; and thefe Courts can_
" not be fo blind to their own proper interefts, as to
" fupport America."

———————

After fome preliminary propofitions, Conrad Gerard, authorifed by a fpecial commiffion from the King
of the French, dated Jan. 30th, 1778, and Benjamin
Franklin, Silas Deane, and Arthur Lee, on the part of
the Congrefs, figned at Paris, on the 6th of February
following, a treaty of friendfhip and commerce between the Crown of France, and the United States of
America.   Thefe plenipotentiaries, at the fame time,
infifted on obtaining an alliance offenfive and defenfive,
by which Louis XVI. was to engage, not only purely
and fimply to recognife the independence of the
United States, but alfo to guarantee and to defend
them : This was refufed by the French cabinet.

The King might readily acknowledge the independence of the colonies as an evident political fact,
but he did not choofe to make himfelf an umpire ; he
could not confequently either guarantee, or undertake
a war, in order to fupport it.

Neverthelefs, as the court of London appeared to
have conceived a defign of attacking France, the
King thought proper to enter into an eventual, but
purely defenfive alliance with the commonwealth
of America.

It

It was agreed, in confequence of this, *that if war
Jhould be declared between France and Great Britain,
during the prefent hoftilities between the United States
and England,* his Moft Chriftian Majefty and the
United States fhould make a common caufe of it,
and mutually aid each other with their counfels and
their forces, according to the neceffity of circumftances, as is ufual between good and faithful allies.

It was alfo declared, by article II. That the effential and direct object of the alliance was effica-
cioufly to maintain the liberty, fovereignty, and abfolute and unlimited independence of the United
States, as well in what related to commerce, as government. In fhort, the King engaged, in cafe war
fhould be declared between France and England,
never to lay down his arms, until after the independence and the fovereignty of the United States of
America fhould be recognifed by Great Britain.

This alliance did not prevent the colonies from
treating with England without the confent of France,
as long as hoftilities were confined to them; and it
left the King and Parliament of Great Britain abfolute mafters of either peace or war.

It never acquired any reality, until the commencement of hoftilities on the part of his Britannic Majefty, who ordered Pondicherry to be befieged, even
before the treaty in queftion was concluded.

It remained, indeed, a profound fecret, becaufe,
being provifional, it was then of no real value whatever; but the treaty of commerce was notified to the
Court of London, by the Count de Noailles, Am-

baffador

Ambaffador from France, on the 13th of March 1775.

On that very evening, Lord North declared in Parliament, that he regarded a war with France as inevitable.

Dr. Franklin, at length, had an interview with his Moft Chriftian Majefty; he was prefented to him, in the gallery of Verfailles, by the Count de Vergennes, Minifter for foreign affairs. On this occafion, he was accompanied and followed by a great number of Americans, and individuals of foreign ftates, who were collected together by curiofity. His age, his venerable appearance, the fimplicity of his drefs on fuch an occafion, every thing that was either fingular or refpectable in the life of this American, contributed to augment the public attention. Clapping of hands, and a variety of other demonftrations of joy, announced that warmth of affection, of which the French are more fufceptible than any other people, and of which their politenefs and civility augments the charm to him who is the object of it.

His Majefty addreffed him as follows :

" You may affure the United States of America of " my friendfhip; I beg leave alfo to obferve, that I " am exceedingly fatisfied in particular with your " own conduct, during your refidence in my king- " dom." When the new Ambaffador, after this audience, croffed the Court, in order to repair to the office of the minifter of foreign affairs, the multitude waited for him in the paffage, and hailed him with their acclamations.

At

At the moment that this illuftrious philofopher was received in this manner in Europe, the fpirit of divifion was introduced among the people of America. General Wafhington began, to be reproached for never having come off victorious in any pitched battle he had fought. The Court of London had emiffaries in its pay, who, with an appearance of zeal in the caufe of America, endeavoured to ruin it, by fermenting the diffenfions that took place between the chief perfons in the legiflature, and the leaders of the army. Some men, the fecret enemies of France, endeavoured to infpire the people with diftruft to government, and with a hatred to the individuals of the nation. Several adventurers, who pretended to be officers in the fervice of his Moft Chriftian Majefty, had, by means of their diforderly and improper conduct, but too much favoured the prejudices conceived againft their countrymen.

They alfo endeavoured to throw doubts upon the fuccefs of Dr. Franklin's miffion; the Congrefs actually refufed to employ fome individuals felected from our beft troops; they even expected but little trade with France, either on account of paft experience in bufinefs, or fome other reafons not eafily fpecified; for, in a country, of which commerce is the life, and which holds up as the firft clafs of citizens, all thofe that practife it with fuccefs, franknefs and good faith form the bafis of negotiations; whereas, among thofe nations in which commerce does not attract the public attention, the merchant

2   neceffarily

neceffarily becomes a man full of tricks, and defpi-
cable manœuvres.   The trade of monarchies is
propagated with great difficulty throughout the
world, whereas, on the contrary, in all ages, commerce has become tributary to republics, and even
to thofe the foil of which affords them but little or
nothing to exchange.

At length, the Court of England refolved to fend
Commiffioners to America, provided with extenfive
powers, in order to offer peace to the colonies, and
to re-eftablifh an union on the fame bafis as it had
exifted in 1763.

The treaty with France had been concluded on
the 6th of February, and the conciliatory bills did
not pafs the Britifh Parliament until the 16th of the
fame month ; but the miniftry hoped, that if their
Ambaffadors fet off inftantly, they would arrive in
fufficient time to divide the fentiments of the people,
and even to prevent the Congrefs from ratifying the
engagement entered into at Paris with its Plenipotentiaries.   Lord Carlifle, a man of gentle manners,
and fome parts ; Mr. (afterwards Commodore)
Johnftone, formerly Governor of Florida, who was
beloved in America on account of his candour, his
knowledge, and his humanity ; and William Eden,
a man of confiderable capacity ; were entrufted with
this delicate miffion.   Several of the Englifh had
actually perfuaded themfelves that the Congrefs
ufurped the authority which they exercifed over the
people, and knowing that the declaration of Independence had not paffed by an unanimous vote, they
thought

thought that it would be eafy to gain over a fufficient number of the members of the Affembly, in order to procure a majority.

The cabinet of St. James's had alfo fent its emiffaries to Paris, to treat with Dr. Franklin, and endeavour either to deceive, or betray him.

But it was now too late to open a negotiation, for Silas Deane had left the capital of France, in order to embark at Toulon on board the fleet commanded by Count d'Eftaing, and M. Gerard was to proceed to America, on the fame occafion, in quality of Minifter Plenipotentiary.

The Court of London, notwithftanding thefe conciliatory bills, did not recall its armies; on the conveftiges of the ravages'd and General Howe among the ferved, by their contraft, to endeavy reafon to believe, pleafures arifing from peace and victory.

---

* CHARACTER OF DR. FRANKLIN.

Humanity and franknefs were the bafis of his morality. A habitual gaiety, a happy facility in regard to every thing refpecting the common concerns of life, and a tranquil inflexibility in affairs of importance, formed the character of Dr. Franklin.— Thefe two latter qualities are eafily united in men, who, endowed with a fuperior mind, and ftrong underftanding, abandon trifling things to doubt and to indifference.

His fyftem of conduct was fimple; he endeavoured to banifh forrow and wearifomnefs, by means of

* By M. Condorcet

temperance

thefe furnifhed occupations for the evening of a
ferene life. But a grievous infirmity at length
troubled his happinefs; from that moment, his in-
clinations were turned towards America, and he
accordingly departed from France, to which, by
way of recompenfe for its fervices, he lefc a great
example, and leffons that could not remain long
without their proper ufe. Soon after his arrival in
the Ifle of Wight, he embarked, once more, for his
native country; he was accompanied to Great Britain by M. le Veillard, who, during his refidence at
Paffy, had conftantly exhibited towards him a degree of attention and refpeft, which filial affeftion
could alone rival. The American philofophe^ ^^^^^^
touched Englifh ground with ^^^^^^^^lory bills did
^^^^^^^^^ ^ ^^^ arnament until the 16th of the
fame month; but the miniftry hoped, that if their
Ambaffadors fet off inftantly, they would arrive in
fufficient time to divide the fentiments of the people,
and even to prevent the Congrefs from ratifying the
engagement entered into at Paris with its Plenipotentiaries. Lord Carlifle, a man of gentle manners,
and fome parts; Mr. (afterwards Commodore)
Johnftone, formerly Governor of Florida, who was
beloved in America on account of his candour, his
knowledge, and his humanity; and William Eden,
a man of confiderable capacity; were entrufted with
this delicate miffion. Several of the Englifh had
actually perfuaded themfelves that the Congrefs
ufurped the authority which they exercifed over the
people, and knowing that the declaration of Independence had not paffed by an unanimous vote, they
thought

tures of a great man, whofe talents, whofe fervices, and whofe virtues, had excited in their hearts the firft raptures of enthufiafm. Having advanced from a port henceforth open to all nations, to a city, the model of all future capitals, he beheld the public fchool which he had founded, in a ftate of fplendour; and faw the hofpital, the eftablifhment of which had been one of his firft fervices, and the increafe of which was owing to his forefight, now fully commenfurate to all his wifhes, by folacing fuffering humanity, and by aiding the progrefs of reafon. He then turned his eyes towards the neighbouring country, embellifhed by liberty, in which, in the midft of public profperity, were ftill to be feen fome veftiges of the ravages of the Englifh; but thefe only ferved, by their contraft, to endear, ftill more, the pleafures arifing from peace and victory.

---

* CHARACTER OF DR. FRANKLIN.

Humanity and franknefs were the bafis of his morality. A habitual gaiety, a happy facility in regard to every thing refpecting the common concerns of life, and a tranquil inflexibility in affairs of importance, formed the character of Dr. Franklin.— Thefe two latter qualities are eafily united in men, who, endowed with a fuperior mind, and ftrong underftanding, abandon trifling things to doubt and to indifference.

His fyftem of conduct was fimple; he endeavoured to banifh forrow and wearifomnefs, by means of

* By M. Condorcet

temperance

. temperance and labour. " Happinefs," he was ufed to fay, " like a body, is compofed of infen- " fible elements."

Without difdaining glory, he knew how to defpife the injuftice of opinion; and while enjoying renown, he could pardon envy.

During his youth, he had carried his *pyrrhonifm* to the very foundations of morality; the natural goodnefs of his heart, and the directions of his con- fcience, were his fole guides; and they very rarely led him aftray.

A little later in life, he allowed that there exifted a morality founded upon the nature of man, inde- pendent of all fpeculative opinions, and anterior to all conventions.

He thought, that our fouls, in another life, re- ceived the recompenfe of their virtues, and the punifhment of their faults; he believed in the exiftence of a God, at once beneficent and juft, to whom he offered up, in the fecrecy of his own confcience, a filent, but pure homage.

He did not defpife the exterior forms of religion; he even thought them ufeful to morality; he, how- ever, fubmitted himfelf to them but feldom.

All religions appeared to him to be equally good, provided an univerfal toleration was the principle of them, and that they did not deprive, of the recom- penfe due to virtue, thofe who were of another be- lief, or of no belief at all.

The application of the fciences to the common purpofes of life, and to domeftic œconomy, was

often

often the fubject of his refearches; he took pleafure to demonftrate, that, even in the moft common affairs of life, cuftom and ignorance are but bad guides; that we were far from having exhaufted the refources of nature; and were only deficient in men capable of interrogating her *.

He never wrote any thing upon politics, except fome tracts required by circumftances, and produced upon the fpur of the occafion.

It was eafy to perceive, that he always endeavoured to reduce all queftions to their fimple elements, and to prefent them in fuch a manner to the public, that the unlearned might be enabled to underftand, and to refolve them. It was to fuch that he always addreffed himfelf. Sometimes it was an error that he attempted to root out and deftroy; and fometimes an ufeful truth, for which he wifhed gently to prepare their minds, that at lengrh they might be enabled to receive, and, above all, to preferve it. It is in vain that we fhall fearch for any fubject, on which he could be fuppofed to have written from the mere impulfe of glory.

* He was occupied a long time, in endeavouring to make the forms of chimnies more perfect, and to introduce œconomy in regard to combuftible fubftances, by regulating the intenfity and the equality of heat, and the renewal of the air in places warmed artificially. Several years before he became fo celebrated as he afterwards was, and at the period when he began to enjoy an independent fortune, it was propofed to him to procure a patent for a ftove of his own invention. This he rejected; faying, at the fame time, " I have profited by the inventions of others, and if is it not juft that they, in return, fhould profit by mine ?"

Sometimes

Sometimes he employed thofe forms, which, in appearance only, difguife the truth, in order to ren, der it more affecting, and which, inftead of difclof, ing, allow the pleafure of divining it.

It was thus that, while feeming to teach the fureft means for diminifhing the extent of a ftate, which is found too difficult to be governed, he lampooned the conduct of the Englifh miniftry in regard to America; thus, alfo, by way of difplaying the injuftice of the pretenfions of Great Britain in regard to her colonies, he fuppofes the King of Pruffia to publifh a proclamation, in which he fubjugates England to the payment of certain taxes, under pretext that the in, habitants of the banks of the Oder had formerly con, quered and peopled it.

His converfation, like his ftyle, was always natu, ral, and often ingenious. In his youth, he had read Xenophon, an author who had infpired him with a tafte for the Socratic method of argument,—and he took pleafure in employing it, fometimes by putting artful queftions, tending to make the advocates of a falfe opinion refute themfelves; fometimes, by an application of their principles to other events, oblig, ing them thus to recognife the truth, when difen, gaged from the clouds within which cuftom or pre, judice had enveloped it; at other times, deciding by means of an apologue, a tale, or an anecdote, thofe queftions which the pride of a ferious difcuffion would have obfcured,

Being employed by fome of the American pro, vinces, to requeft an abolition of the infulting cuftom
of

of tranfporting malefactors to the colonies, the minifter, by way of reply, alleged the neceffity of delivering England of fuch vermin.

" What would you fay to us," rejoined he, " if " we were to export our rattlefnakes ?"

Dr. Franklin had never formed a general fyftem of politics: He examined the queftions exactly as the events prefented themfelves to his obferv-ation, or as his forefight anticipated them; and he decided them all according to the ftandard of thofe principles which originate in a virtuous mind, and in a judgment at once juft and comprehenfive.

In general, he appeared not fond of giving all at once the greateft poffible degree of perfection to human inftitutions; he thought it a more certain way to wait for the effects of time. He was not fond of attacking abufes in front; he thought it more prudent firft to attack thofe errors which are the fource of them.

He had in politics, as in morals, that kind of indulgence which requires but little, becaufe it hopes much, and which forgets, and even pardons the prefent, in favour of the future. He always propofed thofe meafures which feemed to him to be moft proper in order to preferve peace; becaufe he was not fond of delivering up the happinefs of mankind to the uncertainty of events, nor truth to the interefts of a party.

He preferred the good obtained by reafon to that which might be expected from enthufiafm; becaufe

Q   it

it is more eafy to be procured, and infinitely more lafting.

In one word, his politics were thofe of a man who believed in the power of reafon and the reality of virtue, and who afpired to be the teacher of his fellow-citizens before he became their legiflator.

---

* At the name of Franklin, every thing interefting to virtue, freedom, and humanity, rifes to our recollection! By what eulogium fhall we do juftice to his pre-eminent abilities and worth? This would require a pre-eminence of abilities and worth like his own.

His original and univerfal genius was capable of the *greateft* things, but difdained not the *fmalleft*, provided they were ufeful. With equal eafe and abilities he could conduct the affairs of a printing-prefs, and of a great nation, and difcharge the duties of a public minifter of ftate, or the private executor of a will.

Franklin, as a philofopher, might have become a Newton; as a lawgiver, a Lycurgus; but he was greater than either of them, by uniting the talents of both in the practical philofophy of doing good, compared to which all the palms of fpeculative wifdom and fcience wither on the fight. He did not feek to derive his

---

* Selected from Dr. Smith's Eulogium on Benjamin Franklin, L. L. D. delivered March 1, 1791, before the Congrefs, and the American Philofophical Society of Philadelphia.

eminence

eminence from the mere profeſſion of letters, which,
although laborious, ſeldom elevates a man to any
high rank in the public confidence and eſteem ; but
he became great by applying his abilities to things uſeful, and accommodating his inſtructions to the exi-
gencies of the times, and the neceſſities of his country.

Had we no other proof of this, the great and dignified part which he ſuſtained in the American Revolution, one of the moſt important events recorded
in the annals of mankind, would have been alone ſufficient to immortalize his name ; but when we take
into the account his previous labours for half a century, on purpoſe to illuminate the minds of his fellow-
citizens, to prepare them for the mighty event, to
nurſe them into greatneſs by the arts of induſtry and
virtue, to ſhew them the happineſs which lay within
their reach, to teach them to dare, and to bear, and
to improve ſucceſs ;—this accumulation of ſervices
has woven for his head a diadem of ſuch beauty,
as ſcarcely ever adorned the brow of either ancient
or modern worthy.

In the earlieſt ſtages of life he had conceived the
mighty idea of American glory and empire ; but,
like Hercules in the cradle, he was ignorant of his
own ſtrength, and had not conceived the achieve-
ments and the labours that awaited him. He had
not yet conceived that he was one day to contend
with kings and potentates for the rights of his country, to extort from them an acknowledgment of
its ſovereignty, and to ſubſcribe with his name the

Q 2   ſacred

facred inftruments which were to give it a pre-eminent rank among the nations of the earth, and to
affure its liberty and independence to the lateft ages!

Virtus vera nobilitas *, was an adage with which
he was well pleafed. He confidered a defcent from
any of the virtuous peafantry and venerable yeo-
manry of America, who firft fubdued the fturdy oaks
of our forefts, and affifted to introduce culture and
civilization into a once untutored land, as having
more true nobility in it, than a pedigree which
might be traced through the longeft line of thofe
commonly called great and noble in this world. He
rofe from low beginnings, and advanced not only
himfelf but his country by means of the prefs. The
prefs was the great inftrument he made ufe of in
order to draw the attention of Pennfylvania to habits
of virtue and induftry; to the inftitution of focieties
for the promotion of agriculture, commerce, and
the mechanic arts; to the founding of fchools, libraries, and hofpitals, for the diffufion of ufeful knowledge and the advancement of humanity : When you
confider this, you will go and do likewife †; you
will, with profeffional joy and pride, obferve, that from
the torch which Franklin kindled by means of his
prefs, in the new world, " fparks are already ftolen
" which are lighting up the facred flame of liberty,
" virtue, and wifdom, over the entire face of the

---

* Virtue is true nobility.

† This part was addreffed to the printers of Philadelphia, who
attended in a body.

" globe."

globe." Be it your part to feed that torch by means of the prefs until its divine flame reach the fkies.

For the purpofe of aiding his prefs, and increafing the materials of information, one of the firft focieties in America was formed by Dr. Franklin in the year 1728, about the twenty-fecond year of his age, and was called the Junto. The number was limited to twelve members, who were bound together in all the ties of friendfhip, and engaged to affift each other not only in mutual communications of knowledge, but in all their worldly undertakings. This fociety, after having fubfifted forty years, and having contributed to the formation of fome very great men, befides Dr. Franklin himfelf, became at laft the foundation of the *American Philofophical Society,* now affembled to pay the debt of gratitude to his memory. Many of the queftions difcuffed by the members are curious; the following are a few of them:

" Is found an entity or a body?"

" How may the phænomena of vapours be ex-
" plained?"

" Is felf-intereft (the rudder that fteers mankind)
" the univerfal monarch to whom all are tribu-
" taries?"

" Which is the beft form of government, and
" what was that form which firft prevailed
" among mankind?"

" What is the reafon that the tides rife higher in
" the bay of Fundy, than in the bay of De-
" laware?"

Q 3   " Is

" Is the emiffion of paper money fafe?"

" What is the reafon that men of the greateft
" knowledge are not the moft happy?"

" How may the poffeffion of the lakes be improved
" to our advantage?"

" Why are tumultuous, uneafy fenfations united
" with our defires?"

" Whether it ought to be the aim of philofophy
" to eradicate the paffions?"

" How may fmoky chimnies be beft cured?"

" Why does the flame of a candle tend upwards
" in a fpire?"

" Which is the leaft criminal, A *bad* action joined
" with a *good* intention, or a *good* action with
" a *bad* intention?"

" Is it confiftent with the principles of liberty in a
" free government to punifh a man as a libeller
" when he fpeaks the truth?" &c. &c.

But Dr. Franklin did not reft fatisfied with the inftitution of this literary club, for the improvement of
himfelf and a few of his felect friends. He proceeded year after year in the projecting and eftablifhing other inftitutions for the benefit of the community at large. Thus, in 1731, he fet on foot the
" Library Company of the city of Philadelphia,"
a moft important inftitution to all ranks of people,
giving them accefs, at a fmall expence, to books on
every ufeful fubject, amounting in the whole to near
ten thoufand volumes, and the number is daily increafing.

After

After the eſtabliſhment of this company, its founder ſtill proceeded to promote other eſtabliſhments and aſſociations; ſuch as fire companies, the nightly watch for the city of Philadelphia, a plan for cleanſing, lighting, and ornamenting the ſtreets, and an aſſociation for inſuring houſes damaged by fire; to which, as collateral, he ſoon after added his plan for improving chimnies and fire-places, which gave riſe to the open ſtoves now in general uſe, to the comfort of thouſands who aſſemble round them in the wintry nights, and bleſs the inventor's name which they yet bear.

The next inſtitution, in the foundation of which he was the principal agent, was the Academy and Charitable School of the city of Philadelphia, the plan of which he drew up and publiſhed in the year 1749.

The Pennſylvania Hoſpital is alſo a monument of his philanthropy and public ſpirit, for the eſtabliſhment and endowment of which he was happily inſtrumental in obtaining a legiſlative ſanction and grant, by his great influence in the General Aſſembly in the year 1752.

Theſe various inſtitutions, which do ſo much honour to Pennſylvania, he projected, and ſaw completed during the firſt twenty years of his reſidence in this ſtate.

A life ſo aſſiduouſly employed in deviſing and executing ſchemes for the public good could not fail to aid him in his political career. He firſt became

clerk

clerk of the General Affembly, and then a member of the fame for the city of Philadelphia, during the fpace of fourteen years fucceffively. In 1744, a Spanifh privateer having entered the bay of Delaware, afcended as high as Newcaftle, to the great terror of the citizens of Philadelphia. On the occafion of this alarm he wrote his firft political pamphlet, called " Plain Truth," to exhort his fellow-citizens to the bearing of arms, which laid the foundation of thofe military affociations which followed at different times for the defence of the country.

Endowed with a penetrating and inquifitive genius, fpeculative and philofophical fubjects engaged his early attention ; but he loved them only as they were ufeful, and purfued them no farther than as he found his refearches applicable to fome fubftantial purpofe in life. His ftock of knowledge, and the fruits of his inveftigations, he never hoarded up for his own private ufe ; whatever he difcovered, whatever he confidered as beneficial to mankind, frefh as it was conceived, or brought forth in his own mind, he communicated to his fellow-citizens by means of his newfpapers, and almanacks, in delicate and palatable morfels for the advancement of induftry, frugality, and other republican virtues ; and at a future day, as occafion might require, he would collect and digeft the parts, and fet out the whole into one rich feaft of ufeful maxims and practical wifdom. Of this kind is his celebrated addrefs, entitled, " The " Way to Wealth," which is a collection, or a digeft, of the various fentences, proverbs, and wife maxims,

which,

which, during a courfe of many years, he had occafionally publifhed in his " Poor Richard's Alma-
" nack," on topics of induftry, frugality, and the duty
of *minding one's own bufinefs.* Had he never written
any thing more than this admirable addrefs, it would
have infured him immortality; he, befides this, publifhed " The Farmer's Philofopher," " The Rural
" Sage," and " The Yeoman's and Peafant's Oracle."

But greater things lay before him, although, as a
philofopher as well as a politician, he remained un-
confcious of the plenitude of his own ftrength and
talents, until called into further exertions by the
magnitude of future objeêts and occafions.

From the beginning of the year 1746, till about
twenty years afterwards, was the æra of eleêtricity;
no other branch of natural philofophy was fo much
cultivated during that period. In America and in
the mind of Franklin it found a rich bed; the feed
took root, and fprung into a great tree, before he
knew that fimilar feeds had vegetated, or rifen to
any height in other parts of the world.

Anterior to that period philofophers amufed themfelves only with the fmaller phænomena of eleêtricity;
fuch as relate to the attraêtion of light bodies, the di-
ftances to which fuch attraêtion would extend, the lu-
minous appearance produced by the excited glafs
tube, and the firing fpirits and inflammable air by
eleêtricity.

Little more was known on this fubjeêt than Thales,
the Milefian, had difcovered 2000 years before.
Sufficient *data* and experiments were wanting to
reduce

reduce the doctrine and phænomena of electricity into any rules or fyftem, and to apply them to any beneficial purpofes of life. This great achievement, which had eluded the induftry and abilities of a Boyle and a Newton, was referved for a Franklin.

What muft have been his ideas on the fuccefs of his grand experiment by means of his *electrical kite* ? Similar muft his raptures have been to thofe of a Newton, when, by applying the laws of *gravitation* and *projection* firft to the moon, he was enabled to ex-tend them to the whole folar fyftem, as is beautifully defcribed by the poet :

" What were his raptures then ! how fine ! how ftrong !
" And what the triumphs of old Greece and Rome
" With this compar'd—When Nature and her laws
" Stood all fubdu'd by him, and open laid
" Their every latent glory to his view."

His inquiries and difcoveries were confined to no limits or fubjects. Through all the elements, in the fire and in the water, in the air and in the earth, he fought for, and he found, new and beneficial knowledge.

Being on fhip-board in the year 1757, an accident gave him occafion to obferve the wonderful effect of oil in ftilling the waves of the fea. He immediately determined to elucidate this new property of oil, which he did with fuccefs; and the philofophical world is indebted to him for being now fully ac-quainted with a fact which, although not unknown to Plutarch and Pliny, could, for ages paft, have

3 been

been known only among the Dutch fifhermen, and a few feamen of other nations.

He difcovered that unaccountable agitation of the two furfaces in *contaƈt*, when a quantity of *oil* floats on water in a veffel.

He found the pulfe glafs in Germany, and introduced it into England with improvements of his own.

He difcovered that equal and congenial bodies, acquired different degrees of heat from the fun's rays, according to their different colours.

He made experiments to fhew that boats are drawn with more difficulty in fmall canals than in greater bodies of water.

He made and publifhed experiments for improving the art of *fwimming*, and for allaying thirft by bathing in fea water.

He publifhed obfervations on the gradual progrefs of north-eaft ftorms along the American coafts contrary to the direƈtion of the wind; and likewife to afcertain the courfe, velocity, and temperature, of the *gulf-ftream*, for the benefit of navigation.

He contrived experiments, and recommended them to the late Dr. Jngenhouz, for determining the relative powers of different metals for conduƈting heat.

He revived and improved the *Harmonica* or *Glaffichord*, and extended his fpeculations to the fine arts, fhewing that he could tafte and criticife even the compofitions of a Handel!

He

He left behind him fome very curious thoughts, and conjectures, concerning an univerfal fluid, the original formation of the earth, and how far, from attentive obfervations made during the fummer, it may be poffible to foretel the mildnefs or feverity of the following winter.

And to conclude the whole : One of the laft public acts in which he was concerned, was to fanction with his name the memorial prefented to the general government of the United States on the fubject of the *Slave Trade*, by the " Pennfylvania Society, " for promoting the abolition of flavery, and the " relief of the free negroes unlawfully held in bond- " age." Of this fociety he was prefident, and the inftitution and the defign of it could not but be con- genial to the foul of a man, whofe life and labours had been devoted to the caufe of *Liberty* for more than half a century, ardently ftriving to extend its bleffings to every part of the human fpecies, and particularly to fuch of his fellow-creatures as, being entitled to *freedom*, are neverthelefs injuriously en- flaved, or detained in bondage by fraud or violence.

EULOGIUM ON DR. BENJAMIN FRANKLIN,

Read before a Society in Paris, by MONSIEUR DE LA ROCHEFOUCAULT, *Deputy to the National Affembly, on the thirteenth day of June* 1789.

GENTLEMEN,

WHEN this fociety was inftituted, you placed in the lift of its members two names illuftrious in the annals of liberty, thofe of Wafhington and Franklin; and already one of them is no more! Franklin died in the month of April, after fixteen days illnefs, and his memory has received the higheft honours that were ever paid to man, as they were the homage of a free people. All America has wept for him, and the National Affembly of France, by the diftinguifhed act of putting itfelf into mourning, tells the world that a great man belongs equally to every country.

Honoured with the friendfhip of this refpectable man, for whom I entertained profound veneration, permit me to call your attention to him for a few moments.

Benjamin Franklin, born at Bofton in the year of our Lord 1706, was placed at a very early age under one of his brothers, who was a printer, and with whom he made a rapid progrefs in a trade fo ufeful to mankind; indeed he acquired an attachment for it which continued as long as he lived. During his refidence at Paffey, fo celebrated by being the place of his retreat

while

while in France, he frequently invited Meſſieurs Di-
dot, Pierres, and other diſtinguiſhed artiſts of the
capital to viſit him, and contributed, by his penetrating and inventive genius, to the advancement of
a ſcience to which he had ever been fondly attached.

Scarcely emerged from infancy, young Franklin, a journeyman printer, was a philoſopher without
being conſcious of it; and by the continual exercise
of his genius, prepared himſelf for thoſe great diſco-
veries which in ſcience have aſſociated his name with
that of Newton, and for thoſe political reflections
which have placed him by the ſide of Solon and
Lycurgus.

Ill-treated by his brother, he left Boſton, and procured employment firſt in a printing-office at New-
York, and afterwards at Philadelphia, where he ſettled.
America was not then what it is now. Agriculture and a few of the ruder arts almoſt excluſively
occupied the unpoliſhed people by whom it was inhabited. The religious fanaticiſm which had conducted
thither the firſt Engliſh emigrants, left traces that
ſometimes diſturbed its tranquillity, particularly in
the northern provinces, and confined the education
of the inhabitants to a narrow circle, of which ſuper-
ſtition was frequently the centre.

Pennſylvania, however, whoſe legiſlator, although
a fanatic *, cheriſhed liberty, was in this reſpect more
happily ſituated for the reception of improvement.

* This term is ſurely improper when applied to William Penn.

TRANS.

Soon

Soon after his arrival in this province, Franklin, in concert with fome other young men, eftablifhed a fmall club, where every member brought his ftock of ideas, which were fubmitted to difcuffion. This fociety, of which the young printer was the foul, has been the fource of many ufeful eftablifhments, calcu_lated to promote the progrefs of fcience, the mechanical arts, and particularly the improvement of the human underftanding.

A newfpaper that iffued from his prefs was the means he employed to draw the attention of his countrymen. There he hazarded anonymous propofals, t firft loofe, but afterwards more precife and definitive, and he fet on foot fubfcriptions which were the more readily filled, as every fubfcriber might confider himfelf as the head of an undertaking, the author of which was not named.

It was in this manner that public libraries were founded, that feminaries of education, fince become celebrated colleges, arofe; it was in this manner that the philofophical fociety of Philadelphia, no contemptible rival of the academies of Europe, was formed; that affociations for ornamenting, cleanfing, and lighting the ftreets of that city, and for preventing fires, were eftablifhed, and that commercial focieties, and even military bodies for the defence of the country, were incorporated. Nothing was foreign to the genius of Franklin ; and his name, which his modefty endeavoured to conceal, was always placed by his countrymen in the lifts, and frequently at the head

head of thofe different focieties, the members of which were defirous of retaining him as their hono-- rary chief. But higher avocations called him from his country, which he was deftined to ferve more effectually as its agent in the metropolis of England.

He was fent thither in the year 1757. Celebrated for his aftonifhing difcoveries refpecting the nature, effects, and identity, of thunder and electricity, and the means of guarding againft their ravages, his fame had arrived before him. The letters by which he had announced thefe difcoveries remained for a long time unnoticed by the Royal Society of London; but they were at length publifhed, and all the learned of Europe were inform-ed, that in the new world exifted a philofopher who was worthy of their admiration.

The ftamp act, by which the Britifh Minifter wifh-ed to familiarife the Americans to pay taxes to the mother country, revived that love of liberty which had led their forefathers to a country at that time a defert; and the colonies formed a Congrefs, the firft idea of which had been communicated to them by Franklin, at the conferences at Albany in the year 1754. The war that was juft terminated, and the exertions made by them to fupport it, had given them a conviction of their own ftrength; they accordingly oppofed this odious meafure, and the Minifter gave way, but referved the means of renewing his attempts. Once cautioned, however, they remained on their guard; liberty, cherifhed by thefe alarms, took deep root; a falutary fermentation agitated their minds,

and

and prepared for the revolution, men, whofe names it has rendered juftly celebrated. Among thefe were Hancock, Samuel and John Adams, the fage Jeffer-fon *, Jay, Green, and the great Wafhington; and they were not a little obliged for the rapid circulation of ideas to newfpapers, for the introduction of which they were indebted to, the printer of Philadelphia. In the year 1766, this printer, called to the bar of the Houfe of Commons of Great Britain, under-went that famous interrogotary which placed the name of Franklin as high in politics, as it was before in natural philofophy.

From that time he defended the caufe of America with a firmnefs and moderation, becoming a great man, pointing out to miniftry all the errors they had committed, and the confequences they would pro-duce, until the period when; the tax on tea meeting the fame oppofition as the ftamp act had done, Eng-land blindly fancied herfelf capable of fubjecting by force three millions of men determined to be free, at a diftance of two thoufand leagues from her terri-tories.

Every man is well acquainted with the particulars of that war, its fortunate refult to the whole univerfe,

* Mr. Jefferfon was afterwards minifter plenipotentiary from the United States to the court of France, where he fucceeded Franklin. It was he who framed the act of independence of the United States, and the act paffed in Virginia for eftablifhing reli-gious liberty. America has lately recalled him from France, where he is truly regretted, to confer on him the office of Secre-tary of State for foreign affairs.

the

the part taken in it by France under a King who, protector of the liberties of America, has since meritoriously obtained from the French nation the title of restorer of the liberty of his own country ; and the brilliant services of that youth whose name, gloriously connected with that revolution, has acquired fresh lustre in a revolution infinitely more great.

Having asserted their independence, and placed themselves in the rank of nations, the different colonies, now the United States of America, adopted each its own form of government; and retaining almost universally their admiration for the British Constitution, framed them from the same principles variously modelled.

Franklin alone, disengaging the political machine from those multiplied movements and admired counterpoises that rendered it so complicated, proposed the reducing it to the simplicity of a single legislative body. This grand idea startled the legislators of Pennsylvania ; but the philosopher removed the fears of a considerable number, and at length determined the whole to adopt a principle which the National Assembly has made the basis of the French constitution *.

After

---

* The usual progress of the human mind leads man from the complex to the simple. Observe the works of the first mechanics overloaded with numerous pieces, some of which embarrass, and others diminish their effect. It has been the same with legislators, both speculative and practical ; struck with an abuse, they have endeavoured

After having given laws to his country, Franklin determined to vifit Europe once more, in order to ferve it, not by reprefentations to the mother-country, or anfwers at the bar of the Houfe of Commons, but by treaties with France, and fucceffively with other ftates, which, though governed by monarchs

tleavoured to correct it by inftitutions that have been productive of ftill greater abufes. In political œconomy the unity of the legiflative body is the *maximum* of fimplicity. Franklin was the firft who dared to put this idea in practice : The refpect the Pennfylvanians entertained for him induced them to adopt it ; but the other ftates were terrified at it, and even the conftitution of Pennfylvania has fince been altered. In Europe this opinion has been more fuccefsful. When I had the honour to prefent to Franklin the tranflations of the conftitutions of America, the minds of people on this fide the Atlantic were fcarcely better difpofed toward it than thofe on the other fide ; and if we except Dr. Price in England, and Turgot and Condorcet in France, no man who applied himfelf to politics agreed in opinion with the American philofopher. I will venture to affert that I was of the fmall number of thofe who were ftruck with the beauty of the fimple plan he traced, and that I faw no reafon to change my opinion when the National Affembly, led by the voice of thofe deep-thinking and eloquent orators who difcuffed that important queftion, eftablifhed it as a principle of the French Conftitution, that legiflation fhould be confided to a fingle body of reprefentatives. It will not perhaps be deemed unpardonable to have once mentioned myfelf, at a time when the honour I have of holding a public character makes it my duty to give an account of my fentiments to my fellow-citizens. France will not relapfe into a more complex fyftem, but will affuredly acquire the glory of maintaining that which fhe has eftablifhed, and give it a degree of perfection which, by rendering a great nation happy, will attract the eyes and the applaufes of all Europe, and of the whole world.

or defpots, liftened to the voice of an American fpeaking liberty.

Some years previous to this I became acquainted with him during a journey I made to London; and permit me, Gentlemen, to recall to my mind the happinefs I felt when, on his arrival at Paris, I conducted to his houfe Monfieur Turgot, then ex-minifter, and faw thofe two excellent men, both fo deferving of the admiration and regret of mankind, embrace for the firft time. Franklin at leaft completed a long career; but Turgot, taken from the world at the age of fifty-four, faw not his country reftored to freedom. It was he who wrote under the portrait of Franklin that beautiful verfe,

Eripuit cœlo fulmen, mox fceptra tyrannis,

the laft hemiftich of which was a prophecy that was fpeedily accomplifhed.

The viciffitudes of fortune experienced by the Americans fometimes gave confiderable anxiety to their illuftrious negociator; but his great mind, encouraged by the bravery of his countrymen, by the firmnefs of the Congrefs, and, above all, by the genius, talents, and virtues, of the immortal Wafhington, did not give way to fear. He did not, however, flatter himfelf that peace would fo foon finifh the courfe of that happy revolution; and when I embraced him, the day on which he had figned the articles, " My friend," faid he to me with an air of perfect

perfect fatisfaction, " could I have hoped at my age
" to have enjoyed fuch a happinefs ?"

Whatever attractions an abode in France had for
him, whatever pleafure he tafted in the fociety of the
friends he had made, however great was the danger
of fo long a voyage to an old man of feventy-nine
years of age, tormented with the ftone, it was now
neceffary for him to revifit his country. He fet off
in the year 1785, and his return to America, at
length become free, was a triumph of which antiquity
cannot furnifh us with any example.

He lived five years after this period: For three
years he was prefident of the General Affembly of Pennfylvania ; he was a member of the convention that
eftablifhed the new form of fœderal government ; and
his laft public act afforded a grand example for thofe
who are employed in the legiflation of their country.
In this convention he had differed in fome points
from the majority ; but when the articles were ulti-
mately decreed, he faid to his colleagues, " We ought
" to have but one opinion ; the good of our country
" requires that our refolutions be unanimous."

His almoft continual fufferings for the two laft
years of his life had neither altered his temper nor his
difpofition, and to the laft moment he retained the
ufe of all his faculties. His will, which he made
during his refidence here, and which has juft been
opened, begins with a compliment to his profeffion.
Even on his death-bed he did homage to typography,
and the fame fentiment induced him to inftruct his

grandfon,

grand-fon, Benjamin Beach, in this art, who, proud of the leffons of his illuftrious mafter, is now a printer in Philadelphia.

He never wrote a work of any length. Almoft every thing publifhed by him on fubjects of natural philofophy confifts of letters to Mr. Collinfon of the Royal Society of London, and to fome other men of learning in Europe; they have been tranflated into French by Monfieur Barbeu du Bourg ; but perhaps a new verfion hath become neceffary. His political works, many of which are not known in France, confift of letters or fhort tracts; but all of them, even thofe of humour, bear the marks of his obferving genius and mild philofophy. He wrote many things for that rank and defcription of people who have no opportunity for ftudy, and whom it is of fo much confequence to inftruct; and he was well fkilled in reducing ufeful truths to maxims eafily retained, and fometimes to proverbs or little tales, the fimple or the natural graces of which acquire a new value when affociated with the name of their author.

The moft voluminous of his works is the hiftory of his own life, which he commenced for the ufe of his fon, and for the continuation of which we are indebted to the ardent folicitations of Monfieur le Veillard, one of his moft intimate friends. It employed his leifure hours during the latter part of his life, but the bad ftate of his health, and his excruciating pains, which gave him little refpite, frequently interrupted his work; and the two copies, one of which was

fent

fent by him to London to Dr. Price and Mr. Vaughan, and the other to Monfieur le Veillard and me, reach no farther than the year 1757. He fpeaks of himfelf as he would have done of another perfon, delineating his thoughts, his actions, and even his errors and faults ; and he defcribes the unfolding of his genius and ta_ lents with the fimplicity of a great man who knows how to do juftice to himfelf, and with the teftimony of a clear confcience void of reproach and " of offence " towards God and towards man."

In fact, Gentlemen, the whole life of Franklin, his meditations, his labours, have all been directed to public utility ; but the grand object that he had always in view did not fhut his heart againft fociety : He loved his family and his friends ; he was bene- ficent ; the charms of his converfation were inex- preffible ; he fpoke little, but he did not refufe to fpeak, and his communications were always inte- refting, and always inftructive. In the midft of his occupations for the liberty of his country, he had always fome curious experiment near him in his clofet ; and the fciences, which he had rather difco- vered than ftudied, afforded him a continual fource of pleafure.

His memoirs, Gentlemen, will be publifhed as foon as we receive from America the additions he may have made to the manufcript in our poffeffion ; and we then intend to give a complete collection of his works.

His

His name will be celebrated among the different affociations of politics and of literature. Innumerable eulogies will be written or pronounced upon him, and you doubtlefs expect with impatience that of the virtuous orator *, the organ of the Academy of Sciences, in which the moft honourable praife will be beftowed by him who beft knew how to appreciate the worth of Franklin. The eulogium to which I allude, is to forerun the award of hiftory, which will place this illuftrious name among the moft eminent benefactors of his fpecies; which will trace the incidents of his life, pourtray the anguifh of his fellow-citizens at his death, who believed that in him they loft a father and a friend, and which, after recounting the honours that America had confecrated to his memory, will alfo regifter in its calendar the fplendid homage which the National Affembly has juft paid, as an incident equally honourable to the people who thus difplayed their love of virtue, and to the man who thus merited this mark of their attention.

_____

As foon as the above eulogium was concluded, M. de Liancourt made a motion, that the members of the fociety 'fhould wear the mourning decreed by the National Affembly; and that the buft of Franklin fhould be placed in their hall, with the following infcription :

* M. de Condorcet.

" In

*" In teſtimony of the homage rendered by the una-
" nimous vote of the ſociety of the year 1789,
" to Benjamin Franklin, admired and regret-
" ted by all the friends of liberty."

The motion was carried unanimouſly. M. de la
Rochefoucault then preſented to the ſociety a buſt
of Benjamin Franklin, and the ſociety voted him
their thanks.

---

*OBSERVATIONS on the generally prevailing Doctrines
of Life and Death : In a Letter from Dr. BENJAMIN
FRANKLIN to M. DUBOURG, the French Tranſlator
of his Works.*

DEAR SIR,

YOUR obſervations on the cauſes of death, and
the experiments which you propoſe for recalling to
life thoſe who appear to be killed by lightning, de-
monſtrate equally your ſagacity and your humanity.
It appears that the doctrines of life and death, in general, are yet but little underſtood.

A toad buried in ſand will live, it is ſaid, till the
ſand becomes petrified ; and then, being incloſed
in the ſtone, it may ſtill live for we know not how
many years or ages. The facts which are cited in
ſupport of this opinion are too numerous and too
circumſtantial not to deſerve a certain degree of credit.

dit. As we are accuftomed to fee all the animals with which we are acquainted eat and drink, it appears to us difficult to conceive how a toad can be fup- ported in fuch a dungeon; but if we reflect that the neceffity of nourifhment, which animals experience in their ordinary ftate, proceeds from the continual wafte of their fubftance by perfpiration, it will ap- pear lefs incredible that fome animals in a torpid ftate, perfpiring lefs becaufe they ufe no exercife, fhould have lefs need of aliment, and that others, who are covered with fcales or fhells, which ftop perfpiration, fuch as land and fea turtles, ferpents, and every fpecies of fifh, fhould be able to fubfift a confiderable time without any nourifhment whatever. A plant, with its flowers, fades and dies immediately if expofed to the air without having its root immerfed in an humid foil, from which it may draw a fufficient quantity of moifture to fupply that which exhales from its fubftance, and is carried off continually by the air. Perhaps, however, if it were buried in quickfilver, it might preferve for a confiderable fpace of time its vegetable life, its fmell, and colour. If this be the cafe, it might prove a commodious method of tranfporting from diftant countries thofe delicate plants which are unable to fuftain the incle- mency of the weather at fea, and which require par- ticular care and attention.

I have feen an inftance of common flies preferved in a manner fomewhat fimilar. They had been drowned in Madeira wine apparently about the time when

when it was bottled in Virginia to be fent to London. ; At the opening of one of the bottles, at the houfe of a friend where I then was, three drowned flies fell into the firft glafs that was filled. Having heard it remarked that drowned flies were capable of being revived by the rays of the fun, I propofed making the experiment upon thefe : They were, therefore, expofed to the fun upon a fieve, which had been employed to ftrain them out of the wine. In lefs than three hours two of them began by degrees to recover life. This commenced by fome convulfive motions in the thighs, and at length they raifed themfelves upon their legs, wiped their eyes with their fore-feet, beat and brufhed their wings with their hind-feet, and foon after began to fly, finding themfelves in old England without knowing how they came thither. The third continued lifelefs till fun-fet, when, lofing all hopes of him, he was thrown away.

I wifh it were poffible, from this inftance, to invent a method of embalming drowned perfons, in fuch a manner that they might be recalled to life at any period however diftant ; for, having a very ardent defire to fee and obferve the ftate of America an hundred years hence, I fhould prefer to an ordinary death, the being immerfed in a cafk of Madeira wine with a few friends till that time, to be then recalled to life by the folar. warmth of my dear country. But fince, in all probability, we live in an age too early, and too near the infancy of fcience, to hope

to

to fee fuch an art brought in our time to perfection, I muft, for the prefent, content myfelf with the treat which you are fo kind as to promife me of the refur-rection of a fowl or a turkey-cock.

I am, dear Sir,

Your fincere friend,

BENJAMIN FRANKLIN.

LETTER from Dr. BENJAMIN FRANKLIN *to* BENJA-MIN VAUGHAN, ESQ., *on the Criminal Laws, and the Practice of Privateering.*

MY DEAR FRIEND,   *March* 14, 1785.

AMONG the pamphlets you lately fent me was one entitled, "Thoughts on Executive Juftice." In return for that I fend you a French one on the fame fubject, entitled, " Obfervations concernant l'Exécution de l'Article II. de la Declaration fur le Vol." They are both addreffed to the judges, but written, as you will fee, in a very different fpirit. The Englifh author is for hanging all thieves; the Frenchman is for propottioning punifhments to of-fences.

If we really believe, as we profefs to believe, that the law of Mofes is the law of God, and the dictates of divine wifdom infinitely fuperior to human ; on what principles do we ordain death as the punifh-ment of an offence which, according to that law,

was

was only to be punifhed by a reftitution of fourfold? To put a man to death for a crime which does not deferve death, is it not a murder? And as the French writer fays, " Doit-on punir un délit contre " la fociété par un crime contre la nature?"

Superfluous property is the creature of fociety. Simple and mild laws were fufficient to guard the property that was merely neceffary. The favage's bow, his hatchet, and his coat of fkins, were fufficiently fecured, without law, by the fear of perfonal refentment and retaliation. When, by virtue of the firft laws, part of the fociety accumulated wealth and grew powerful, they enacted others more fevere, and would protect their property at the expence of humanity. This was abufing their power, and commencing a tyranny. If a favage, before he entered into fociety, had been told, " Your neighbour by this " means may become owner of an hundred deer; but " if your brother, or your fon, or yourfelf, having no " deer of your own, and being hungry, fhould kill " one, an infamous death muft be the confequence;" he would probably have preferred his liberty, and his common right of killing any deer, to all the advantages of fociety that might be propofed to him.

That it is better an hundred guilty perfons efcape, than that one innocent perfon fhould fuffer, is a maxim that has been long and generally approved, and never, that I know of, controverted. Even the fanguinary author of the " Thoughts, &c." agrees to it, obferving, " that the very thought of injured " innocence, and much more that of fuffering inno-

" cence,

" cence, muſt awaken all our tendereſt and moſt
" compaſſionate feelings, and, at the ſame time,
" raiſe our higheſt indignation againſt the inſtru-
" ments of it. But," he adds, " there is no dan-
" ger of either from a ſtrict adherence to the laws."
Really ?—Is it then impoſſible to make an unjuſt law ?
And if the law itſelf be unjuſt, may it not be the
very " inſtrument" which ought " to raiſe the au-
" thor's and every body's higheſt indignation?" I ſee,
in the laſt newſpapers from London, that a woman
is capitally convicted at the Old Bailey, for privately
ſtealing out of a ſhop ſome gauze, value fourteen
ſhillings and three-pence, and the puniſhment of an
human creature for this offence is by death on a
gibbet! Might not that woman, by her own labour
and induſtry, have made the reparation ordained by
God in paying fourfold ? Is not all puniſhment in-
flicted beyond the merit of the offence, ſo much
puniſhment of innocence ? In this light how vaſt is
the annual quantity of not only injured but ſuffering
innocence, in almoſt all the civilized ſtates of
Europe !

But it ſeems to have been thought that this kind
of innocence may be puniſhed by way of preventing
crimes. I have read indeed of a cruel Turk in Bar-
bary, who, whenever he bought a new Chriſtian
ſlave, ordered him immediately to be hung up by
the heels, and to receive an hundred blows of a
cudgel on the ſoles of his feet, that the ſevere ſenſe
of the puniſhment, and fear of incurring it there-
after,

after, might prevent the faults that fhould merit it. Our author himfelf would hardly approve entirely of this Turk's conduct in the government of flaves, and yet he appears to recommend fomething like it for the government of Englifh fubjects.

He applauds the reply of Judge Burnet to the convicted horfe-ftealer, who being afked what he had to fay, why judgment of death fhould not be paffed againft him? and anfwering, that it was hard to hang a man for only ftealing an horfe, was told by the judge, " Man, thou art not to be hanged only for " ftealing a horfe, but that horfes may not be " ftolen."

But the man's anfwer, if candidly examined, will, I imagine, appear reafonable, as being founded upon the eternal principles of juftice and equity, that pu-nifhments fhould be proportioned to offences, and the judge's reply brutal and unreafonable, though the writer " wifhes all judges to carry it with them " whenever they go the circuit, and to bear it in " their minds, as containing a wife reafon for all " the penal ftatutes which they are called upon to " put in execution. It at once illuftrates (fays he) " the true grounds and reafons of all capital punifh- " ments whatfoever, namely, that every man's pro- " perty, as well as his life, may he held facred and " inviolate."

Is there then no difference in value between pro-perty and life? If I think it right that the crime of murder fhould be punifhed with death, not only as

4 an

an equal punifhment of the crime, but to prevent
other murders, does it follow that I muft approve of
inflicting the fame punifhment for a little invafion on
my property by theft? If I am not myfelf fo barbarous, fo bloody-minded, and revengeful as to kill a
fellow-creature for ftealing from me fourteen fhillings
and three-pence, how can I approve of a law that
does it?

Montefquieu, who was himfelf a judge, endeavours to imprefs other maxims. He muft have
known what humane judges feel on fuch occafions,
and what the effects of thofe feelings are; and fo far
from thinking that fevere and exceffive punifhments
prevent crimes, he afferts, as quoted by our French
writer, that

" *L'atrocité des loix en empêche l'exécution.*

" *Lorfque la peine eft fans mefure on eft fouvent obli-*
" *gé de lui préférer l'impunité.*

" *La caufe de tous les relâchemens vient de l'impu-*
" *nité des crimes, et non de la moderation des peines.*"

It is faid by thofe who know Europe generally,
that there are more thefts committed and punifhed
annually in England, than in all the other nations
put together. If this be fo, there muft be a caufe
or caufes for fuch grofs depravity in the common
people. May not one be the deficiency of juftice
and morality in our national government, manifefted
in our oppreffive conduct to fubjects, and unjuft wars
on our neighbours? View the long-perfifted-in, un-

juft,

juft, monopolizing treatment of Ireland at length acknowledged.

View the plundering government exercifed by our merchants in the Indies, the confifcating war made upon the American colonies, and, to fay nothing of thofe upon France and Spain, view the late war upon Holland, which was feen by impartial Europe in no other light than that of a war of rapine and pillage, the hopes of an immenfe and eafy prey being its only apparent and, probably, its true and real motive and encouragement.

Juftice is as ftrictly due between neighbour nations, as between neighbour citizens. An highwayman is as much a robber when he plunders in a gang as when fingle; and a nation that makes an unjuft war is only a great gang. After employing your people in robbing the Dutch, is it ftrange, that being put out of that employment by peace, they ftill continue robbing and plundering one another?

Privaterie, as the French call it, or privateering, is the univerfal bent of the Englifh nation, at home and abroad, wherever fettled. No lefs than feven hundred privateers were, it is faid, commiffioned in the laft war! Thefe were fitted out by merchants to prey upon other merchants, who had never done them any injury. Is there any one of thofe privateering merchants in London, who were fo ready to rob the merchants of Amfterdam, that would not as readily plunder another London merchant of the next ftreet, if he could do it, with the fame impunity? The

s   avidity

avidity, the *alieni appetens*, is the fame: It is the fear alone of the gallows that makes the difference.

How then can a nation, which, amongft the honeft-eft of its people, has fo many thieves by inclination, and whofe government encouraged and commiffioned no lefs than feven hundred gangs of robbers, how can fuch a nation have the face to condemn the crime in individuals, and hang up twenty of them in a morning! It naturally puts one in mind of a New-gate anecdote: One of the prifoners complained that in the night fomebody had taken his buckles out of his fhoes; " What the devil!" fays another, " have " we then thieves amongft us? It muft not be fuffer-" ed; let us fearch out the rogue, and pump him " to death."

There is, however, one late inftance of an Eng-lifh merchant who would not profit by fuch ill-gotten gain. He was, it feems, part owner of a fhip, which the other owners thought fit to employ as a letter of *marque*, and which took a number of French prizes. The booty being fhared, he has now an agent here inquiring by an advertifement in the Gazette, for thofe who fuffered the lofs, in order to make them, as far as in him lies, reftitution. This confcientious man is a Quaker.

The Scotch Prefbyterians were formerly as tender; for there is ftill extant an ordinance of the town-coun-cil of Edinburgh, made foon after the Reformation, forbidding " the purchafe of prize goods, under pain " of lofing the freedom of the burgh for ever, with " other

" other punifhment at the will of the magiftrates, the
" practice of making prizes being contrary to good
" confcience, and the rule of treating Chriftian bre-
" thren as we would wifh to be treated ; and fuch
" goods are not to be fold by any godly men within
" this burgh." The race of thefe godly men in Scotland is probably extinct, or their principles abandoned,
fince, as far as that nation had a hand in promoting
the war againft the colonies, prizes and confifcations
are believed to have been a confiderable motive.

It has been for fome time a generally received
opinion, that a military man is not to inquire whether a war be juft or unjuft ; he is to execute his
orders. All princes, who are difpofed to become
tyrants, moft probably approve of this opinion, and
are willing to eftablifh it ; but is it not a dangerous
one ? fince on that principle, if the tyrant commands his army to attack and deftroy not only an
unoffending neighbour nation, but even his own
fubjects, the army is bound to obey. A negro flave
in our colonies, being commanded by his mafter to
rob or murder a neighbour, or do any other immo-
ral act, may refufe, and the magiftrate will protect
him in his refufal. The flavery then of a foldier is
worfe than that of a negro ! A confcientious officer,
if not reftrained by the apprehenfion of its being imputed to another caufe, may indeed refign, rather
than be employed in an unjuft war ; but the private
men are flaves for life ; and they are, perhaps, incapable of judging for themfelves. We can only lament
their fate, and ftill more that of a failor, who is often

dragged

dragged by force from his honeſt occupation, and compelled to imbrue his hands in, perhaps, innocent blood. But methinks it well behoves merchants (men more enlightened by their education, and perfectly free from any ſuch force or obligation) to conſider well of the juſtice of a war, before they voluntarily engage a gang of ruffians to attack their fellow-merchants of a neighbouring nation, to plunder them of their property, and, perhaps, ruin them and their families if they yield it, or to wound, maim, and murder them, if they endeavour to defend it. Yet theſe things are done by Chriſtian merchants, whether a war be juſt or unjuſt ; and it can hardly be juſt on both ſides. They are done by Engliſh and American merchants, who neverthelefs complain of private theft, and hang by dozens the thieves they have taught by their own example.

It is high time, for the ſake of humanity, that a ſtop were put to this enormity. The United States of America, though better ſituated than any European nation to make profit by privateering (moſt of the trade of Europe with the Weſt Indies, paſſing before their doors), are, as far as in them lies, endeavouring to aboliſh the practice, by offering, in all their treaties with other powers, an article, engaging ſolemnly that, in caſe of a future war, no privateer ſhall be commiſſioned on either ſide ; and that unarmed merchant ſhips ſhall purſue their voyages unmoleſted *.

This

* This offer having been accepted by the late King of Pruſſia, a treaty of amity and commerce was concluded between that

Monarch

This will be an happy improvement of the law of
nations. The humane and juſt cannot but wiſh general ſuccefs to the propoſition.

With unchangeable eſteem and affeſtion,
I am, my dear friend,
Ever your's,
BENJAMIN FRANKLIN.

Monarch and the United States, containing the following humane
philanthropic article, in the formation of which Dr. Franklin, as one
of the American plenipotentiaries, was principally concerned, viz.

ARTICLE TWENTY-THIRD.

IF war ſhould ariſe between the two contraſting parties, the
merchants of either country then reſiding in either, ſhall be allowed to remain nine months to collect their debts, and ſettle their
affairs, and may depart freely, carrying off all their effects without moleſtation or hindrance ; and all women and children, ſcho-
lars of every faculty, cultivators of the earth, artizans, manufacturers, and fiſhermen, unarmed, and inhabiting unfortified towns,
villages, or places, and in general all others whoſe occupations
are for the common ſubſiſtence and benefit of mankind, ſhall be
allowed to continue their reſpective employments, and ſhall not be
moleſted in their perſons, nor ſhall their houſes or goods be burn-
ed, or otherwiſe deſtroyed, nor their fields waſted by the armed
force of the enemy, into whoſe power, by the event of war, they
may happen to fall ; but if any thing is neceſſary to be taken
from them for the uſe of ſuch armed force, the ſame ſhall be paid
fɔr at a reaſonable price. And all merchants and trading veſſels,
employed in exchanging the products of different places, and thereby
rendering the neceſſaries, conveniencies, and comforts of human
life more eaſy to be obtained, and more general, ſhall be allowed
to paſs free and unmoleſted ; and neither of the contracting powers ſhall grant or iſſue any commiſſion to any private armed veſſels,
empowering them to take or deſtroy ſuch trading veſſels, or inter-
rupt ſuch commerce.

LETTER

LETTER from Dr. FRANKLIN *to Madame* B***.
Written at Paſſey, near Paris.

YOU perhaps recollect, Madam, when we lately
ſpent ſo happy a day in the delightful gardens of
Moulin Joli, with the amiable ſociety who reſided
there, that I ſtopped in one of the walks, and permitted the company to paſs on without me.

We had been ſhewn an infinite number of dead
flies of the ephemeron ſpecies, the ſucceſſive generations of which, it is ſaid, are born and die in the
ſame day.

I happened to perceive, on a leaf, a living family
engaged in converſation. You know, Madam, I
underſtand the language poken by every ſpecies of
animals inferior to our own; and the very cloſe application I give to the ſtudy of them, is perhaps the
beſt excuſe I can offer for the little proficiency I have
made in your charming language.

Curioſity led me to liſten to the converſation of
theſe little creatures; but, from the vivacity peculiar
to their nation, three or four of them ſpoke at once,
and I could ſcarcely learn any thing from their diſcourſe. I underſtood, however, from ſome broken
ſentences which I caught now and then, that they
were warmly diſputing about the merit of two foreign
muſicians, a drone and a gnat; and that they appeared to ſpend their time in theſe debates with as
little

little concern for the brevity of life, as if they had been fure of living for a whole month. " Happy " people!" faid I to myfelf, " you certainly live un- " der a wife, equitable, and moderate government ; " fince no public grievances call forth your com- " plaints, and your only fource of difpute is the per- " fection or imperfection of foreign mufic."

, I left them foon after, in order to obferve an aged ephemeron with grey hairs, who, perched folitary on a leaf, was talking to himfelf. His foliloquy will, I believe, amufe that amiable friend to whom I am in- debted for the moft agreeable of my recreations, the charms of animated converfation, and the divine har- mony of mufical execution.

" It was the opinion," faid he, " of the learned " philofophers of our race, who lived and flourifhed " before us, that this vaft world itfelf could not fub- " fift more than eighteen hours ; and that opinion to, " me appears to have fome foundation, fince, by the " motion of the great luminary that gives life to the " whole nation, and which in my time has, in a " perceptible manner, declined confiderably towards " the ocean that bounds the earth, it muft ne- " ceffarily terminate its courfe at that period, be " extinguifhed in the waters that furround us, and " deliver up the world to cold and darknefs, the in- " fallible forerunners of death and univerfal deftruc- " tion. I have lived feven hours in thefe eighteen ; " it is a great age, amounting to no lefs than four

" hun-

" hundred and twenty minutes. How few of us live
" fo long!

" I have feen whole generations fpring up, flou-
" rifh, and difappear. My prefent friends are the
" children and grandchildren of the friends cf my
" youth, who, alas! are no more, and whom I muft
" foon follow; for, in the ordinary courfe of nature,
" I cannot expect, though in good health, to live
" more than feven or eight minutes longer.

" What avail at prefent all my labours, all my fa-
" tigues, to accumulate a provifion of fweet dew
" which I fhall not live long enough to confume?
" What avail the political difcuffions in which I am
" engaged for the fervice of my countrymen, the in-
" habitants of this bufh; or my philofophical inqui-
" ries, devoted to the welfare of the fpecies in ge-
" neral? In politics, what are laws without man-
" ners?

" A courfe of minutes will render the prefent ge-
" neration as corrupt as the ancient inhabitants of
" other bufhes, and, of confequence, as unhappy.
" And in philofophy, how flow is our progrefs! Alas!
" art is long, and life is fhort! My friends would con-
" fole me with the name which, they fay, I fhall
" leave behind me. They tell me I have lived long
" enough for glory and for nature. But what is fame
" to an ephemeron that will be no longer in exift-
" ence? What will hiftory become, when, at the
" eighteenth hour, the world itfelf will be drawn to

5 " a clofe,

" a clofe, and be no longer any thing but a heap of
" ruins?

" For myfelf, after having made fo many bufy re-
" fearches, the only real bleffings that remain to me,
" are, the fatisfaction of having fpent my life with
" the view of being ufeful, the pleafing converfation
" of a fmall number of good lady ephemeras, and
" now and then the captivating fmiles of Madame
" B**, and the fweet founds of her *forte piano.*"

E·U L O G I U M

ON

Benjamin Franklin, LL.D. &c.

DELIVERED IN THE ROTUNDA,

ON THE 21ST OF JULY, 1790,

IN THE NAME OF THE COMMONS OF PARIS;

In presence of the Deputies to the Legislative Assembly, and of all the Departments in the Kingdom, the Mayor, the Commandant-General of the National Guards, the Representatives of the Commons, the Presidents of the Districts, and the Electors of the Capital. -

---

BY THE ABBE FAUCHET,

NOW CONSTITUTIONAL BISHOP OF THE DEPARTMENT OF CALVADOS,
AND A MEMBER OF THE NATIONAL CONVENTION.

ADVERTISEMENT.

THE Reprefentatives of the Commons of Paris paffed a vote on the twenty-fecond of July 1790, in confequence of which it was ordered, that this Eulogium fhould be printed, and prefented to the National Affembly of France, and the Congrefs of America.

EULOGIUM

ON

BENJAMIN FRANKLIN;

Pronounced by the Abbé FAUCHET, *in the Name of the Commons of Paris.*

A SECOND creation has taken place; the elements of fociety begin to combine together; the moral univerfe is now feen iffuing from chaos; the genius of Liberty is awakened, and fprings up; fhe fheds her divine light and creative powers upon the two hemifpheres: A great nation, aftonifhed at feeing herfelf free, ftretches her arms from one extremity of the earth to the other, and embraces the firft nation that became fo: The foundations of a new city are created in the two worlds; brother-nations haften to inhabit it; it is the city of mankind!

One of the firft founders of this univerfal city was the immortal Franklin, the deliverer of America.

The fecond founders, who accelerated this great work, made it worthy of Europe—the legiflators of France have rendered the moft folemn homage to his memory. They have faid—" A friend of humanity " is dead; mankind ought to be overwhelmed with " forrow! Nations have hitherto only worn mourning " for Kings; let us affume it for a Man, and let the " tears of Frenchmen mingle with thofe of Ameri-

5 " cans,

" cans, in order to do honour to the memory of one
" of the Fathers of Liberty !"

The city of Paris, which once contained this philosopher within its walls, which was intoxicated with
the pleasure of hearing, admiring, and loving him;
of gathering from his lips the maxims of moral legis-
lation, and of imbibing from the effusions of his heart
a passion for the public welfare, rivals Boston and
Philadelphia, his two native cities (for in one he was
born as it were a man, and in the other a legislator),
in its profound attachment to his merit and his glory.

It has commanded this funeral solemnity, in order
to perpetuate the gratitude and the grief of this third
country, which, by the courage and activity with
which it has profited of his lessons, has shewn itself
worthy of having him at once for an instructor and a
model.

In selecting me for the interpreter of its wishes, it
has declared, that it is less to the talents of an orator,
than the patriotism of a citizen, the zeal of a preacher
of liberty, and the sensibility of a friend of men, that
it hath confided this solemn function. In this point
of view, I may speak with a holy confidence; for I
have the public opinion, and the testimony of my own
conscience, to second my wishes. Since nothing else
is wanting than freedom, and sensibility, for that spe-
cies of eloquence which this eulogium requires, I am
satisfied; for I already possess them.

My voice shall extend to France, to America, to
posterity; I am now to do justice to a great man, the

founder

founder of trans-Atlantic freedom; I am to praife him in the name of the mother-city of French liberty; I myfelf alfo am a man; I am a freeman; I poffefs the fuffrages of my fellow-citizens: This is enough; my difcourfe fhall be immortal!

PART I.

THE academies, the philofophical focieties, the learned affociations, which have done themfelves honour by infcribing the name of Franklin in their records, can beft appreciate the debt due to his genius, for having extended the power of man over nature, and prefented new and fublime ideas, in a ftyle fimple as truth, and pure as light.

It is nòt the naturalift and the philofopher that the orator of the commons of Paris ought to defcribe; it is the *man*, who hath accelerated the progrefs of focial order; it is the *legiflator*, who hath prepared the liberty of nations!

Benjamin Franklin was born at the commencement of the prefent century, in Bofton, the capital of New England.

His father, perfecuted in his own country on account of his religious opinions (for the Englifh, fo wavering in regard to religion, and who have fo often changed it by *act of Parliament*, at the nod of corrupt

rupt Kings, or fanatical chiefs, have always been, and are at this very day, perfecutors); his father, I fay, took refuge in the new world, where the church of England, not having as yet intruded her intolerant folicitude, permitted the liberty of confcience.

His profeffion was obfcure; but it is from this very obfcurity that it is glorious for him to have elevated himfelf to the head of his nation, and to become the chief, as it were, of mankind.

He who was deftined to be the founder and the prefident of the Philofophical Society of Philadelphia, the creator and the foul of the congrefs of America, was at firft brought up to the trade of a tallow-chandler. The celebrated orator Flechier began life among ourfelves precifely in the fame manner: It may be confidered as a prodigy that, under the feudal ariftocracy, he fhould have ever become a rich Bifhop! The hereditary Nobles, the titled families (it is but yefterday as it were they have ceafed to exift in France), regarding his elevation with a degree of furprife, mingled with fcorn, were unable to conceive how a Minifter dared to confer a Bifhopric upon a plebeian. "Duke," replied the Bifhop of Nifmes to one of his contemporaries, who reproached him with the occupation of his father, "this is in truth what diftin- "guifhes us from each other: If you had been born "in the fame ftation that I was, you would have ftill "remained a maker of candles!"

Gentlemen, I have mentioned this anecdote, becaufe it is fomething in the manner of Franklin. He might

might have faid the fame thing to the Englifh Nobility, and all thofe infulters of merit, who think themfelves difpenfed from poffeffing any, becaufe, in
virtue of their family, they occupy the firft employments in the ftate, and obtain, even through the folly
of their titles, all the honours of fociety.

A very limited bufinefs, and one which prefented;
no opportunity for the developement of the human
faculties, could not be deemed worthy of the genius
of Franklin. The art of printing had been fcarce
eftablifhed in America; he turned his views towards
this polite art, to which the deftiny of the human genius is attached.

He laboured affiduoufly in this profeffion, firft at
Bofton, afterwards at Philadelphia, and at length at
London, where, while he acquired a confiderable degree of perfection in this art, his mind, always of a
thinking turn, made a variety of obfervations on the
vices of the Englifh government, and accumulated in
filence the means of making typography more ufeful
to his country, and to human kind.

On his return to the capital of Pennfylvania, he was
able to work at, direct, and even to fupply matter
for thofe preffes, whence were to iffue that knowledge
deftined to be the harbinger of the glorious day of
liberty.

Englifh America was defigned, in the eternal views
of Providence, and in the combinations already ripe
in the mind of Franklin, to fee the fun of juftice firft
elevated above its horizon, a fun who was pro-

T   greffively

greffively to fpread his rays over all parts of the world. Its colonies were formed of men, who did not find themfelves fufficiently free in England; who would not depend, in regard to religion, but upon Heaven and their own confcience; in their morals, but upon civil equality and good laws; in their happinefs, but upon domeftic fociety and the fimplicity of virtue.

Penn, the firft man who arofe out of that focial chaos in which the nations had been plunged, founded Philadelphia, the City of Brethren; and which, in confequence of this title, which it hath ever fince fo amply juftified, merits the appellation of the *capital of the human kind.* It is opened to human nature, without reftriction; for the law which prohibits the entrance of the atheift and the fluggard, as not being men, does not prefent, as Franklin himfelf has very juftly obferved, any more than a threatening exception, which cannot poffibly be carried into execution.

" If," fays he, " an atheift exifted in any other
" part of the univerfe, he would be inftantly con-
" verted on entering into a city where every thing is
" fo admirably conducted; and if there was a flug-
" gard, having the three amiable fifters, Riches, Sci-
" ence, and Virtue, who are the daughters of Labour,
" continually before his eyes, he would foon con-
" ceive an affection for them, and endeavour to ob-
" tain them from their father."

Delightful idea! worthy of a fage philofopher, the object of our prefent homage! It, at one and the fame time, defcribes both Franklin and Philadelphia.

A Catholic

A Catholic prieft, I fhall doubtlefs be reproached for delivering an eulogium on the Quakers, as I have heretofore been reproached for praifing the Janfenifts; as I am reproached at this very moment for pronouncing a funeral oration on a Proteftant, who himfelf profeffed religious principles different from thofe that were fpread over the face of his country.

Thefe reproaches do me honour, for they iffue from fanaticifm, the greateft fcourge of fociety. Yes, I have praifed, and I now praife again in the name of the commons of Paris, both with eagernefs and affection, that philanthropic Janfenift, if they pleafe, but, at the fame time, very catholic and very holy preceptor of thofe who are born deaf and dumb;—the virtuous Philadelphians, fimple and fublime obfervers of univerfal fraternity;—the principal philofopher of Proteftantifm, the fage Franklin, who, without being perfect in his faith, yet poffeffed the perfection of evangelical benevolence.

And here, Gentlemen, fince the queftion of univerfal toleration prefents itfelf, and enters of its own accord into the chain of ideas, which are fucceffively to complete the character of the great moralift whom I now attempt to defcribe, permit me to ftop. After developing the principles of this fage, I fhall purfue my fubject, and fulfil the tafk you have impofed upon me.

Men cannot be brethren, and, confequently, cannot be focial creatures, while one part reprove the other for the opinions which they have formed, and

T 2 think

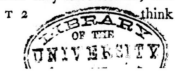

think themfelves, on account of this imaginary difference, to be feparated and divided from each other,
as far as heaven is diftant from hell.

No one can judge the confcience but God alone.

He who affirms that man ought to believe, or
not believe, this or that doctrine, often renders himfelf guilty of injuftice, and always of temerity.

The firft genius of the univerfe, although inflamed
with the moft ardent love for truth, might embrace a
religious error, and think himfelf bound by his confcience to defend it. Who is the audacious mortal,
that pretends to have been able to calculate all the
lights and fhades, which might have intervened between the moft fimple or the moft fublime minds,
and who dares to fay—" all ought to believe like
" me?"

Thefe are invincible prejudices to an uniformity of
faith: The effects of education, the ideas inftilled
into the human mind, during infancy and youth,
thofe religious defcriptions which infpire the imagination with awful terrors, the cuftomary practice of
adoration, the fanction of felf-love in behalf of received dogmas, a thoufand acts of virtue practifed
by fincere believers in a particular faith; all thefe may
inevitably detain the moft righteous and juft men in
the religion of their fathers, although it may be
mingled with error.

The fage himfelf, who by means of the activity of
his mind, and the force of his reflections, raifes himfelf, while he implores the divine affiftance, above
vulgar

vulgar ideas and popular fuperftitions, only floats in the immenfity of eternal conceptions, and redefcends, with a holy fear, to the elements of his primitive faith; he does nothing more than feparate it from that impure mixture, by which fanaticifm, in his eyes, has evidently altered its venerable fimplicity. Undoubtedly, the indolence that precludes reflection, the animal paffions, the abufe of our faculties, may retain, or draw us, in refpect to religion, into thofe errors which are imputable to us. But it appertains to us, and to Him only, who reads the heart, and probes the thoughts, to mark them down for reprobation, and to punifh them at the day of judgment.

Thofe actions alone, which are manifeftly contrary to the laws of univerfal morality, are fubmitted to the infpection of men, and the fentence of fociety. The vicious, the bafe, the wicked, even when they profefs the true faith, are the enemies of humanity. The virtuous, the good, the benevolent, even while their faith is erroneous, are the friends and the benefactors of mankind.

Such, Gentlemen, were the doctrines of the fage, whofe memory we are now doing honour to; and, if this were the place, it would be eafy to prove, as he himfelf has demonftrated, that the true fpirit of the gofpel confifts in indulgence, charity, brotherly love, concord, peace, and univerfal unity.

Notwithftanding this, " out of the pale of Catholic " faith," fays one, " there is no falvation for man " kind !"

This maxim is true, Gentlemen; but thofe who deduce from it the reprobation of all thofe who are of a different religion, and a frightful intolerance towards nearly the whole human race, are fanatics and impoftors.

It is one of the avowed principles of the Catholic faith, that all thofe who ftrictly obferve the natural law, that is to fay, all virtuous men, appertain to the true church, and have Jefus Chrift, the light of fouls, for their mafter and infpector.

I pronounce this facred name with fo much more fatisfaction in this difcourfe, as Franklin was accuftomed to invoke it with the moft refpectful awe. But thofe who do not know, and who " practife natu-" rally," as the Apoftle fays, his divine law, fhall be judged after the teftimony of their own confciences, and arrive, by means of the miracles wrought through his grace, at the true light. Thus according to the principles of our religion, no one can pronounce upon the reprobation of a fingle man, becaufe all men are in the hands of a Father who can, and who wifhes to, fave all; he has exprefsly told us fo; and, although his juftice may profcribe incorrigible finners, he has left to himfelf the final determination of their doom, that fo our hearts may not be tortured in regard to any of our brethren, who purfue along with us the paffage to eternity. A doctrine truly Catholic, which places all men in the communion of our love, and points out to us the fages of all the countries in the world who have done honour to their lives by a feries of ufeful

virtues,

virtues, and thus become the friends of God, and the adopted children of the univerſal church.

This religion of virtue, by which we are inſtructed to love God and man, and which, according to the ſacred Scriptures, is the only one pure and ſpotleſs, was viſible in the heart of Franklin, and in all his works.

He preached it in the inſtructions which he com-poſed, and which he printed at Philadelphia. He adorned them by means of a ſimplicity, a plainneſs, and, at the ſame time, an intelligence, a ſenſibility, and a happy air of calmneſs and tranquillity, which affected every boſom. He excelled in thoſe religious parables, of which the Scriptures furniſh ſo many amiable and ſublime examples.

Permit me, Gentlemen, to quote one compoſed by him againſt intolerance and perſecution. In it he de-ſcribes, in the ſame ſtyle in which Geneſis is written, the Patriarch Abraham exerciſing hoſpitality towards an old man, who refuſes to join him in thankſgiving to the Almighty God, the Creator of heaven and earth.

The ſtranger tells him, that he will not adore any one but the God of his own country, and that he will on no account participate in any other worſhip. On this, the zeal of Abraham is kindled, he puſhes the man out of his tent, in the dead of night, and chaſes him into the deſert. In a ſhort time, the voice of the Almighty is heard: " Abraham, where is the " ſtranger?" On this, Abraham replies—" Lord,

" he

"he refufed to adore thee, and I chafed the infidel
"away!" And God faid—"for one hundred four
"fcore and eighteen years I have bore with this unbe-
"liever; I have nourifhed and clothed him all this
"time, notwithftanding his rebellion againft me,
"and yet thou, who art thyfelf a finner, could not
"bear with him for one night!"

On this, Abraham cried out—"I have finned, O
"Lord! let not thy anger fall upon me!" And he
arofe, and ran to the defert; he fought the old man;
he found him; he brought him to his tent; he
treated him with kindnefs, and fent him away next
morning with many prefents!

How much does this, Gentlemen, refemble the ftyle
of the holy Scriptures! every perfon participates in the
infpiration with which it is written; we are tempted
to fearch the book of Genefis, and wifh to believe
that we fhall find it there! Another allegory, compofed
by Franklin, and borrowed from the art which he
exercifed, offers a convincing teftimony of his belief
in the immortality of the foul, the purification of
it in another life, and the refurrection of the body;
I allude to his epitaph, written by himfelf*. How
admirable, how fhort, and yet how full of fentiment,
are the expreffions contained in every line; evangelic
faith and religious hope are here evident, and they
forcibly point out the end of life, and the prize of
virtue.

* See page 192.

It

It was thus that Franklin, in his periodical works, which had a prodigious circulation on the Continent of America, laid the facred foundations of focial morality. He was no lefs inimitable in the developement of the fame morality, when applied to the duties of friendfhip, general charity, the employment of one's time, the happinefs attendant upon good works, the neceffary combination of private with public welfare, the propriety and neceffity of induftry, and to that happy and blifsful ftate which puts us at eafe with fociety and with ourfelves. The " Proverbs of Old " Henry," and " Poor Richard," are in the hands both of the learned and the ignorant; they contain the moft fublime morality, reduced to popular language and common comprehenfion, and form the catechifm of happinefs for all mankind.

Franklin was too great a moralift, and too well acquainted with human affairs, not to perceive that women were the arbiters of manners. He ftrove to perfect their empire, and accordingly engaged them to adorn the fceptre of virtue with their graces. It is in their power to excite courage, to overthrow vice by means of their difdain, to kindle civifm, and to light up in every heart the holy love of our country.

His daughter, who was opulent, and honoured with the public efteem, helped to manufacture and to make up the clothing for the army with her own hands, and fpread abroad a noble emulation among the female citizens, who became eager to affift thofe by means of the needle and the fpindle,

who

who were ferving the ftate with their fwords and their guns.

With the charm ever attendant upon true wifdom, and the grace ever flowing from true fentiment, this grave philofopher knew how to converfe with the other fex, to infpire them with a tafte for domeftic occupations, to hold out to them the prize attendant upon honour unaccompanied by reproach, and inftil the duty of cultivating the firft precepts of education, in order to teach them to their children, and thus to acquit the debt due to nature, and fulfil the hope of fociety! It muft be acknowledged that, in his own country, he addreffed himfelf to minds capable of comprehending him.

Immortal females of America! I will tell it to the daughters of France, and they only are fit to applaud you! You have attained the utmoft of what your fex is capable; you poffefs the beauty, the fimplicity, the manners, at once natural and pure—the primitive graces of the golden age. It was among you that liberty was firft to have its origin. But the empire of freedom, which is extended to France, is about to carry your manners along with it, and produce a re-volution in morals as well as in politics.

Already our female citizens (for they have lately become fuch) are not any longer occupied with thofe frivolous ornaments, and vain pleafures, which were nothing more than the amufements of flavery; they have awakened the love of liberty in the bofoms of fathers, of brothers, and of hufbands; they have

encou-

encouraged them to make the moſt generous ſacrifices; their delicate hands have removed the earth,
dragged it along, and helped to elevate the immenſe
amphitheatre of the grand confederation. It is no
longer the love of voluptuous ſoftneſs that attracts
their regard; it is the ſacred fire of patriotiſm.

The laws which are to reform education, and with
it the national manners, are already prepared; they
ſhall advance, they ſhall fortify the cauſe of liberty by
means of their happy influence, and become the
ſecond ſaviours of their country!

Franklin did not omit any of the means of being
uſeful to men, or ſerviceable to ſociety. He ſpoke
to all conditions, to both ſexes, to every age. This
amiable moraliſt deſcended, in his writings, to the
moſt artleſs details, to the moſt ingenuous familiarities,
to the firſt ideas of a rural, a commercial, and a civil
life; to the dialogues of old men and children; full
at once of all the verdure and all the maturity of wiſ-
dom; in ſhort, the prudent leſſons ariſing from the
expoſition of thoſe obſcure, happy, eaſy virtues,
which form ſo many links in the chain of a good
man's life, derived immenſe weight from that reputation for genius which he had acquired, by being
one of the firſt naturaliſts and greateſt philoſophers in
the univerſe.

At one and the ſame time, he governed nature in
the heavens and in the hearts of men.

Amidſt the tempeſts of the atmoſphere, he directed
the thunder; amidſt the ſtorms of ſociety, he directed
the

the paffions. Think, Gentlemen, with what attentive docility, with what religious refpect, one muft
hear the, voice of a fimple man, who preached up human happinefs, when it was recollected that it was
the powerful voice of the fame man who regulated
the lightning.

He electrified the confciences, in order to extract
the deftructive fire of vice, exactly in the fame manner as he electrified the heavens, in order peaceably
to invite from them the terrible fire of the elements.
He thus exercifed (O power immenfe of wifdom and
of genius!) two attributes of the Deity.

Figure to your own minds, this fage with the celeftial phyfiognomy which he poffeffed, with that calm
and auguft forehead, reuniting, in his own perfon,
an authority over the natural and focial world; does
he not refemble a beneficent God defcended upon
earth, in order to extinguifh the wrath of heaven and
teach virtue to mankind?

The leifure hours of Franklin were fo many acts of
goodnefs, which, if they were not too numerous,
would form the chief charm of this oration. His
amufements confifted in experiments which refembled
prodigies, and of which a fingle inftance will fuffice to give fome idea. He himfelf, in a letter to one
of the moft learned Members of the Royal Society of
London *, has prefented the defcription of a feftival,
which he gave to his friends and the public upon the
borders of the Schuylkill.

* Mr. Collinfon.

An

An electric fpark, without any other conductor than the water, ferved to light the volatile fpirit prepared to illuminate both banks of the river, at one and the fame moment. The invifible fhock of the electric matter, appeared, to the ravifhed eyes of the fpectators, to kill the game and wild fowl prepared for the treat; culinary inftruments turned and dreffed the viands by means of the heat arifing from the ethereal flame, while the goblets, as if filled by magic, became replenifhed with the choiceft wines of Europe.

In the mean time his guefts, compofed of the moft learned men in Philadelphia, accompanied by a difcharge of artillery from an electric battery, drank the healths of all the famous philofophers of France, of England, of Switzerland, of Holland, of Italy, and of Germany, by turns, while the echoes arifing from the neighbouring fhores fpread abroad and multiplied thefe folemn falutations. The joyous acclamations of the people of a country formerly favage and deferted, but at prefent inhabited by numerous nations of new men, who have formed an alliance between fcience and morality, reached to the fkies.

You may eafily conceive, Gentlemen, what a mild, but fure afcendant, this fage, who infpired his citizens with a tafte for fuch noble pleafures, exercifed over their minds! Not a fingle moment did he lofe in the courfe of his whole life; not one of his thoughts but what tended to the public welfare; not one of his laborious or of his leifure hours which did not fay to

men,

men, " It is thus that exiftence becomes valuable,
" it is thus that mankind become happy !"

I have not as yet attempted to paint any thing more
than the philofopher, who, by the force of his ideas,
and the communication of his fentiments, beftowed
a charm unknown before, and a new activity upon
focial morality.

Franklin had formed men : He had conceived ftill
more noble projects—he wifhed to create citizens.
He had already completed the bafis, which is morality ; he determined upon this to elevate the column
of legiflation.   It is now the legiflator whom I muft
exhibit, it is the electrician of nations that is about
to begin his operations ; it is. he who compofed and
completed the moft charming model of liberty that
was ever prefented to the univerfe; and it is to France,
now become free, it is before her firft legiflature
that I am ambitious of exhibiting this picture ; it
will awaken flaves, it will tranfport Frenchmen!

PART II.

" TRAVELLER, inform Sparta that we have died
" in obedience to her holy laws."

This infcription over the bodies of thofe who pe-
rifhed at Thermopylæ, is the moft fuperb monument
that was ever erected to the honour of Greece : It

proves

proves that antiquity recognized citizens in an angle of the world.

The city of Lacedemon, the only one which merits that appellation, on account of the feparation of the three powers which organifed its government (for the anarchy of Athens, and the war of civic elements in Rome, prohibit them, although in other refpects immortal, from enjoying this fingular honour), the city of Lacedemon was deftined to endure but a fhort time, for it had not humanity for its bafis. Mankind themfelves were not as yet acquainted with it. It was neceffary that whole ages fhould firft elapfe; and the Spartans, citizens without being men, were to be annihilated by the force of Nature, who does not long tolerate whatever contradicts her laws.

Methinks I now behold a more noble monument erected between the old and the new world : It rifes out of the bofom of the Atlantic ocean ; it looks on one fide towards Europe, and on the other towards America : The image of the auguft Franklin furmounts it, and points to the following infcription : "Men, love your fellow-men! Be free! Promote "commerce and the arts ; but, above all, cultivate "humanity."

Legiflator of mankind! thy countrymen, the Americans, obey thee ; France liftens to thy voice, fhe repeats thy accents ; the univerfe awakes at the found !

The light fcattered over the world by the philofo-pher of nature, from the city of Philadelphia, not only excited the fcintillations of private, but it alfo
kindled

kindled the fire of public, virtue, which compofes the life of nations.

From the banks of the Delaware and the Schuyl-kill, Franklin attentively furveyed the conduct of England, marked her errors and her imprudence, aroufed that juft difcontent which her cruelties infpir-ed, obferved how far the patience of the people could be ftretched, reinforced the principles of li-berty, but yet preached up peace and moderation, until that day fhould arrive, in which violence and injuftice were no longer to be fuffered, and a revolu-tion was to be expected as an inevitable event. His wifdom prophecied the approach of liberty, and accom-plifhed it; his fellow-countrymen, the Americans, who felt the iron hand of defpotifm, but yet fcarcely dream-ed of independence, were already, in the calculations of his genius, the firft free citizens of the univerfe.

The minifters of England were well acquainted with the afcendency of this great man, and were alarmed at his influence. In conformity to their fyftem of corruption, they were determined to bring him over to their views, and were perfuaded that, by beftowing one of the lucrative employments upon him, which they had the difpofal of in the colonies, his private intereft would induce him to affift them in fubjugating his countrymen.

He was accordingly appointed Director General of the Poft Office belonging to the Englifh colonies in America*.

* He was entrufted with the fouthern department only. TRANS.

In

In this employment he perceived that he could be uſeful to the people and to himſelf; for it furniſhed him with a better opportunity of communicating his principles throughout the continent. He well knew that his labours would accelerate the freedom of America; he was authoriſed by his office to viſit all the provinces without the leaſt fuſpicion whatever; he thus was enabled to found the diſpoſitions of the inhabitants, to augment their horror for oppreſſion, and to induce them to reconquer the rights of man and of citizens.

Franklin undoubtedly foreſaw, while deſtroying an oppreſſive government, the favours of which he turned to the public advantage, that he ſhould make great ſacrifices in regard to his own private intereſt; but his natural ſimplicity and prudent œconomy had enabled him to accumulate a fortune ſufficient to inſure his independence; and he always dreaded great opulence, either to himſelf or his fellow-citizens.

He had always two great ideas in contemplation: The firſt was, to elevate England and all her colonies to the principles of civil liberty; and if that did not happen, at leaſt to give freedom to his native country. Had the former ſcheme ſucceeded (and it gave him the greater degree of pleaſure), the parliament of England was to have had a full national and colonial repreſentation. The King was to have carried the legal wiſhes of the fellow-citizens of the two continents into execution, and the perfect combina-

U   tion

tion of the legiflative power of all, and the executive power of one, would have realized to Great Britain that noble conftitution deftined to form the happinefs of France.

But if it were impoffible thus to infure the felicity of the whole empire, and if the fyftem of colonial oppref-fion was to be continued, then he thought that a grand example ought to be fet by America to the world, that the caufe of the people ought to be avenged, and that Liberty ought to hoift her ftandard in another hemifphere.

Thus all the views of this great man were in per-fect coincidence with the principles of truth and of juftice; for whatever might be the laft determination of the oppreffors, they themfelves would either be-come citizens, or enable their fellow flaves to become fo, by eftablifhing the firft free government that ever exifted in the world.

Such was the pofition of public affairs when Frank-lin was fent to England by the Affembly of Pennfyl-vania, in order to defend the colonies againft the en-terprifes of the court. He did not diffemble his opi-nions to the Englifh miniftry, who, at that period, were employing their ufual perfidious arts of bribery and corruption, in order to exact feveral new and vexatious impofts from his countrymen.

Franklin announced to them the infallible refult of their proceedings.

The Americans were alarmed, and protefted with one accord againft this act of tyranny. Their conduct

duct appeared to the generous patriots of England
(where there are many good citizens, although they are
not fuffered to rule the nation) to be dictated by the
juft rights derived from oppreffion ; but it feemed to
be the revolt of flaves, who wifhed to free themfelves
from the authority of a mafter, in the eyes of the fervile
minions of the fovereign, who are more numerous,
and who are always employed by the government.

Amidft thefe important conjunctures, Franklin is
ordered to the bar of the Houfe of Commons. he obeys.
How great appeared that man, the defender of liberty,
before an ariftocracy who monopolize the independence of a nation! He was unacquainted with the
queftions which were to be put to him, but his mind
was ever prepared. Not a fingle vague idea, not an
ufelefs or unneceffary word ; thoughts fimple, but
yet vaft ; fentiments loyal, but yet generous ; the
boldeft affertions ; the moft convincing reafons ; the
moft pofitive denials, afforded no triumph to his enemies. With a mafculine eloquence and undifguifed
truth, he proved all the firft acts of the American
infurrection to be legitimate, and afferted that all the
projects that could be fuggefted by Englifh violence,
would be abortive and without effect.

" Either let us be free together," fays he, " or
" we fhall be fo without, and even in fpite of you.
" If you do not annul your oppreffive laws, we fhall
" continue to make new ones independent of you.
" If you endeavour to fubjugate us, we fhall tri-
' umph. Your armies? They are not numerous

" enough,

" enough. Your navy? All the navies upon earth
" are not capable of making us fubmit to your will.
" Make your election between our love and our
" hate; we have already made our choice between the
" liberty that is to combine us, and thofe chains with
" which we are to be manacled."

This affords but a feeble image of the dignified
conduct of Franklin in the face of all England. Cy-
neas beheld at Rome, in that fenate which governed
Italy, an affembly of gods, and trembled! Franklin beheld at London, in that fenate which commanded the feas of the two worlds, a corrupted legiflature, and was undifmayed. The ambaffador of
Theffaly fpoke in the name of a King; and what was
a King before the Roman people? But the agent of
Philadelphia fpoke as a man in the name of men,
whom he was about to render free; and free men
have ever been refpected as the firft of human beings
by the Englifh!

He retired honoured by the nation, but detefted
by the Court, convinced that a parliament fold to
the miniftry would fmite America with the fceptre of
defpotifm, and fupport their wrongs by the fwords of
mercenaries; that his countrymen would be forced to
defend their own rights, to confummate their independence, and to vindicate the caufe of human
nature.

Returned to his native continent, he revolved all
thefe ideas in his bofom at Philadelphia. Wafhington and Adams enter into his views; the firft congrefs

grefs is convoked and affembled ; Franklin, or rather the Genius of Liberty, prefides at it; every thing is refolved upon; new laws are enacted, but the principles of them already exift ; all the colonifts are citizens ; the patriot troops are about to be called forth ; they are already formed——all the citizens are foldiers !

The philofopher of humanity, the friend of peace, Franklin had upwards of ten years before prepared all the plans of the infurgent army. The number and order of the regiments and companies, the pay, the inftructions, all the military details, written by his own hand two *luftres* before the infurrection, and depofited in the archives of Philadelphia, atteft at once the extent and forefight of his ideas.

Advance, Englifhmen ; arm your fleets; pour in the warriors of your three kingdoms ; tranfport the mercenaries of Germany to America, now become free ; for Franklin prefides in her councils, and Wafhington regulates her armies ! Wifdom, and at length victory, declare againft you.

By means of thofe manœuvres which difplay at once the fkill and the ferocity of your bands of robbers, you redouble the energy of freemen, add to the horror againft tyrants, and enfure to the United States but greater triumphs. The contraft exhibited by the humanity of the citizens of America in the midft of moft of your moft difgraceful defeats, and the fury of your fervile troops in their flight but impious fucceffes, fhall change your glory to opprobrium, and the blood of a few peaceable men, immolated to your

rage,

rage, fhall furnifh the feeds of victory for the combatants of liberty!

I fhall not here enter into the expofition of the fagacious conduct, the profound combinations, the unexpected refources, the invincible refiftance, the decifive actions, the prodigies of glory, which have immortalifed the campaigns of the armies of Independence.

They did not poffefs any metal, but iron; any military knowledge, but courage; any experience in combats, but a genius fitted for victory; any difcipline proceeding from long previous preparation, but a General, who was all of a fudden the creator of an army.

From men who wifh to become free, from Franklin who directs, from Wafhington who commands, what is not to be expected?

However, even iron at laft is wanting; it is procured from Europe. Officers are not in fufficient abundance; they are invited from France.

Franklin, now in the feventieth year of his age, had juft returned from Canada, where he had been drawn, during the moft rigorous feafon of the year, by the interefts of the revolution, and, in the courfe of his journey, had traverfed, in company with Montgomery, the rivers and the lakes, at that time covered with ice. He is now appointed to proceed to France, in order to affift the efforts of Deane, and invite thofe fuccours which they were to procure from a generous people, who had fubmitted, during a difhonourable peace, to all the haughty pride, and all the intolerable outrages, of the Englifh miniftry.

He

He departs inftantly, although he did not poffefs a fingle piece of gold; for his country was deftitute of money. He arrives at Paris with a cargo of tobacco, in the fame manner as when Holland determined to become free, her deputies arrived at Bruffels with a convoy of herrings, in order to pay their expences.

Admiration preceded, attachment followed him. Every tongue celebrated his name; every look was fixed upon, every heart leaped at the fight of him : He fpoke, he was liftened to, and he fucceeded. The treaty of commerce with the infurgents is proclaimed; ammunition and warlike inftruments are fent from our ports—America receives them with gratitude; the free men of the new have now allies in the old world; they are foon alfo to have rivals, emulous to imitate, and, if poffible, to excel them.

At the voice of Franklin, at the voice of glory, appear, young Fayette, or rather difappear to Europe! Shew thyfelf to America, aftonifhed at thy noble daring; France fhall not learn thy flight, but with the news of thy firft victory in the country of liberty.

The furious Englifh every-where attacked our veffels; but they no longer poffeffed the advantage of thofe perfidious ftratagems which they had formerly made ufe of, before a declaration of war.

Our naval armaments were in readinefs; Orvilliers and Eftaing command them. In one quarter * of the globe the Englifh fleet experiences an invinci-

* This alludes to the engagement off Ufhant.

- ble

ble refiftance, and finds its only refource to confift in flight; in another† it meets with a fignal defeat; and the Weft-India iflands ‡ are obliged to receive into their ports thofe troops which were deftined to conquer them. Paul Jones §, an American commander, takes feveral prizes upon the very coafts of Great Britain; Rochambeau leads the French legions in the United States; La Fayette ¶ is the hero of the two nations; Wafhington is the arbiter of victory.

The independence of America is confummated; England, in its turn, is conftrained to fue for peace. The fovereignty of a great people is acknowledged, and from the banks of the Seine, Franklin, the harbinger, the director, and the very foul of this fublime novelty in the univerfe, conferring all the glory upon thofe who had the heroifm of acquiring it by means of arms, receives, with the calmnefs of a philofopher, the felicitations of America, of France, of the Englifh patriots themfelves, and of all thofe men who feel the godlike workings of humanity.

The fovereignty of the nation is eftablifhed; this then is the moment to perfect their laws. The ambaffador of America was its legiflator: He had already prepared, and he now tranfmits to his fellow-citizens

† At Granada.

‡ Tobago, &c.

§ This officer, fo celebrated during the American war, died lately in great poverty at Paris.

¶ The fubfequent conduct of this General has converted the eulogiums of the patriot Bifhop of Calvados into *anathemas*.

the

the conftitution of Pennfylvania, which connects it
with all the eftablifhments of the confederated ftates.

The rights of man are developed, for the firft time,
in laws fimple and beneficent as thofe of nature;
the rights of citizens are elevated on the fundamental
bafis of fociety. The organization of the public
power is combined with the private intereft of every
man, and the univerfal good of humanity, with the
individual advantage of every patriot, and the general
profperity of the country.

The inftitutions of Franklin are unanimoufly hailed
as the code of wifdom and beneficence. We have
adopted them into the new laws of France, and we
ought to regard their author as one of the founders
of this facred conftitution, which is about to attain
all the elevation of reafon and of juftice, all the perfection of focial and natural order, and which will
one day be the Pharos of the human kind.

Here, Gentlemen, the intereft of this difcourfe
becomes augmented. It is my intention to compare America become independent, with France now
free, and to prefage, from thefe circumftances, the
deftinies of the univerfe.

I have already faid, and I repeat it again—The
Anglo-Americans were the firft great people who
poffeffed the plenitude of liberty; the firft that prepared itfelf to enjoy the perfection of freedom is the
French nation; and in both thefe points of view
Franklin is the firft legiflator of the world. Let
the prefent and future generations hear and judge!

In

In Switzerland a fenatorial ariftocracy domineers; in Holland the Stadtholderate tends towards defpot- ifm; in England the people poffefs a corrupt, and but an inadequate, reprefentation: The Minifter re- gulates the elections; a Houfe of Peers arrefts every thing at its will; the Court, by means of money, ob- tains money; by money, fuffrages: In fhort, in what- ever point of view you are pleafed to confider the public welfare, the King hath an abfolute power over it. If there is a country in the world where there is a phantom of liberty idolifed by the people, and no real liberty which they can love, it is there. But this very phantom had hitherto fomething venerable in it. The imaginations of the Englifh, exalted by the temporary glory of their country, beholding around her nothing but nations of flaves, who wifhed to continue fuch, they, with good reafon, have looked upon themfelves, until now, as the people who poffeff- ed the firft rank in the univerfe.

Franklin once faid to the Englifh nation, " Admit
" all the men who belong to your government in the
" different parts of the globe, to a free competition
" for, and an equal reprefentation in, your legifla-
" ture; let the King alone fway the executive fcep-
" tre, and never be permitted to ftretch it forth but
" in the name of thofe laws made by the reprefenta-
" tives, and confented to by the colonies and pro-
" vinces; you will then poffefs the fupreme focial
" unity, and the grand monarchy of liberty. The
" univerfe will all affimilate to your empire, or at
" leaft

" leaft all the earth will be eager to imitate fuch a
" beautiful model; you will thus have the glory
" of commencing the happinefs of the world, and
" enfuring the fraternity of the human kind."

He fpoke to thofe who were refolved to be deaf,
who would not hear him, and who embraced
nothing but a chimera of liberty in their own ifland,
which they obftinately perfifted in fupporting by a
tyrannical domination abroad.

But America inclined her head, and liftened to his
voice. France, although ftill crouching under her
old and heavy fetters, ruminating even then in her
thoughts the great leffons of Mably and of Rouffeau,
lent an attentive ear, and faid—" The moment will
" arrive, it faft approaches, when that which Eng-
" land had not the wifdom to undertake, I fhall have
" the glory to execute."

In the mean time, the new States organize themfelves into a federate republic. Every other fpecies
of government was impracticable. The perfection
arifing from *unity* could not be expected from a multitude of independent provinces, of which each poffeffed the fovereign right of adopting whatever form
it pleafed.

The mutual neceffity of allying and connecting
itfelf together, fo as to form but one people, gave
rife to the Congrefs, which is deftined to regulate
thofe vaft objects that intereft the whole of the States.
Each province poffeffes its own proper legiflative affembly,

fembly, and alfo an independent power of executing its own decrees.

I repeat it once more, the Genius of Liberty reigns there in her full plenitude of glory; the union is happy, but the unity is not abfolute, and cannot be fo. How is it poffible to inftitute a fupreme chief? Each of the United States has an equal right to it; and moft horrid diffenfions would inevitably refult from the fole idea of a *King*.

The creation of a free monarchy, the moft perfect of all poffible governments, was referved for us.

Hail, France! vaft, yet united, country; rear up thy immenfe body; break thy chains; let the thunder of thy liberty fnap them in twain; let the Baftile and all the fortreffes of defpotifm fall and difappear; let Fayette prefent himfelf as the foldier of his country; the fon of France, the pupil of Wafhington; he fhall continue a citizen until his death: Let the elected reprefentatives of all the claffes of the empire, no longer form feparate orders, and let there be an abfolute equality, and, with the free competition of voices, a fole legiflature. Let them fpeak in the name of the whole nation, and let the nation reply—" This " is our will!"

Beloved chief of the French! Monarch, who, in fpite of thyfelf, haft hitherto poffeffed but the falfe grandeur of the nation, ceafe to be the powerlefs idol of a fmall and abhorred *caft* of oppreffing defpots, and become the refpected fovereign of twenty millions of freemen

freemen. Afcend, and thou wilt be the firft Prince in the world, who ever poffeffed that glory—afcend the throne of the laws; and fee not, within the large horizon of this empire, aught but that liberty which gives and maintains thee in full poffeffion of thy all-powerful fceptre. Thou governeft citizens ; thou ruleft over men ; thou art a King, and the only one upon earth !

This perfection of human genius has hitherto been wanting ; it was neceffary that France fhould arife, in order to refolve the problem of ages, to organize focial order, in abfolute unity, and to prefent to her a chief impaffible as a Divinity, and, like him, invariable in his juftice !

Eternal Ruler of human occurrences ! who, according to thy promife, wilt difpofe every thing in favour of our infant liberty *, it is thou who haft accumulated in filence thofe remarkable, prodigious, and miraculous events, in order to operate the creation of our happinefs.

But, in the combination of all thy benefits, the greateft is, that thou haft given us a Franklin, and connected us with an America ; the moft propitious is, that thou haft placed in the balance of the deftinies, the genius of the National Affembly, and the patriotifm of Bailly † and La Fayette ; the moft happy is, that thou haft in one day given liberty to

* Tu autem dominator virtutis .... cum magnâ reverentiâ difponis nos. Sap. 12. 18.

† Then Mayor of Paris.

the

the capital and the provinces, and difpofed a King to embrace it.

O memorable fuccefs! The furrounding nations can fcarce give credit to the truth of it; but they begin to be moved at the fight; their doubts feem to evaporate, and they at length believe that they may be happy.

Tyrants tremble; their reign has paffed away; we have now brothers in fentiment over all the earth. But a little longer, and, in a mutual independence and equal affection, the nations of the univerfe will be aftonifhed at being happy, and at finding themfelves Frenchmen!

Venerable old man, auguft philofopher, legiflator of the felicity of thy country, prophet of the fraternity of the human race, what extatic happinefs embellifhed the end of thy career! From thy fortunate afylum, and in the midft of thy brothers, who enjoyed in tranquillity the fruit of thy virtues, and the fuccefs of thy genius, thou haft fung fongs of deliverance. The laft looks which thou caft around thee, beheld America happy, France, on the other fide of the ocean, free, and a fure indication of the approaching freedom and happinefs of the world.

The United States, looking upon themfelves as thy children, have bewailed the death of the father of their republic; France, thy family by adoption, has honoured thee as the founder of her laws; and the human race has revered thee as the univerfal patriarch

triarch who has formed the alliance of nature with
fociety. Thy remembrance belongs to all ages; thy
memory to all nations; thy glory to eternity *!

* M. Veillard, Intendant of the waters at Paffy, who was very
intimate with Franklin, has been kind enough, as well as the celebrated M. Fleury, to give me a variety of information relative to
him; and this has ferved as the bafis of the prefent Eulogium. I
myfelf have alfo had the happinefs of being perfonally known to
this great man, having often dined in company with him at the
charming little villa belonging to M. Roy de Chaumont, at Paffy.
He affifted at fome of my fermons, and has afforded me many teftimonies of his efteem.   I might multiply the notes which authen-
ticate the facts mentioned by me in this difcourfe; but I rather
choofe to add, by way of appendix to this publication, a juftifica-
tory memorial, which M. le Roy, a Member of the Academy of
Sciences, of the Royal Society of London, of the Philofophical
Society of Philadelphia, and Keeper of the King's Cabinet of Natural Hiftory, has been fo kind as to fend me.   It arrived too late
to be ufed in the body of the prefent work; but it confirms all I
have advanced; it contains a number of details I was ignorant of,
and it cannot fail to intereft the public, and give additional fuppor
to my labours.

TRANSLATION of a Letter from M. LE ROY *to the* Abbé FAUCHET (*now conſtitutional Biſhop of Cal-* *vados*), *relative to the late* Dr. FRANKLIN.

I AM enchanted to hear, Sir, that, elevating your mind above the vain prejudices of the vulgar, you have formed the noble deſign of pronouncing, in the metropolis of France, the funeral oration of my illuſ-trious friend, who was born a Proteſtant.

Flattered with the confidence which you have been pleaſed to repoſe in me, I have endeavoured to comply with your wiſhes by tranſmitting you ſome particulars of the life of this great man; collected partly from what I can recollect in regard to him, and partly from what he himſelf has told me, in the numerous converſations we have had together.

It is neceſſary that the claſs of men, equally vain and imbecile, who wiſhed to eſtabliſh a privileged *caſt* among us, to whom alone the command of the ar-mies, the venerable departments of juſtice, and the councils of the Sovereign were to be open; it is ne-ceſſary they ſhould learn that Franklin, like the illuſ-trious Flechier, was the ſon of a tallow-chandler; that he was born in Boſton; that he left it at fourteen years of age, much in the ſame manner as thoſe young men who, being impatient under the yoke of pater-nal authority, leave their fathers houſe in order to ſeek their fortune elſewhere; that he happened to go to Philadelphia, where, having preſented himſelf to

2   the

the only printer then refiding in that city, he took a fancy to the boy; in whom he difcovered a natural genius, and inftructed him in the art of printing *.

I know that M. de la Rochefoucault, in the difcourfe which he read before the fociety of 1789 †, on the 13th of June laft, gives us to underftand that he was a journeyman printer in Bofton, and that he left it in order to feek for employment at New York and Philadelphia.

But, as well as I can remember, both from what he and his countrymen have told me, he arrived at Philadelphia in 1720, a period when the art of printing, fo very curious in itfelf, was almoft unknown to a great part of the country.

I have alfo learned, that the farmers who frequented that city, and who were fond of whatever was interefting, were accuftomed to vifit the printing-houfe in which young Franklin worked, and, being aftonifhed at his activity and addrefs, prefented him with many marks of their liberality.

Avaricious of knowledge, and poffeffing an infatiable defire after inftruction, he eafily perceived that, at the diftance of two thoufand leagues from England, it was by books alone that he could gain information: But how could he procure them, when, at this pe-

---

* It may be neceffary to obferve here, that this and a number of other little miftakes are corrected in Dr. Franklin's firft and fecond letters, Part. I.—*Note by the Tranflator.*

† See page 237.

riod,

riod, there were not more than perhaps four or five hundred volumes in all Philadelphia?

By way of attaining knowledge, he formed a club confisting of some young men, who were of a similar disposition with himself, and, in order to have the advantage of each other's books, it was agreed that they should place them in one common library. As this resource was not attended with all the advantages at first expected from it, it was resolved to subscribe a small sum every month, to enable them to import all the new works from London.

The young people of Philadelphia having learned that this society possessed a great number and variety of books, were exceedingly desirous to borrow them; this was most readily consented to, on condition of paying a trifle for the use of them, in order to augment their number. In short, this new scheme was attended with so much success, that their little collection swelled into a library; and the other colonies, perceiving the immense advantages arising from such an establishment, began to form similar ones at Boston, New York, Charlestown, and several other places. Thus originated a number of the first libraries in America; and that at Philadelphia may, at this day, dispute its consequence with many of the most celebrated in Europe.

Pardon me, Sir, for entering into these details; for to me they appear interesting, and even necessary, in order to point out how my illustrious friend has

not

not only been the founder, but, as it were, the fchool-mafter, of American independence.

Thinking, however, that all the inftruction he could acquire in his own country, was not fufficient to conduct him to that point of perfection at which he wifhed to arrive, he determined to vifit England, and accordingly arrived there about the year 1724 or 1725.

This much is certain, that he was there during the life of Newton, whom he told me he had feen feveral times, and who did not die until 1727 *.

He worked at his bufinefs as a printer in London; and it appears to me that he lived in very great ob-fcurity.

After a fhort refidence in the metropolis of Eng-land, he returned to America. It was at that period, if I am not greatly miftaken, that he perfuaded the printer with whom he had formerly refided to publifh a newfpaper, in imitation of thofe he had feen in London. This fcheme was attended with fuccefs, and the printer, to whom it brought in a large fum, after having, out of gratitude, taken him into co-partnerfhip, gave him his daughter in marriage †.

From this marriage fprung Mr. (commonly called Governor) Franklin, one of the principal Ame-rican Loyalifts, and Mrs. Beach, his favourite daugh-ter, to whofe family he has left the greateft part

* March 20, 1726-27.
† This is another miftake. See Chap. I. and II. Part I.

of

of his fortune *, having bequeathed but one or two
farms to Mr. William Franklin, the fon of the Loyalift, whom you have feen here.

Devoted

* Dr. Franklin's will was made during his refidence in the village
of Paffy, near Paris.

It begins as follows:

" I Benjamin Franklin, printer, at prefent Minifter Plenipotentiary from the United and Independent States of America to his
Moft Chriftian Majefty Louis XVI. King of France, hereby declare my laft will and teftament," &c. &c.

The following articles will evince that this great man was not
unmindful of pofterity:

" I was born in Bofton, New England, and owe my firft inftructions in literature to the two grammar-fchools eftablifhed there. I
have, therefore, confidered thofe fchools in my will.

" But I am alfo under obligations to the State of Maffachufets,
for having, unafked, appointed me formerly their agent in Eng.
land, with a handfome falary, which continued fome years: And
although I accidentally loft in their fervice, by tranfmitting Governor Hutchinfon's letters, much more than the amount of what
they gave me, I do not think that ought in the leaft to diminifh
my gratitude.

" I have confidered that, among artifans, good apprentices are
moft likely to make good citizens; and having myfelf been bred
to a manual art, printing, in my native town, and afterwards
affifted to fet up my bufinefs in Philadelphia by kind loans of money from two friends there, which was the foundation of my fortune, and of all the utility in life that may be afcribed to me; I
wifh to be ufeful even after my death, if poffible, in forming and
advancing other young men that may be ferviceable to their country
in both thofe towns.

" To this end, I devote two thoufand pounds fterling; of which
I give one thoufand to the inhabitants of the town of Bof-

ton

Devoted entirely to his profeffion during a large portion of his life, it appears that, foon after the treaty

ton in Maffachufets, and the other thoufand to the inhabitants of the city of Philadelphia, in truft, to and for the ufes, intents, and purpofes, hereinafter mentioned and declared.

" The faid fum of one thoufand pounds fterling, if accepted by the inhabitants of the town of Bofton, fhall be managed under the direction of the felect men, united with the Minifters of the oldeft Epifcopalian, Congregational and Prefbyterian churches, in that town, who are to let out the fame upon intereft at five per cent. per annum, to fuch young married artificers under the age of twenty-five years, as have ferved an apprenticefhip in the faid town, and faithfully fulfilled the duties required in their indentures, fo as to obtain a good moral character from at leaft two refpectable citi_ zens, who are willing to become their fureties in a bond with the applicants for the repayment of the monies fo lent, with intereft, according to the terms hereinafter prefcribed ; all which bonds are to be taken for Spanifh milled dollars, or the value thereof in current gold coin. And the managers fhall keep a bound book or books, wherein fhall be entered the names of thofe who fhall apply for and receive the benefit of this inftitution, and of their fureties, together with the fums lent, the dates, and other neceffary and proper records, refpecting the bufinefs and concerns of this inftitution. And, as thefe loans are intended to affift young married artificers in fetting up their bufinefs, they are to be proportioned by the difcretion of the managers, fo as not to exceed fifty pounds fterling to one perfon, nor to be lefs than fifteen pounds.

" And if the number of appliers fo entitled fhould be fo large as that the fum will not fuffice to afford to each as much as might otherwife not be improper, the proportion to each fhall be diminifhed, fo as to afford to every one fome affiftance.

" Thefe aids may therefore be fmall at firft ; but, as the capital increafes by the accumulating intereft, they will be more ample.

" And, in order to ferve as many as poffible in their turns, as well

treaty of Aix-la-Chapelle, he found himfelf enabled, by the fortune he had acquired, to gratify his paffion for

as to make the repayment of the principal borrowed more eafy, each borrower fhall be obliged to pay, with the yearly intereft, one tenth part of the principal; which fums of principal and inte reft fo paid in, fhall be again let out to frefh borrowers.

"And as it is prefumed, that there will be always found in Bof-ton virtuous and benevolent citizens, willing to beftow a part of their time in doing good to the rifing generation, by fuperintend-ing and managing this inftitution gratis, it is hoped that no part of the money will at any time lie dead, or be diverted to other pur-pofes, but be continually augmented by the intereft; in which cafe, there may in time be more than the occafion in Bofton fhall require, and then fome may be fpared to the neighbouring or other towns in the faid State of Maffachufetts, which may defire to have it; fuch towns engaging to pay punctually the intereft and the proportions of the principal annually to the inhabitants of the town of Bofton.

" If this plan is executed and fucceeds as projected, without in-terruption, for one hundred years, the fum will then be one hundred and thirty-one thoufand pounds; of which I would have the ma-nagers of the donation to the town of Bofton then lay out, at their difcretion, one hundred thoufand pounds in public works, which may be judged of moft general utility to the inhabitants, fuch as fortifications, bridges, aqueducts, public buildings, baths, pave-ments, or whatever may make living in the town more convenient to its people, and render it more agreeable to ftrangers reforting thither for health, or a temporary refidence.

" The remaining thirty-one thoufand pounds I would have conti-nued to be let out on intereft in the manner above directed, for another hundred years, as I hope it will have been found that the inftitution has had a good effect on the conduct of youth, and been of fervice to many worthy characters and ufeful citizens.

" At the end of this fecond term, if no unfortunate accident has prevented the operation, the fum will be four millions and fixty-one

for ſtudy. From that period he alſo began to diſtin-guiſh himſelf by the ſervices he performed to his native country.

The famous Leyden experiment having excited the attention of all the learned men in Europe; Mr. Col-linſon, a Quaker of London, who was a Member of the Royal Society, tranſmitted ſome glaſs tubes to Mr. Franklin, and the other inſtruments neceſſary for making experiments in electricity. He employed theſe with ſo much ability and ſucceſs, as to be able, by means of their aſſiſtance, to accompliſh thoſe diſ-coveries which have immortalized his memory.

Two of them particularly characteriſe his genius: The firſt is, the unèqual diſtribution of the electric fluid in the human body; whence ariſe thoſe electri-cal *phenomena* which preſent themſelves to us. The other, which is more grand, and more likely to afford aſtoniſhment, is the *para-tonnere*, or conductor.

It may not be unneceſſary here to ſay a few words on this ſubject, in order the better to develope the genius of my illuſtrious friend, and to aſcertain in what manner he contrived to make the moſt advan-tageous applications of certain *phenomena*, the conſe-quences to be deduced from which had eſcaped the penetration of other naturaliſts.

one thouſand pounds ſterling; of which I leave one million and ſixty-one thouſand pounds to the diſpoſition and management of the inhabitants of the town of Boſton, and three millions to the diſpoſition of the government of the State, not preſuming to carry my views further, &c.".

X 4

Mr.

Mr. Gray, an Englishman, had said, a little before his death, that, if it were permitted to compare small things with great, he dared to affirm that electricity and thunder were one and the same thing. It was in 1735 that this Gentleman, to whom electricity is under great obligations, hazarded this bold comparison. The more the *phenomèna* multiplied, the better did this theory appear to be founded.

But how was it possible to pass that immense interval between us and the clouds? It had been discovered in America that pointed substances drew the electric fluid from electric bodies, from a much greater distance, than the bodies which have other shapes. Mr. Franklin instantly reasons upon this idea, and says—if the cause of thunder be the same as that of electricity; if the clouds, during a tempest, are replete with this fluid; there is nothing more to be done than to present a pointed substance upon an elevated place, and this will infallibly be electrified during a storm.

This great and superb conjecture appeared extravagant to those who do not know how to raise themselves above vulgar opinions.

Notwithstanding this, a man was found in France (M. Dalibard), who had the courage to attempt the verification of this experiment; and, on the tenth of May 1752, a tempest which took place at Marly-la-Ville, where the apparatus was erected, justified, at one and the same time, the hardy conjecture of my illustrious friend, and the courage of M. Dalibard,

who

who had been tempted to try whether it was well founded or not.

In a fhort time, this new and grand experiment was difclofed to all Europe, and a variety of obfervations confirmed what M. Dalibard had firft feen. Thus I am of opinion, Sir, that, if you fhould think proper to mention this fublime difcovery in your difcourfe, you can fay, it was in France that this.experiment was made for the firft time, and that it was confequently an honour referved for us.

From this difcovery to the conduƈtor, or *para-tonnere*, there is but a fingle ftep; for if points, in preference to all other figures, attraƈt eleƈtric matter from the clouds, it will inconteftably follow, that a pointed conduƈtor, elevated above a building, will poffefs this advantage; and that if this could tranfmit, immediately and without any obftacle, this eleƈtric matter to the·earth, its common refervoir, by means of a metal chain, no accident could refult from it, and a houfe might, by thefe means, be entirely preferved from the ravages of the thunder.

The new and hardy ideas conceived by Mr. Franklin found much oppofition in England. Notwithftanding this, when he revifited that country in 1755, ample juftice was done to his merits, and the Royal Society decreed him the golden medal, which it awards annually to the authors of thofe memoirs containing interefting and ufeful difcoveries. On this occafion, he was received with great attention and refpeƈt; and, much about the fame period, he was

5 admitted

admitted Doctor of Laws at one of the Englifh Uni-
verfities *. War having broke out in the fucceeding
year between England and France, he returned to
America, and was much employed in public bufinefs.

He has often mentioned to me that, having been
appointed a captain of artillery, the matroffes who
ferved under him infifted upon doing him honour by
firing a falute before his door, which broke all the
china in his houfe.

We are now arrived at that moment when he may
be confidered as a public man. Having been nominated
agent for the province of Pennfylvania, he returned
to England about the year 1761. At this period
there was a prodigious fermentation in the minds of
the people of America.

The act enforcing a duty on tea had irritated them
exceedingly; and the Bofton-port bill, which was
enacted foon after, entirely completed the difcontent
of the Colonies.

At length it was refolved that the agent of Pennfylvania, as well as the agents of the other provinces,
fhould be called to the bar of the Houfe of Commons,
in order to anfwer certain interrogatories concerning
the population of America, the difpofition of the
people in regard to the Parliament of England, and
the reafons of their refiftance to the late impofts.

It was on this occafion that my illuftrious friend
diftinguifhed himfelf, by the clearnefs, the force, and
the precifion of his reafons, and made himfelf known

* Oxford,

to

to all ..urope as a great man. I faw him a few months after in Paris; and M. Malefherbes very juftly remarked, when I prefented him to that gentleman, that he was the firft learned man who had difcovered extraordinary talents for politics. This was an advantage he derived from the nature of the government under which he lived, as it permitted the efforts of the human mind to be directed towards thofe important objects which have for their object the happinefs and the felicity of the people.

Had this man been born in Paris, under our ancient fyftem, he would have remained for ever in obfcurity: How would it have been poffible to have employed the fon of a tallow-chandler? Indeed, if his genius for the fciences had forced the barriers oppofed by his birth, he might have been elected a member of an academy!

· Ought it not to be readily allowed by every body, that population being one of the moft important objects for a State, a too great competition and rivalfhip for employments can never be dreaded; and that the probability of poffeffing citizens capable of worthily prefiding in the different departments, augments always in proportion to the number of candidates who afpire to the honour of filling them?

I now return to my illuftrious friend: I have only permitted myfelf to make this digreffion on account of the indignation with which an abfurd ariftocratical tyranny, that defignated and confined the employments of a kingdom to a particular *fect*, has ever infpired me.

me. What renders this ftill more infufferable is, that this very fect was much lefs capable, and lefs inftructed, than that of the *third Eftate*, which had been fo much defpifed.

The replications of Franklin added new force to the refolutions of the Colonies, and augmented the number of the partizans which they already had in Parliament. But fuch was the obftinacy of the men who furrounded the King of Great Britain, that they infifted on laying impofts upon the Americans, in direct oppofition to the fpirit of that very law, which fays that the citizens can never be taxed but by their own confent.

At length the Americans determine to affemble a Congrefs.

About this time, my illuftrious friend, who had formerly poffeffed great influence with the Englifh Miniftry (for he had been able to procure the appointment of Governor of New Jerfey for his fon), began to lofe all his intereft at Court; and Mr. Wedderburne (now Lord Loughborough), who was at that time Attorney General, and a true *ariftccrat*, permitted himfelf to treat him with great infolence and haughtinefs. It was even faid, that there was an intention of imprifoning him.

Perceiving at length that his refidence in England could be no longer ufeful to his countrymen, he refolved to leave it, and concerted his meafures with fo much addrefs, that he had embarked and was actually at fea, in the beginning of the vear 1775, at the very time

time that he was thought, by his enemies, to be ſtill in England.

The events of that period are well known. Every body recollects that, in June or July 1776, America declared herſelf independent; and that ſhe took all the meaſures in her power to aſſert and ſecure her ſovereignty. I beg leave to obſerve, however, that it was towards the cloſe of July, or the beginning of Auguſt, that Mr. Deane, who came from America in order to negotiate with the Court of France, and Mr. Bencroft, who came from England to aſſiſt him in his labours, met at my houſe.

, Franklin, as every body knows, was one of the moſt ſtrenuous ſupporters of American liberty, and was perpetually buſied in preparing every thing for that great revolution which was about to give freedom to his country.

The Congreſs ſent him to Canada in the autumn of 1776, to negotiate with the inhabitants, and engage them to make a common cauſe with the Colonies, in order to throw off the yoke of England. But the Canadians were ſo diſguſted with the exceſſes committed by their neighbours, the Preſbyterians of New England, who had deſtroyed and burnt ſeveral of their chapels, that they could never be prevailed upon to liſten to the propoſitions of the Colonies, although ſupported with all the energy which he knew how to give to every thing with which he was entruſted.

Fana-

Fanaticifm is an enemy to the happinefs of man-kind, and is to be found in all religions; the Prefby-. terians of the Englifh Colonies have preferved, from their very original, a certain gloominefs and fpirit of tyranny in their character, which they not only dif-played then againft the Canadians, but upon many other occafions.

Having failed on this occafion, Dr. Franklin re-turned to Philadelphia, and the Congrefs knowing the confideration which he enjoyed in Europe, and the reputation which he had acquired by his philofo-phical difcoveries, entrufted him with a miffion to France, where he was to put the laft hand to the ne-gotiations which Mr. Deane had already commenced in a fecret manner.

Although now in the feventy-firft year of his age, he accepted this delicate and important commiffion, and arrived at Paris about the fixteenth of December 1776.

The fuccefs of the Americans in the northern pro-vinces, and the defeat of General Burgoyne by Gene-ral Gates, in the autumn of 1777, at length deter-mined our Court to give a more favourable hearing to the propofitions of the Congrefs; and, either towards the end of this year, or the beginning of 1778, the treaty of alliance and commerce with the States of Ame-rica was figned, a circumftance which led us into a war with England.

I flatter myfelf, that I in fome meafure contributed towards the figning of this treaty; for, knowing the

efforts

efforts made by the Englifh in order to induce the infurgents to return under the yoke of the mother-
country, I informed M. Maùrepas of this circumftance, by means of one of my particular friends,
telling him, at the fame time, that there was not a
moment to be loft, if he wifhed to preferve the alliance of the Americans, and detach them from Great
Britain.

Never did I fee a mortal fo happy, fo joyous, as
Fränklin, on the day when Lord Stormont, Ambaffador from England, left Paris, on account of the
rupture with our Court. We dined together; and
he who was ufually very calm and tranquil, appeared
to me, on that day, to be quite a new man.

At length, in confequence of a feries of the moft fortunate events, in lefs than feven years, North America
became free, and my illuftrious friend had the happinefs and the glory, in 1783, of figning, along with the
Englifh Commiffioners, that peace which recognifed
the independence of his country.

Until that period, he had enjoyed a good ftate of
health, and was free from any complaint whatever,
except that he was fubject to the gout. In 1782, he
had a very violent fit, which was accompanied with
a very grievous nephritic colic. This appears to have
been the origin of the ftone, with which he was afterwards tortured; for, in the courfe of the year 1783,
he fuffered feveral very violent attacks, and, from
that epoch, they continued daily to augment.

As

As his mind was full of refources, and calculated for every fituation in life, he found means, in fome meafure, to alleviate the violence of his pains, and render his malady more fupportable.

His wifhes being now fully accomplifhed, and peace concluded, he fighed after the moment when he might once more revifit his native country. He accordingly requefted feveral times to be recalled by Congrefs: But how was it poffible to replace him? However, that illuftrious body, on his reiterated applications, nominated Mr. Jefferfon Minifter to our Court; and certainly they could not have made a better choice, nor appointed a man more worthy to fucceed my illuftrious friend.

His fucceffor having at length arrived*, he refolved to depart. It was not an eafy matter to repair to Havre,

in

* " I found the Minifters of France (fays Mr. Jefferfon) equally
" impreffed with Dr. Franklin's talents and integrity. The Count
" de Vergennes, particularly, gave me repeated and unequivocal de-
" monftrations of his entire confidence in him.

" When he left Paffy, it feemed as if the village had loft its *pa-*
" *triarch.* On taking leave of the Court, which he did by letter,
" the King ordered him to be handfomely complimented, and fur-
" nifhed him with a *litter* and *mules* of his own, the only kind of
" conveyance that the ftate of his health could bear.

" The fucceffion to Dr. Franklin, at the Court of France, was
" an excellent fchool of humility to me. On being prefented to
" any one as the Minifter of America, the common-place queftion
" was, *C'eft vous, Monfieur, qui remplacez le Docteur Franklin?*—
" ' Is it you, Sir, who replaces Dr. Franklin?' I generally an-
" fwered

In order to embark; he, however, made a shift to reach the place of his destination in carriages supplied by the Court. From that port he set sail for Newport, in the Isle of Wight, and, after a short and agreeable passage, he arrived at Philadelphia in September 1785, amidst the acclamations of an immense crowd of spectators, who were eager to see him, and who accompanied him from the place where he landed to his own house.

· A few days after his arrival, the Members of the Congress, and all the eminent people in Philadelphia, and the adjacent country, waited upon him. In a short time, he was elected, for two years following, Presi-

" swered—' No one can replace him, Sir; I am only his suc-
" cessor.'

" A little before my arrival in France, Argand had invented
" his celebrated *lamp*, in which the flame is spread into a hollow
" cylinder, and thus brought into contact with the air, within as
" well as without. Dr. Franklin had been on the point of the
" same discovery. The idea had occurred to him; but he had
" tried a bull-rush as a wick, which did not succeed. His occu_
" pations did not permit him to repeat and extend his trials to the
" introduction of a larger column of air than could pass through
" the stem of a bull-rush.

" About this time, also, the King of France gave him a signal
" testimony of respect, by joining him with some of the most
" illustrious men of the nation, to examine that *ignis fatuus* of phi-
" losophy, the *animal magnetism* of the *maniac* Mesmer; the pre-
" tended effects of which had astonished all Paris. From Dr.
" Franklin's hand, in conjunction with his brethren of the learned
" committee, that compound of fraud and folly was unveiled, and
" received its death-wound."

Y   dent

dent of the Affembly of Philadelphia; but at length
his great age, and the malady with which he was attacked, precluding him entirely from the adminiftration of public affairs, he demanded and obtained
leave to retire, in order to pafs the remainder
of his life in tranquillity amidft his fellow-citizens,
to offer up vows for their profperity, and to occupy
himfelf entirely with his beloved ftudy, which was
natural hiftory.

There is one thing which I have forgotten to mention to you, Sir; it is, that, during his paffage to
America, he wrote a long memorial, addreffed to my
brother, full of excellent ideas relative to the improvement of fhip-building.

You have heard of the honours that were paid to
him after his death. They are fuch as he merited,
and fuch as a free people ought to render to the memory of a man, who had made them fo by the pains
he had taken to elevate their minds, and to inftruct
them relative to their own rights. I have a variety
of facts to add; but this letter is already too long. I
beg leave to tell you truly, and by way of excufe, that I
have not had time to fhorten it, having a thoufand other
things to do at the prefent moment; as to the reft, I
beg you will look upon this as the Sylva Sylvarum of
Bacon, in which he had affembled every thing that
he thought could be ferviceable to his great edifice of
philofophy. As for me, I have endeavoured to collect
all the facts that may contribute to the oration you are
about to pronounce in honour of my illuftrious friend.

I cannot

I cannot avoid adding a few words more, relative to the character of his genius, and the temper of his mind.· Tranquil, calm, and circumfpect, like the generality of his countrymen, he could never be reproached during his refidence here, and amidft the moft delicate and embarraffing circumftances, with having uttered a fingle word, or expreffion, which could be quoted againft him. This is a very uncommon circumftance, when we confider the part he acted, and the number of fpies who watched every look and every fentence.

He poffeffed all the courage neceffary for great events; and it was that firm courage which appertains to elevated minds, which, after having confidered every thing, looks upon events as the neceffary and inevitable confequence of the order of human affairs.

In regard to his mind, it had this peculiar characteriftic, which has not hitherto been fufficiently attended to; I mean the faculty of obferving and exa_ mining things, in the moft fimple manner poffible. In his philofophical and political inquiries, he always looked at the queftion, in its moft natural point of view. This was invariably the fame, whether the fubject was philofophical or mechanical.

In fine, while the bulk of mankind arrive only at what is true and fimple, by a circuitous road and multiplied efforts, the fuperiority of his genius enabled him, by the moft eafy means, to explain the *phenomena* under difcuffion, to conftruct a machine for which he had occafion; or, in fhort, to

dif-discover the most proper expedients for the success of those plans, projects, and experiments, with which his thoughts were so frequently occupied.

I have the honour to be, with the utmost respect,

SIR,

Your very humble, and

Most obedient servant,

LE ROY.

FINIS.

E
302
.6
,F7
A2
1793a

CPSIA information can be obtained at www.ICGtesting.com
Printed in the USA
BVOW080519021012

301853BV00002B/30/A